Oral
Communication

Oral Communication

Fourth Edition

Message and Response

Larry A. Samovar
San Diego State University

Jack Mills
San Diego State University

ωcb
Wm. C. Brown Company Publishers
Dubuque, Iowa

wcb

Wm. C. Brown
Chairman of the Board

Larry W. Brown
President, WCB Group

Book Team

**Wm. C. Brown Company Publishers
College Division**

Thomas W. Gornick
Editor

Lawrence E. Cremer
President

William J. Evans
Designer

Raymond C. Deveaux
Vice President/Product Development

Rus Caughron
Production Editor

David Wm. Smith
Assistant Vice President/
National Sales Manager

Matt Coghlan
National Marketing Manager

David A. Corona
Director of Production Development
and Design

William A. Moss
Production Editorial Manager

Marilyn A. Phelps
Manager of Design

Mary M. Heller
Visual Research Manager

Chapter opening illustrations by Fred Womack.

Contents

2
Your Ideas
77

3
Having an
Influence
145

**4
Changing
Environments
205**

**Appendixes
239**

Contents

Contents

Preface

We first recorded our philosophy of the principles of good speech communication in 1968. In successive editions that philosophy has been preserved and enriched by the incorporation of suggestions from users of the book. Our hope for this fourth edition is that its usefulness will remain undiminished.

Brevity, consistent with clarity, has always been one of our aims. We believe that students of oral communication can profitably spend the greater share of their time in message preparation. Thus, we have provided the essential theoretical principles while leaving students time to engage in those steps of preparation necessary for effective communication. Such an approach also affords instructors greater latitude in explaining and applying speech principles.

We continue to believe that the effective message is listener-oriented, that the integral parts of that message are ideas, language, voice, and action, and that every communication situation is unique and not bound by a set of universally applicable rules of effectiveness. Accordingly, we have attempted to provide students with an even wider range of choices through the addition of new concepts and illustrations and the recasting of those features that have gained reader acceptance in previous editions.

We have arranged the chapters to provide students with a steadily mounting supply of building materials as they move from their first speeches to greater levels of complexity. In the process, we have tried to remember that we are writing for students, not for our colleagues.

Among the features added to this fourth edition is a treatment of the job interview, in Appendix A. In a period of increasing competition for employment, awareness of factors contributing to a successful interview is a definite asset.

The study of oral communication continues beyond enrollment in a single speech class and the reading of a single textbook. Each communication situation we encounter is unique and provides a special learning experience. The study of oral communication is, indeed, a lifetime endeavor.

Larry Samovar   Jack Mills

Preliminary Considerations

Part 1

Communication
Overview and Preview

This book is based on the contention that communication is an activity. It is something persons do with each other, and as such can be improved. Therefore, it is the purpose of this book to improve your communication ability—your ability to have an influence over your environment. We hope to help you solve your communication problems more easily and effectively. You have been exchanging ideas, emotions, and experiences with others almost since birth; hence, you have been solving communication problems with some measure of success. No doubt you will continue to do so with or without the aid of formal training. But the chances are, if you are like most people, your communication activities have become matters of habit. It is only through conscious study that you can improve your communication patterns, and it follows that you will improve from this study and practice only if you are motivated to improve. You must personally see a real need for communication if you are to gain and grow with this training experience. Reaffirm the axiom that **speech is important for our everyday existence.**

You need only take stock of your waking hours to see the importance of communication. Reflect on what you consider a normal day and you will discover that most of that day was taken over by communication. You were engaged in activities that attempted to share your internal state, at a given instant, with another human being. Studies estimate that we spend up to eighty percent of our waking hours engaging in some communication act.

The uses you make of communication range from the therapeutic to the pragmatic. You tell a friend how you are suffering because you failed an important examination, knowing full well your friend cannot change the results of the test. Yet the sharing of that information seems to have some therapeutic effect. On the job you use communication so that you can make a sale, explain a product, or persuade a client. After hours you use communication to persuade others to your point of view, such as trying to convince the County Board of Supervisors not to put the proposed trailer park in the middle of a wilderness area. Your use of communication here is pragmatic.

Our gift of speech, and the fact that we make great use of it, does not benefit us much unless we have the ability to speak with reasonable effectiveness. History has been correctly called the story of persons and governments trying to resolve their problems. To date we have but two methods of resolving our conflicts: we can talk them out or we can fight them out. The method of bullets and bombs, although used many times in recent history, is far inferior to the method of words and reason. A democracy needs and uses the spoken word.

Whether on the public platform, on the job, or in conversation, we use speech as the central means of sharing our feelings and passing on our ideas. We can tell and we can be told. Communication is the link between what is inside us and what goes on outside us. Without speech we are isolated, unable to share thoughts, wishes, needs, or feelings with family, friend, or foe.

This is a book on *how* to communicate. We are primarily concerned with the efficiency with which you share your opinions and ideas with other people. However, it is our contention that understanding the processes in which you are involved is the first step to improvement. Therefore, this chapter is predicated on the assumption that *understanding* and *doing* are two sides of the same coin—they are interrelated. In this chapter we seek to point out that interrelationship by examining what communication is and how it works.

The Communication Process

To understand the nature and function of speech, we must examine the process of which speech is but one manifestation—the process of communication. We use the terms *communication, oral communication,* and *speech* synonymously in this text simply because a speaker is primarily engaged in communication—that is, in affecting the behavior of others. We ask and answer questions, we take part in conversation, we exchange ideas in committees, and we take part in class discussions; we participate in situations for which we are prepared and in some for which we are not prepared. In short, we use *oral communication* and *speech* interchangeably because **the skills and concepts of successful communication are the same principles that apply to effective speech making**.

You will notice that part of the final sentence in the preceding paragraph is in bold-faced type. This added emphasis should suggest to you that speech communication commonality is important. As we have indicated, the components of communication are essentially the components of public speaking. In both cases, credibility, interest, motivation, clarity, and types of responses, must be considered. Even the assumed differences begin to fade upon close examination. For example, although only one person tends to talk during public speaking, the "other person," is still sending messages. Nonverbal communication is present in all public speaking situations. The way the audience responds is a type of message. There is even commonality in preconceived purposes. In both public and private interaction we have a purpose that has triggered our role in the communication process. We seldom engage in random behavior. So, although the number of persons involved may vary, and the time allowed for preparation may shift from occasion to occasion, public speaking and communication basically include the same elements. And as we have already indicated, we are concerned with improving your use of those elements—both on and off the public platform.

What Is Communication?

In its broadest sense, the term *communication* includes all methods of conveying any kind of thought or feeling between persons. The telegraph operator communicates when he taps out code meanings that are responded to by other individuals. Actors, artists, writers, and musicians communicate with their audiences by various methods including spoken and written words, actions, forms, and colors; and audiences participate in the communication process by responding to the symbols sent by each communication source. The tired student who yawns in an early morning class communicates something to the professor and to those who sit around him. A smile is a communication act, and so is a frown.

The term *communication* is indeed enigmatic. Communication is something we all do, yet it is so very broad as to make it difficult to define. A recent article in the *Journal of Communication* revealed no less than fifteen working definitions of human communication. The problem of defining becomes even more difficult when we realize that in one sense inanimate as well as animate objects can communicate. Therefore, in any definition we must allow sufficient latitude to include the processes as well as the functions of the act. One such definition would suggest that communication is the process of sharing with another person, or persons, one's knowledge, interests, attitudes, opinions, feelings, and ideas. There is still another definition that would broaden the scope of the process to include verbal and *nonverbal* messages. Other definitions pose the issue of whether or not the message must be intentional on the part of the speaker.

Whatever definition is analyzed, a number of crucial characteristics emerge. When understood, they can help us know what communication is and tell us something about how it operates.

1. *Communication is a two-way process.* More than one person must be involved in any act of communication. Speech writers, authors, and musicians may compose in solitude, but there is no actual communication until an audience has reacted to the composition. Granting this communication axiom, you can see that you must keep your communication partner foremost in your mind at all times. You are not alone when you communicate (as we are defining it); one person has decided to involve another person. Hence, communication is a two-way process. Both parties are sending and receiving messages; each is responding to the messages of the other.
2. *Communication seeks to elicit a response.* Speakers communicate to accomplish a purpose. They know what reactions they want from listeners, and this awareness of purpose helps them determine what to say and how to say it. Communication is not random, it is a purposeful activity. Whether you are asking someone for the correct time, or trying to get a large group of people to support legislation outlawing the use of steel traps, you have a reason for engaging in communication—you want to elicit a response.
3. *Communication is a symbolic process.* All communication entails the use of symbols of some kind to express ideas and feelings. When you use language to communicate your ideas, you do not simply transfer them to the passively receptive mind of your listener. Rather, you cause the listener to develop ideas that are approximately, but never exactly, the same as yours. The

degree of resemblance between the ideas you want to express and the ones your listener develops depends largely upon how effectively both of you, as partners in the communication act, use language symbols.

Words are the basic symbols in linguistic communication; however, nonverbal elements also play an important part. For example, the sound of the speaker's voice, his or her appearance, and actions are often as important as the choice of words. Communication calls for the use of a highly complex set of symbols including both verbal and nonverbal elements.

Improving your ability to communicate means improving your faculty to use verbal and nonverbal symbols. These symbols represent your internal state, what you know and feel, and what you select to share. How you manipulate your words and actions will help determine how well you transmit your ideas and feelings to others. After all, your listeners cannot get inside you—that is a personal and private place. Others receive only your symbolic account of that place. To tell someone that you have a headache is not the headache, it is a symbol of your pain. The actual pain, inside you, is all yours! Therefore, communication must rely on the symbolic process. If you are successful as a communicator, the transmission of those symbols has enabled another person to understand approximately what you mean and how you feel.

4. *Communication is a real-life process.* The outcome of any attempt to communicate always depends upon how well you adapt to the environment that surrounds and involves that communication situation. Among the factors that you must try to keep in mind are the occasion that calls forth your attempt to communicate; your relationship to the person with whom you are communicating; your appearance, mood, character, and personality; the knowledge, skill, and perception of the receiver of your communication; the most suitable style and form of speaking; the channeling system you use to bring that expression to your receiver's attention; and the response from that receiver that will achieve your purpose as a communicator.

To communicate is to do more than just send words. To communicate is to adapt your whole personality to the effort of arousing certain thoughts and feelings in the mind of another.

5. *Communication is a receiver phenomenon.* Although this book places special emphasis on the role of the speaker, in reality it is what the receiver does with the speaker's message, how he or she responds, that is at the heart of the communication process. Communication does not take place unless another person receives and responds to someone else's symbolic behavior. The speaker must keep the receiver in mind at all times. In the speech communication situation, the sender of the message knows the desired response *before* sending the message. The goal of attaining a predetermined response underscores the idea that communication is a receiver phenomenon. One test of your effectiveness is whether or not you obtained your desired response.

6. *Communication is a process.* During the last few pages we have talked about the *communication process* as often as we have talked about communication.

Process implies that sender, message, and receiver do not remain constant before, during, or after the message is sent. Communication is not static. Past, present, and future blend together as do all of the ingredients of communication. To touch one aspect of communication is to touch them all. We would be incredibly naive to assume that our listeners are passively waiting for us to come into their lives—simply waiting for us to influence them. You know from your own experiences that if you are talking to yourself, or talking to someone else, you cannot abruptly stop and begin something new. What usually happens is that past, present, and future are fused together.

Successful communicators are well aware of the fact that their receivers are engaged in some other activity moments before becoming listeners. The implications of this situation remind the communicator that a listener's mood prior to interaction is often as significant as his or her attitude toward the topic. Being cognizant of the process approach to communication keeps a speaker from taking the listener for granted; at the same time it alerts the speaker to the issues of motivation, language, interest, and material.

7. *Communication is complex.* We can say unequivocally that as authors we have failed if, after you have read this first chapter, you do not agree with the axiom that communication is complex. It is a process that calls for the simultaneous production of a number of intricate and interdependent activities. If communication were a linear phenomenon, with one action producing one response, the issue of complexity would not arise.

Furthermore, communication contains many variables. In a sense this chapter attempts to catalog a few of those variables, such as the many aspects of personality that each person brings to an encounter, the diverse forms that messages can take, and the influence of context on communication. Each of these components, when analyzed, offers ample evidence for the assertion that communication is a complicated process.

The Ingredients of Communication

Although each communication situation differs in some ways from every other one, we can isolate certain elements that all communication situations have in common. Every time you talk to your neighbor, or every time you deliver a speech, these ingredients of communication are present. What are they?

The communication act has to originate from a *source.* You, as the source, want to express yourself—to pass on your feelings, to convey information, to give directions, to obtain agreement, to get something done, or to relate an idea. You have something *within yourself* that you want to share with others.

The communicator's idea, which to this point has been privately held, is now *encoded*—put into a code, a systematic set of symbols that can be transferred from person to person. The procedure of translating ideas, feelings, and information into a code is called encoding.

The idea, now represented by a set of symbols, is the source's *message.* The message is the essential part of the communication process—the subject matter to be communicated. It is the message, in written or spoken language, that is the symbolic representation of the source's idea.

The message must now be sent from the source. The carrier or medium of the message is called the *channel*. Channels can appear in such forms as graphic signs, light vibrations, and air vibrations.

Even though the message at this point has been sent, communication has not yet taken place, for there must be another ingredient, someone to whom the message is directed, the *receiver*.

For the receiver to understand the message, to react, he or she must *decode*, or retranslate, the source's message, putting it into a code that the receiver can use.

Communication takes place within a particular *context* and *setting*. As you know from personal experience, the place of an act often controls many aspects of that act. The same words spoken at a party may take on different meanings if uttered in a classroom. The locale of communication, be it hallway or church, can influence such things as which channels we employ (speaking, writing), our purpose (persuasion, information, enjoyment), and the roles we play (student at school, nurse at hospital, boss at work). Even the number of people present in the communication environment can have an effect. We often talk differently to one person than we do to one hundred.

As senders of messages we usually perceive the response people make to the messages we generate. They can respond with words, silent actions, or both. It matters little; what is important is that our message, as a stimulus, produces a response that we take into account. The perception of the response created by our message is called *feedback*.

The term *feedback* applies directly to (1) the reactions you obtain from your listeners and (2) your efforts in adapting yourself to these perceived reactions. The term was originally used only in the literature of engineering and cybernetics to designate the return of information to the machine so that the machine could adjust itself to changing conditions. A thermostat is an example of a device that employs feedback. As information related to the original message (heat) is returned to the machine, an act is performed enabling the machine to readjust—to shut off the heater when the air is hot and to turn it on when the air is cold. The source is making adjustments because of the information it is receiving.

Feedback provides the communicator with essential information concerning his or her success in accomplishing desired objectives. In so doing, feedback controls future messages. Whether talking to one or one hundred, the speaker has the two-fold task of (1) observing and interpreting audience reactions and (2) readjusting the next message in light of observations and interpretations.

Dean C. Barnlund, in his book *Interpersonal Communication: Survey and Studies,* offers the most succinct statement concerning the value of and the need for effective feedback in human communication. He writes,

> The timing and amount of feedback, the positive or negative value it carries, and the interpretation made of it—all affect the degree of understanding achieved through communication. The data suggests that when receivers are encouraged to respond with questions, comments, correc-

tions, or even counter arguments, greater confidence and mutual respect are likely to result.

The sender is not the only source sending messages to the receiver. Each situation is also characterized by what we call *competing stimuli*. Competing stimuli are all those other messages vying for the listener's attention. Noise or talk coming from another source are examples of competing stimuli. Most of us as listeners are constantly attending to many messages at the same time. The successful communicator is one who realizes he or she is competing with other stimuli and works to overcome these obstacles.

Our final item for discussion is not an ingredient of communication, but an observation regarding how communication actually works. An accurate description of human communication must allow for the fact that the responses people make to messages do not occur as single, one-dimensional entities. There are *levels of responses*. This means that we usually respond in more than one way. Let us assume that someone tells you that driving a motorcycle is dangerous and that you should not purchase one. At one level—the cognitive level—you agree with the person. Yet while that person is talking, you discover that you have some bad feelings about him or her—feelings that you keep to yourself. This is a type of conscious unstated response. When the person is finished, you reply that perhaps you should think the entire issue over. Here we have a verbally expressed response. A few weeks later you find that you have still other feelings about motorcycles. This is another level of response—your subconscious is reacting.

Let us construct a very transparent situation and observe all of the ingredients of communication in operation. Suppose you, as the *source,* enter a professor's office (*context*) and attempt to persuade her that you should have received a higher grade on your last examination. (You have a reason for engaging in communication.) Your nervous system orders your speech mechanism to construct a message to gain the support you want. At the same time the professor's phone rings (*competing stimuli*), your speech mechanism, serving as part of the *encoding process,* produces the following *message*, "If you have some free time I would like to talk to you about my last examination." The message is transmitted via sound waves through the air so the *receiver* can hear it. The sound waves constitute the *channel*. Your professor hears your message and, employing her nervous system, tries to find meaning in what you said (*decoding*). She now *responds* to you by saying "Please come in and sit down." (She gives *feedback* based on your message.)

Our enumeration of the ingredients of communication could extend for the remainder of this book, for communication is highly complex and multidimensional—it is not subject to simple analysis. Factors such as perception, motivation, communication skills, knowledge level, and social systems, all play a role in the process. We have merely isolated the factors that are common and dominant in the final response made by the receiver of the message. We will return to these elements, and others, as we weave our way through the principles and skills needed in successful communication.

Ethics—The Responsibility of Communication

It may have become evident during the last few pages that there is a direct relationship between communication and ethical responsibilities. We have repeatedly stressed that communication is something that persons do with each other, and that this behavior produces a response that has an effect. Perceiving any message, because of the nature of our complex nervous systems, involves in varying degrees changes of behavior on the parts of both sender and receiver. Each party is gaining entry into the other's life. Ordway Tead, in his book *Administration: Its Purpose and Performance,* observes:

> Tampering with personal drives and desires is a moral act even if its upshot is not a far-reaching one, or is a beneficial result. To seek to persuade behavior into a new direction may be wholly justifiable, and the result in terms of behavior consequences may be salutary. But the judgment of benefit or detriment is not for the communicator safely to reach by himself. He is assuming a moral responsibility. And he had better be aware of the area with which he concerns himself and the responsibility he assumes. He should be willing to assert as to any given new policy, "I stand behind this as having good personal consequences for the individuals whom it will affect." That judgment speaks a moral concern and desired moral outcome.

What Tead, and we, are talking about is ethical standards related to the production of messages that influence other persons. By ethics we mean a mode of conduct based on high moral standards. As members of a culture that has given us various moral values and principles, most of us are aware of the constituents of these high standards, and the responsibilities that go with carrying out these moral principles. These responsibilities are compounded as the group we are addressing grows in size. Our audience may range from a handful of friends to a large conference or convention. This social responsibility was never more important than in our own time, when television and radio make it possible for a single speaker to influence the actions and the thinking of millions of persons.

The power of speech to influence minds has for centuries caused grave apprehensions. The crux of the worry is this: the means of changing behavior are so potent that, in the hands of evil or ignorant people, they may be used to induce an audience to act in ways that are unwise or unjust. One of the most astute rebuttals to this position was written by Aristotle over two thousand years ago. In *The Rhetoric,* Aristotle asserts that the art of persuasion (changing behavior) is good in itself, but can be used either for good or bad ends:

> If it is urged that an abuse of the rhetorical faculty can work great mischief, the same charge can be brought against all good things (save virtue itself), and especially against the most useful things such as strength, health, wealth, and military skill. Rightly employed, they work the greatest blessings; and wrongly employed, they work the utmost harm.

The Sender

While discussing the ethics of communication we must understand that the evils, if they occur, are brought forth by humans, not by the processes of communication. The devices and means used by speakers are indeed their own responsibility. The issue becomes one of speakers realizing that they have an obligation to their listeners as well as to themselves.

Accordingly, a number of indispensable questions should be considered each time you initiate a communication act.

1. *Have you investigated the subject fully before expressing opinions about it?* In your speech class and in this textbook you will discover that serious research and analysis is an important part of successful, effective, and ethical speaking. Because you should speak only from a sound background, you have an obligation to be silent if you do not understand what you are called upon to discuss. "I don't know" is a valuable and too rarely used phrase. When you do speak, you have a duty to be morally thoughtful—to know what you are talking about before you try to influence the thinking of your associates.

2. *Do you respect the intelligence of the people with whom you are speaking?* You should never distort or "adjust" the truth because you think the audience will not notice the distortion. Any misrepresentation can easily cause an audience to reject you and your cause. The audience's perception of you as a good person will greatly influence the success or failure of your communication act. Volumes of experimental research indicate that what the audience thinks of you as a person can either hinder or aid your cause. Aristotle, Quintilian, and Cicero, the great speech theorists of classical Greece and Rome, agree—the speaker whose prestige is high in the eyes of the audience has a better chance of gaining acceptance for ideas presented than the speaker whose prestige is low.

3. *Have you been ethical in the treatment of content?* Half-truths, outdated information, lies, and unsupported assertions are some of the devices used by the unethical speaker. Unethical speakers seek acceptance of their ideas but are unwilling to have them tested by the rules of logic.

4. *Are you aware that what you say will influence others?* You are altering and adjusting the attitudes and feelings of others. A constant awareness of this fact will allow you to reevaluate your language and your goals.

5. *Have you tried to be interesting?* We do not mean to imply that all speakers, at all times, must be humorous and entertaining, but we do mean that all attempts at communication should be worthy of the receiver's time and energy. It is important to remember always that you are asking someone to stop whatever they are doing and give you one second or one hour of their time. Try to deserve that time.

The Receiver

Ethical responsibility in the speech act is not borne by the speaker alone. The listener as well as the speaker shares in the moral issues of the speech act. Much ethical responsibility lies in listening itself. If one is to judge, evaluate, accept, and respond to the remarks of others, he or she must first of all hear and understand those remarks. It is indeed unfair, as well as unethical, for us to act on a message to which we have not fully attended. Therefore, a listener's first obligation is to offer full attention to the speaker. Admittedly this is much easier to write about than to carry out. Each communication act is characterized by countless distractions, but these must be overcome if we are to fairly analyze what we hear. We will have much more to say about listening in chapter 4, but now our appeal to the reader is simply *try to pay attention*.

Once you have paid attention, you are better able to locate the techniques and devices of the unethical speaker. You will also be able to make valid decisions on what is being proposed.

A Preview of Principles

Although we may appear to make a rather sudden shift in emphasis, we are only moving from theory to practice. Up to this point, we have tried to explain some of the theory behind human communication so that you might have an understanding of what communication is and how it works. But as we have said, *communication is an activity that persons engage in; it is something we do.* Therefore, we shall now focus our attention on that doing. We shall look at those aspects of communication concerned with the practical phases of human communication. This function of theory and practice should be perceived as a natural and orderly progression rather than as a major philosophical leap. Everything we have said thus far about communication and ethics leads to the conclusion that becoming a more effective communicator is the goal of everyone sharing ideas and information with other persons. In short, we take part in communication so that we can have an influence. Let us now talk about how you can develop those skills that will contribute to greater efficiency in carrying out that influence.

Organizing Your Ideas

Effective speaking, whether to one person or to a large group, demands careful thought and preparation. In your speech class you may face the problem of having to give speeches in the first few days of the semester before you have had an opportunity to study and absorb all the principles treated in this book. For this reason, we shall briefly look at some steps you should take in preparing your first speeches. *The steps of speech preparation to be examined at this point constitute the basic themes of entire chapters later in the text.* The order of the steps is not nearly as rigid as our listing might suggest. You may, for example, discover situations where analysis of the audience precedes analysis of the purpose of the speech. But regardless of the order in which you consider the six items, a thorough preparation should include them all.

1. *Determine the purpose of your speech.* All communication is purposeful—it seeks to elicit a response from the person receiving the message. This reaction can range from enjoyment at one extreme to direct, specific action at the other. Do you want your listener to understand a concept, agree with a concept, or act upon a concept? Think of your speech as an instrument of utility—a means of getting a reaction. A considerable amount of valuable energy and time can be saved by keeping your purpose clearly in mind.

Knowing what you want your audience to do or feel will influence what you say and how you say it.

2. *Choose and limit the topic.* In speech class you may, on occasion, be assigned a subject area, but in most cases your instructor will let you make your own selections. In speaking situations outside the class, you may be asked to speak on a specific subject, or you may simply be asked to speak. In all of these situations observing a few basic principles will enable you to choose the proper subject and limit its scope to meet the demands of the audience, the occasion, and your purpose.

   a. Select a topic worthy of your time and the time of your audience. No listener enjoys hearing about a subject that is insignificant or trivial. Talk about subjects, issues, and controversies that affect the lives of your listeners.

   b. Select a topic that interests you. Unless you are interested you will not be sufficiently motivated to accomplish your purpose. Preparation will be a tedious task, and the delivery of your speech may mirror an apathetic attitude. Pick a topic in which you are interested (or in which you can *become* interested), and you will find that the results are apt to be contagious.

   c. Choose a subject your listeners will find interesting or one you can make interesting to them. Think about your listeners, what they like, how they feel, and what they know. The effective speaker can, by knowing the audience, select topics that will interest them and also adapt new information to their interests.

   d. Select a topic you can deal with adequately in the time you have at your disposal. It is obvious that the subject area of "Peace in the World" cannot be intelligently discussed in a five- or six-minute speech.

3. *Analyze your audience and the occasion of your speech.* The listener is as much a part of the communication process as the speaker. A good speaker discovers all he or she can about the people who make up the audience and the occasion that has brought them together. The speaker then prepares, adapts, and adjusts his or her speech to the specific communication situation.

   The process of analyzing the audience and occasion is discussed more thoroughly in the next chapter. However, we may draw a few guidelines to assist you in your early speeches.

   a. Learn all you can about the place where the communication will occur. How will the audience be seated? Interaction will be influenced by the position you take in regard to the other members of the gathering, the size of the room, its shape, and other physical conditions as well.

   b. Learn the purpose of the gathering. Is it a regular weekly meeting, is it a special meeting, or is it a spontaneous gathering?

   c. Learn as much as you can about the people to whom you will speak. Knowing their age, sex, educational background, occupation, needs, and attitudes enables you to adapt your remarks to the demands of the specific listeners you are facing.

4. *Find the material for your speech.* There are basically two places to look for materials—within yourself for what you already know, and outside yourself to discover what you do not know. What you know, in many instances, may not be enough to accomplish your objective. In addition, two individuals seeing the same situation may interpret what they see in different ways. It is therefore necessary to augment your observations with those from other sources. In chapter 5 we talk about finding materials in books, magazines, newspapers, and other storehouses of information. At this point it is important to remember that the successful speaker is seldom the one who "talks off the top of his head."

5. *Organize and arrange the speech.* Now that you have the ingredients of your message—the materials—you must arrange them so that they make sense to your listener. In most instances, if you are thorough in your search for materials, you will find far more than you can possibly use in the time allotted to you. You will therefore be faced with two problems. First, you will have to decide what material you want to use. Second, you will have to make a decision concerning the organization of that material.

The purpose of your speech determines the selection and arrangement of materials you choose to include. You will want to include material that directly relates to and supports the main idea of your talk as well as materials that add interest to your ideas.

Arrangement of materials centers around the three parts of the speech—introduction, body, and conclusion. The body of the speech should be planned first. This includes marshalling all the supporting material designed to establish the central idea of the speech. The specific problems of selecting and arranging the ideas that constitute the body of the speech will be discussed in detail in chapter 6.

The main purpose of the introduction is to gain the attention and interest of the listeners, to put them at ease, and to help them focus their attention upon your speech. The material you select should accomplish those objectives.

The conclusion ends the speech gracefully and in a compelling manner. It may take the form of a summary, an illustration, an appeal, a challenge, or several other endings depending upon the purpose of your speech.

One of the chief organizational aids is the outline. It enables you to visualize your material in a clear and logical order. It lets you see what materials you have and aids you in sorting the relevant from the irrelevant. An outline helps you avoid the aimless, disorganized thinking characteristic of many speeches.

6. *Practice your speech aloud.* If you desire to have your message understood and your purpose accomplished, you must practice aloud. You should deliver your speech three or four times before you present it to the audience. It is important that you avoid memorizing while you practice. *Learn* the main ideas of the speech, rather than trying to memorize, word for word, large sections of the body. Practice your speech aloud and allow time for changes if, after hearing it, you decide that you need to make alterations.

Presenting Your Ideas

In chapter 3 some very specific principles and skills will be suggested for improving the delivery of your ideas. At this early point we shall simply suggest some general practices useful to you as you begin speech training.

1. *Have a good mental attitude.* A good mental attitude toward the presentation of your ideas will make the job of delivering your speech much simpler and much more pleasurable to you and your audience.

    Do not be unduly alarmed about stage fright. Nervousness is a common trait among beginning speakers. But even the "expert" experiences shaking knees, wet palms, shortness of breath, throat tightness, or increased pulse rate. The following suggestions may help to allay your apprehensions.
    a. Realize that some nervousness is normal and this may, in itself, help to reduce nervousness.
    b. Recognize that the audience is your friend and that, in speech class, you can be well assured that everyone is working for you.
    c. Come before your audience fully prepared. If you have a doubt about your speech and your preparation, it is likely to manifest in nervousness.
    d. Try to feel confident. Your attitude toward yourself is the single most important variable in successful communication. Do not rush through your speech; have the notion that you are talking with your audience. Feel free to pause whenever you desire. Do not be too embarrassed if you find that some of your words are not coming out as you wish. In many instances you may be the only one to realize what is happening. Oftentimes the acknowledgment of a "flub" will relax you and your audience.
    e. Nervous tension can be reduced by having some meaningful physical action in your speech. Try walking during your talk as a method of relaxing and releasing nervous strain.
    f. Remember, even if you are nervous you will be able to finish your speech. Too many speakers tell themselves during their speech that they are just too nervous to go on, only to find out at the conclusion of their talk, that the presentation went very well. So keep on going.
    g. Take comfort in the fact that there is a relationship between improvement, practice, and nervousness. Our students tell us that as they become more proficient in speech making their nervousness, and all of its outward manifestations, seems to lessen. In short, the more you speak, the less you will be nervous.
2. *Be direct.* Looking directly at your audience serves two vital functions. First, directness adds to a lively sense of communication. It tells your listeners that you care about accomplishing your purpose and that you care about them. You know from personal experience that the speaker who gazes at the floor or out the window reflects a lack of interest in his topic and a lack of concern for the audience and the entire speech situation. As in casual conversation, it is helpful to look at the person with whom you are talking. Establishing rapport between sender and receiver is necessary if there is to be fruitful communication. Second, by looking directly at the audience you gain valuable insight into how your message is being received. Successful communi-

cators use the information they receive by observing their audience and making adjustments based on the audience's reactions. Whether you are talking to one person or a large group, your perception of their response to your original message (feedback) will play a significant role in selecting, arranging, and sending future messages.

3. *Be physically animated.* Try to avoid stiffness and a rigid appearance. Your posture should be comfortable and natural. Many beginning speakers develop mannerisms such as shifting their weight from leg to leg or resting on the podium. These activities call attention to themselves and direct attention away from the speech.

Gestures are quite useful in conveying thought or emotion or in reinforcing oral expression. They increase the speaker's self-confidence, ease nervousness, aid in the communication of ideas, and help to hold attention. Relax and be yourself, and you will learn that gesturing comes naturally.

4. *Use vocal variety.* Just as movement and gesture help reinforce ideas, so does an animated voice. If there is sameness of rate, pitch, loudness, and quality, we have full-fledged monotony. Vary as many of these elements of voice as you can, consonant with conveying the full meaning of your ideas and emotions.

Avoid unpleasant and distracting mannerisms such as "and-a," and "uh." These and other meaningless vocalizations call attention to themselves and detract from your message.

Good delivery is simply direct, friendly, conversational, animated, and enthusiastic.

Preview of the Book

Determining the sequence of chapters for this book might well have been our most difficult task, for any sequence we selected would have to be linear. Words and ideas must be uttered one at a time, with each waiting its turn. However, in speech communication many things are going on at the *same time.* For example, you are using *evidence* that is *interesting, appealing,* and *well-organized* while you are employing your *audience analysis* and good *delivery.* In the best of worlds, we would present all of the chapters and all of the principles at the same time. But we cannot. Forced to make the choice of which principles would be presented first and which would have to wait, we based our decisions on the philosophy stated in the preface of this book—to meet the student at his or her current stage of communication development. That development, like most evolutionary stages or learning processes, reflects a movement from the uncomplicated to the intricate. Thus we shall progress from the materials needed in the early stages of your training to the ideas and content necessary for more advanced instruction.

The book is divided into four closely related sections, with each section separated into several chapters. The first section, "Preliminary Considerations," is divided into four chapters dealing with materials germane to your initial exposure to training in speech communication. Underlying chapter 1 is the assumption that successful doing rests firmly upon understanding. Hence, the chapter opens with an explanation of what communication is and how some of its basic components function during interaction. In addition, we preview some basic steps in preparing and presenting a speech so that you may begin your practical training at once.

Chapter 2 offers some initial information on how to select a general and specific purpose, how to choose a method of speaking, and how to analyze the people with whom you are to talk. Very likely your classroom instructor will offer other guidelines that relate to your specific group.

Chapter 3 looks at how your message is affected by the distance between you and your listeners, by your dress, appearance, and other visual factors, by your actions and movements, and by the way you manage your voice.

Chapter 4 looks at another activity fundamental to human communication—listening. Knowing that you will be listening from the first day of your training onward, we have placed our discussion of this activity early in our text.

Part 2, "Your Ideas," assumes that you have begun to master many of the skills discussed in part 1 and that you are now ready for more advanced concepts and activities. Chapter 5 maintains that we need valid and concrete evidence if we are to affect the beliefs, attitudes, and actions of others. How, for example, can we convince an audience that vitamin C helps arrest the common cold if we have not researched and documented our claim?

Chapter 6 considers the organization of messages. Even the best ideas, if poorly organized, will not hold an audience's attention at the desired level.

The final chapter of this section, chapter 7, focuses on language. Recognizing its capabilities and limitations is central to any substantial improvement in the quality of our oral communication. We must learn to use language so that it accurately represents reality and does so in a vivid and compelling way.

By the time you have completed the first two sections of the book, you should be ready to cope with the complexities of two very specific communication situations in which you exercise an influence over other persons. The concern of part 3 is informing and persuading. Chapter 8 investigates those occasions when our purpose is to increase someone's knowledge. Chapter 9 explores those situations when our influence changes someone's beliefs, attitudes, or behavior.

Part 4, the final section of the book, deals with unique communication environments. Chapter 10 examines those instances when we present speeches on special occasions, such as after-dinner speeches and impromptu speeches. Chapter 11 concentrates on small group communication, dealing with those situations in which we interact with several others in searching for solutions to problems.

Appendix A discusses one of the most important communication situations you will ever face, the job interview; and Appendix B provides some of the common fill-in forms used in individual and group evaluations.

Having previewed the main features of the book and having suggested the rationale for the chapter sequence, we are now ready to accomplish the main purpose of this text—to make you a more effective communicator.

Summary

In this chapter we introduced the fields of communication and speech and presented a few elementary principles as a means of providing you with the essential tools of effective speech-making.

Communication, in its broadest sense, is the process of sending and receiving messages. All communication involves the following ingredients: a source, encoding, a message, a channel, a receiver, and decoding. When these ingredients are combined in human communication, certain working principles emerge: (1) communication is a two-way process, (2) communication seeks to elicit a response, (3) communication is a symbolic process, (4) communication is a real-life process, (5) communication is a receiver phenomenon, (6) communication is a process, (7) communication is complex.

The responsibility and seriousness of communication are so great that communicators must be of the highest ethical character. They should know the subject, respect the intelligence of their listeners, treat their content in an honest manner, and realize that they are changing behavior—both theirs and the receiver's.

In preparing early speeches, remember to determine the purpose of the speech, choose and limit the topic, analyze the audience and the speaking occasion, gather material, organize and arrange the material, and practice aloud.

In delivering speeches it is essential that you have a good mental attitude, that you be direct, that you be physically animated, and that you use vocal variety.

Suggested Readings

Berlo, David K. *The Process of Communication*. New York: Holt, Rinehart and Winston, 1960. Chapters 1–2.

Brooks, William D. *Speech Communication*. 3d ed. Dubuque, IA: Wm. C. Brown Company Publishers, 1978. Introduction.

Burgoon, Michael, and Ruffner, Michael. *Human Communication*. New York: Holt, Rinehart and Winston, 1978. Chapter 1.

Nilsen, Thomas R. *Ethics of Speech Communication*. 2d ed. Indianapolis: Bobbs-Merrill, 1974.

Verdeber, Rudolph F. *Communicate!* Belmont, CA: Wadsworth Publishing, 1975. Chapter 1.

Webb, Ralph, Jr. *Interpersonal Speech Communication*. Englewood Cliffs, NJ: Prentice-Hall, 1975. Chapter 1.

Zacharis, John C., and Bender, Coleman C. *Speech Communication*. New York: John Wiley and Sons, 1976. Chapters 1–2.

Your First Speeches
Getting Started

Every thought which genius and piety throw into the world alters the world.
  Ralph Waldo Emerson

In chapter 1 we noted that most communication is initiated because an individual seeks to accomplish a purpose or fulfill a goal. In public speaking, which is simply a specialized form of human communication, the speaker wants a specific response from the audience and communicates in order to secure that response. However, one major characteristic of public speaking often sets it apart from other types of interaction. In public speaking, the speaker has a *preconceived* purpose—a purpose that has been decided *before* the talk begins. Although many interpersonal situations also contain this element, it is not nearly as conspicuous as it is in public speaking. Imagine, if you will, trying to talk to an audience without having a clear idea of what you wanted them to know. By the time you concluded your remarks, they, as well as you, would be frustrated and confused as you drifted from point to point. What is needed is a unifying thread weaving all the pieces together. That thread is the preconceived purpose. Therefore, to be a successful speaker you must decide upon and clarify your purpose before you send your message. By deciding upon the response you want from your audience, you can better select the ideas, organizational patterns, language, and delivery methods that will enable you to reach your goal.

Given this principle—that the public speech should be purposive—let us turn our attention to the initial stages of speech preparation. An obvious question at this point is, "What shall I talk about?" There are several ways of answering that question.

Taking an Inventory

First, in many instances *you are asked to speak on a particular subject*. On those occasions subject selection has been done for you. If your professor says to you, "Please give a talk on the history of rhetoric," or your employer asks you to "explain the company's new computer billing system to the persons in your department," your questions regarding subject selection are answered. Your job, then, is to narrow the subject to fit the specific audience and the various constraints imposed by time.

There will also be speaking situations when *the occasion itself dictates the subject area*. A political rally for a specific candidate or a eulogy are instances where the occasion is instrumental in picking the topic.

As you might suspect, in many instances *you alone must select the subject*. Potential subjects should, as you now know, be screened with an eye to their value and interest to the audience and the speaker, and with the occasion and the time limits in mind. But where do we locate those potential subjects in the first place? Many beginning speakers are overwhelmed at the prospect of talking on any subject they want. Most speech instructors spend many of their office hours trying to help students pick a topic. Yet if the student would not panic, would slow down, and reflect for a little while, the task of topic selection would not be such drudgery. Let us suggest a few procedures to follow that will help you make intelligent choices regarding the general subject of your talks.

Begin your search for a topic by reviewing your personal interests and convictions. Many students find it helpful to begin by taking an inventory of their experiences and attitudes. This inventory often comes early in the semester and is best carried out by listing some information about yourself. For example:

Personal Experiences
    travel
    employment
    education

Abilities
    artistic
    athletic
    intellectual

Hobbies
    politics
    CB radio
    sports cars
    animals
    camping
    drama
    sports

Beliefs
    abortion
    capital punishment
    drinking
    wildlife preservation
    pollution
    race relations
    taxes
    foreign investments
    urban decay
    crime
    education
    space travel
    general education requirements

If you find that your personal inventory does not yield a topic, there are a number of other things you might try. For example, turn to sources outside yourself—read news magazines and local newspapers to assess current events. Ask questions of your friends and professors. In addition, most college campuses have a variety of activities that can help generate topics—guest speakers, controversial debates, career opportunity lectures, and the like, are just a few events that can produce subjects. However, in the final analysis, it is usually your personal decision that serves as the stimulus for your talk. You must determine, and eventually formulate, your reason and purpose for engaging in communication.

Formulating a General Purpose

The classification of speech purposes has long been a subject of controversy among rhetoricians and teachers of communication. Since ancient times disagreements have arisen over the number and the nature of these purposes. However, critical study of the historical arguments leads us to conclude that there are three general speech purposes—to *inform,* to *persuade,* and to *entertain.* These three purposes apply equally to public and private communication.

We should remember as we discuss these speech purposes that we are in reality talking about responses we *desire* from our audience. We must take into account the obvious fact that all individuals are different, and therefore what is intended by the speaker as a speech to *inform* may well *persuade* or *entertain* certain members of the audience. Although all three types of speeches will be treated in greater detail later in the book, they are introduced now to offer you some working principles early in your speech training.

Informative Speeches

The purpose of informative communication is to increase the receiver's knowledge and understanding of a subject. Informative speeches may also entertain or change beliefs. A speaker whose immediate purpose is to impart information often uses amusing or dramatic illustrations to entertain his or her audience, thus holding their attention. Moreover, information, even if it consists only of "facts," may lead to changes of belief and eventually to physical action, although such results may not be a part of the speaker's purpose.

In informative speaking, the speaker's main concern is having the audience learn and remember the information presented. The teacher talking to a class or the manager of a department store explaining the duties of a job to staff members are both engaged in informative speaking. How much the listener knows at the conclusion of a talk is the real test of the speech to inform.

Some examples of informative subjects would be:

1. The procedures to be followed for adding new courses to the college curriculum.
2. How to grow vegetables in an organic garden.
3. The workings of a pollution-free engine.
4. An explanation of California's marijuana laws.
5. A review of the life of Martin Luther King.
6. An analysis of the problem of mental illness on the college campus.

Persuasive Speeches

The major function of the persuasive speech is to induce the audience to think, feel, or act in a manner selected by the speaker. You may want your listeners to discard old beliefs or form new ones, or you may want merely to strengthen opinions that they already hold. You may even want them to take some action. The salesperson uses the speech to persuade as a means of getting the customer to buy a coat. The person asking for a raise, the young college student asking for a date, the wife trying to get her husband to mow the lawn, the Red Cross volunteer pleading for funds, the teacher trying to get his or her class to study— all are trying to persuade someone to do something. An analysis of your own daily life will disclose the frequent need for effective persuasion.

The following are examples of persuasive subjects:

1. Final examinations in our colleges should be abolished.
2. Students should be given college credit for campaigning in behalf of political candidates.
3. Birth control pills should be distributed by the college Health Services Department.

4. All college courses on this campus should be on an elective basis.
5. The United States should condemn the actions of Nicaragua's government.
6. There should be a national law legalizing abortion.

Entertaining Speeches

The third major type of speech has the purpose of entertaining the audience. We are using the word *entertainment* in its broadest sense to include anything that stimulates a pleasurable response, whether it be humorous or dramatic.

The speaker wants the persons present to have an enjoyable time listening to the speech. There is no concern that they learn a great deal or that they change their mind in one direction or another. Entertainment is the purpose of many after-dinner speeches and a favorite type of speech for the comedian.

Some subjects that lend themselves to humorous treatment are:

1. My first day as a college student.
2. My favorite method for securing a blind date.
3. The gourmet food served in the college cafeteria.
4. How to "see" San Francisco on fifty cents a day.
5. How to write a political speech.
6. The best way to avoid giving a speech.

Formulating the Specific Purpose

The general reaction you want to secure from your audience may be stated in terms of informing, persuading, or entertaining. But the particular and immediate reaction that you seek must be precisely formulated into a *specific purpose*. *The specific purpose describes the exact nature of the response you want from your audience.* It states specifically what you want your audience to know, feel, believe, or do.

There are three requirements a good specific purpose should meet. It should contain *one central idea.* It should be *clear and concise.* And most important, it should be *worded in terms of the audience response desired.*

When your general purpose is to *inform*, your specific purpose might be:

1. To have the audience understand the important aspects of student government.
2. To have the audience understand the fundamentals of boating safety.
3. To have the audience understand the history of the modern women's rights movement.

If your general purpose is to *persuade*, your specific purpose might be:

1. To get the audience to give money to a college fund to beautify the campus.
2. To get the audience to agree that the United States should withdraw all its troops from Germany.
3. To get the audience to agree that we should have a Department of Black Studies on campus.

If your general purpose is to *entertain,* your specific purpose might be:

1. To hear the audience laugh at the "clear" statements of some political leaders.

2. To have the audience enjoy hearing about the best ways to stay out of college.

3. To have the audience enjoy, vicariously, your trip to the Jazz Music Festival.

You might find it helpful to write down your specific purpose on a sheet of paper. This will give you a constant target at which to aim. It allows you, at a glance, to see if the material you have gathered, and the organization of that material, directly relates to your specific purpose.

We remind you that we shall return to the speech to inform in chapter 8, the speech to persuade in chapter 9, and the speech to entertain in chapter 10. For now our purpose has been simply to make you cognizant of the importance of deciding on an audience response early in your preparation.

Choosing the Method of Speaking

Regardless of your background, knowledge, or skill, each time you speak is a unique experience. An effective communicator will recognize these differences and prepare specifically for each particular occasion. Included in his or her thought and preparation will be an analysis of the type of delivery best suited for the subject, audience, and occasion.

There are four fundamental ways of presenting a speech: (1) reading it from a manuscript, (2) delivering it from memory, (3) delivering it in an impromptu manner, and (4) delivering it extemporaneously. Many speaking situations may call for a combination of two or three of these types.

Speaking from a Manuscript

In this form of delivery you read your speech directly from a manuscript. In some instances this type of delivery is essential and appropriate. For example, on radio and television many speakers have to be accountable for their remarks and must be extremely accurate in what they say and in the amount of time they take to say it. Indeed, all speakers should be accountable and accurate, but the mass-media speaker has to be able to make instant referrals to sources and materials. At conventions and business meetings the manuscript is helpful for the speaker who would like a speech to be circulated.

There are certain advantages to manuscript speaking in addition to those cited above. The obvious advantage is that it puts no strain on your memory. Your speech is before you and you need only read it. A second advantage is that the manuscript, having been written well in advance of the speech situation, enables you to be very selective and meticulous in your style and choice of materials. The manuscript speech should be free from vague phrases, rambling sentences, and inappropriate colloquialism.

There are also serious disadvantages to this type of delivery. One marked disadvantage is that you often lose sight of the importance of communication. You read your remarks and many times fail to establish rapport with your listeners. The manuscript becomes more significant than the audience. When this happens all eye contact and all sense of spontaneity are forgotten.

For the beginning speech student trying to acquire the ability of sharing personal ideas and feelings, the manuscript type of delivery is not nearly as helpful—nor is it likely to be as effective—as the impromptu and extemporaneous methods. But if you find occasions for the manuscript, remember to (1) write your speech for listeners and not for readers, (2) practice reading aloud, (3) use eye contact and other techniques of effective delivery, and (4) concentrate on getting your *ideas* across, not just the *words*. (We will have more to say about the manuscript speech in chapter 10.)

Speaking from Memory

The memorized speech, much like the manuscript speech, allows you the advantage of a carefully thought out and well-worded speech. Every single word is committed to memory and this, of course, frees you from the manuscript. One problem of the memorized speech is that this "freedom" often leads to mechanical delivery and the presentation of what often appears as a "canned" speech.

The memorized speech is also dangerous because you are apt to forget the entire speech. It is often difficult to recall the exact wording; and if you forget one word, you may forget the entire speech.

Even though the memorized speech permits a careful ordering of your thoughts and materials, it should nevertheless be avoided by the beginning speaker. Training in the other methods will offer the beginning student practice in speech situations that more closely resemble real-life occasions.

Impromptu Delivery

When you are asked to speak on the spur of the moment, without advance notice or time for specific preparation, you are engaging in impromptu speaking. Much of our conversation is nothing more than a series of short, impromptu talks.

In facing an impromptu situation you must quickly tie together all of your thoughts in a few seconds or minutes. The best preparation for impromptu speaking is being well informed and having practice in the prepared speaking situations. The speaker who knows how to prepare a speech when time is *not* a factor in preparation will have little trouble in making the transition to the spur-of-the-moment occasion. We will examine the problems, principles, and skills of impromptu speaking in an individualized manner in chapter 10. However, because many speech classes start with some impromptu speaking, you might want to turn to that chapter early in the term.

Extemporaneous Delivery

The extemporaneous delivery is often referred to as the "middle course." This particular speech form is by far the most desirable of the four we have listed. Therefore, we will examine it in some detail.

Extemporaneous speaking has a number of characteristics that help explain both its uniqueness and its attractiveness. Extemporaneous speaking calls for the speech to be (1) researched, (2) outlined, (3) practiced, and (4) delivered in a conversational manner.

When you choose the extemporaneous method you are also making a decision concerning *research* and *preparation*. Because you know about your speaking assignment beforehand, you have time to gather the necessary information. This investigation should be complete and thorough.

Once the data is gathered, you must *organize* and *outline* the material into a clear and systematic pattern. A major advantage of the extemporaneous speech is that it is prepared in advance, and is therefore well organized. You are not asked to speak off the "top of your head," but rather are granted the luxury of time to prepare.

This time factor not only affords you an opportunity for research and organization, it also means you can practice the speech and clarify your thinking. The exact language for delivery is not memorized; instead, you must *learn the organizational pattern*, main points and subpoints. The focus, during practice, is on ideas, not specific words. Too much practice can give your speech the appearance of a formal stage performance rather than a conversation. "Canned" or artificial speeches usually seem to lack sincerity, and often the artificiality calls attention away from the content of the speech. Learning your outline does not mean memorizing your speech.

The delivery style of the extemporaneous approach is perhaps its most attractive feature. Because preparation stops short of memorization and because note cards may be used, the speaker does not have to worry about forgetting key sections of the talk. Instead, attention can be given to establishing rapport with the audience, directness, eye contact, spontaneity, and a general conversational tone.

Using Note Cards When using note cards in your extemporaneous speech, you should follow a few guidelines. First, your notes should be on small stiff cards, rather than on long sheets of paper. Small cards should not impede any of your gestures, and they will allow you to maintain eye contact with the audience. When using a sheet of paper, some speakers find themselves reading, and in so doing they may break the crucial link between sender and receiver.

Second, you should not write the entire speech on your note cards. A good rule of thumb says that you should only write down what it takes to remind you of your main points and subpoints. For example, if your topic is water pollution, your note card on the causes of the problem might say:

Water Pollution—Causes
　　1. Overpopulation
　　2. Poor Waste Disposal Methods
　　3. Lack of Concern
　　　　a. Industry
　　　　b. Public
　　　　c. Government

Third, you might want to write long quotations and statistics on your note cards. You have probably heard speakers present false or misleading information because they tried to remember a long quotation or a series of numbers and failed.

Fourth, your handwriting on the notes should be clear and easy to read. Over the years we have observed many speakers unable to use their cards, often becoming frustrated, simply because their writing was illegible. Some speakers also make the mistake of writing on both sides of their cards, therefore constantly having to flip their cards in a distracting manner.

Fifth, you may find it useful to insert a card containing a helpful hint or an important reminder. For example, speakers who talk too fast might include a card that says SLOW DOWN!!!

The shortcomings of the extemporaneous method are probably obvious to you now that we have discussed three other styles. The extemporaneous method takes time—research, outlining, and practice cannot be done in haste. And, because the speech is not written out word for word or memorized, the beginning speaker often becomes careless in his choice of language—there is a tendency to rely completely on inspiration for one's vocabulary. This particular indictment is really directed more at the misapplication of the method than at an inherent weakness in the method itself; for there is nothing in the explanation of this form of speaking that should allow you to believe that language is unimportant. In fact, the notion of preparation and practice implies that all phases of the communication process are of equal significance.

Analyzing the Audience

Most of us can remember when we first received our driver's license. "The family car" became an issue of great importance. Reflect on the intrigue and plotting that went into your securing permission to use the car. You had a multitude of methods and devices you could use on your father as a means of gaining your desired end—the keys to the car. Arguments ranging from "Dad, I'll wash the car" to "All my friends are driving" were used on those occasions. But when it came time for you to plead your case before your mother, you most likely brought forth an entirely new set of techniques. You discovered at an early age that what accomplished your purpose with Dad often failed with Mom. When talking to your parents on topics ranging from the car to staying out late at night, you had to adjust your position, and hence your message, from person to person.

While you were considering your parents' attitude toward cars, driving, responsibility, etc., you were conducting an audience analysis. And as you changed your message on each occasion you were using the material you gained from your analysis. *Audience analysis* means, in a very practical sense, *finding out all you can about the people you are talking to or will be talking to.*

Audience analysis is at the core of all human communication. Since communication involves a type of reciprocal relationship wherein each party needs and depends on the other, you must understand the other person or persons so that you can make the necessary adjustments to your language, arguments, appeals, and evidence. Who are they? What are they like? What will they think of me and my message? These questions must be foremost in your mind during the preparation and presentation of the speech. Understanding your listeners will better enable you to adapt your message to them. As Oliver, Zelko, and Holtzman noted in their book *Communicative Speaking and Listening*, "The most significant characteristic of communication is that it must be adaptive." The speaker who presents a speech without considering the audience has very little chance of being understood or gaining support.

Audience analysis enables you to establish rapport *with* your listeners and to promote rapport *among* listeners. This you do by discovering some common denominators that exist in spite of individual and group differences. Central to this idea, and to the entire process of communication, is the concept of identification. In his *Rhetoric of Motives*, Kenneth Burke suggests, "you persuade a man only insofar as you can talk his language by speech, gesture, tonality, order, image, attitude, idea, identifying your ways with his." Successful communication must necessarily ask the speaker to "talk the language" of those he or she hopes to influence. Audience analysis allows you an opportunity to learn the language of your receivers so that you will be able to fuse your goals and purposes with theirs.

Your Listeners— What Do They Bring to Communication?

Thus far we have been discussing your potential receivers in rather abstract terms. You may even have asked yourself whether or not audience analysis is possible. In chapter 1 we noted that each individual is different from every other individual—that a person's uniqueness is his or her most universal trait. Placed in this context, your question regarding the possibility of audience analysis is indeed a valid one.

Admittedly the concept of "the audience" is an abstraction. No such creature exists. In reality what you are faced with is a group of individual auditors— who in combination make what we call an audience. Your task, if you are to be a successful speaker, is to locate their commonalities and formulate your message accordingly.

To predict audience responses to your message demands that you ask the crucial question: To what extent are the members of the audience *similar*? It is in this area of *similarities* that you must focus your energy and attention.

Perhaps the best way to begin our analysis of "similarities" is by discussing what people bring to a communication encounter, for what they bring influences how they behave during and after that encounter. You know from your own experiences that you and a friend can leave a classroom or a movie theatre together and reach different conclusions concerning the worth and merit of the event. You found the communication dull and hard to pay attention to. Your companion, receiving the same messages, was greatly entertained and completely captivated for the entire period. Or think of those occasions when you heard a speaker discussing "race relations" and decided he or she was a bigot. Yet when you shared the speaker's remarks with another member of the audience, you were surprised to hear the speaker branded a "flaming liberal." These examples, and the countless others we face each day, give credence to the notion that our backgrounds determine how we receive and respond to the remarks of others.

As you might well imagine, it is quite difficult to investigate the impact and influence of what each of us brings to a communication experience. What is manifested might be as current as what the receiver was doing *one minute before* you sent your message (for example, persons receiving bad news as they were about to walk into the room to listen to you). This "mood of the moment" could affect their response to you and your message. On the other hand, what happened to them *ten years earlier* could also have an effect on how they responded to you. We are once again left with trying to locate the essential similarities existing among the members of our audience. It is the isolating of these personality and cultural parallels that will be the main concern of this section. Once we have examined the role of personal backgrounds in communication we will discuss some areas of audience analysis that must be dealt with before each specific speaking situation.

General Concepts Because we cannot know everything about each person we meet, we must learn how to use the information we do have. What we have at the end of our audience analysis is some general information about a person's culture, group affiliations, educational level, occupation, sex, age, and the like; we do not have a long list of highly personalized characteristics. However, the general information, if we know how to use it, can tell us a great deal about the people we shall be talking to. The usefulness of this information is based on the assumption that as members of a culture or a group we share a set of norms, perceptions, attitudes, and interests with the other members of that culture or group. The task of the speaker, therefore, is to discover the affiliations of his or her audience, to make some valid generalization about those affiliations, and to adapt the material to meet the conclusions.

Many scholars of human behavior believe that most of our actions are a product of our culture and our individual experiences. These two forces, working in combination, help determine not only how we act, but also what we believe and pay attention to. Therefore, any discussion of audience analysis must include a discussion of cultural and individual determinants.

Cultural Determinants Culture is best described as the totality of learned and accumulated experience that is socially transmitted from generation to generation. Our culture gives each of us, in both conscious and subconscious ways, modes of behavior, patterns of thought, ideas and values, and many of our habits. For the communicator, the ramifications of this definition should be obvious. To understand our co-participants in the encounter, we must know something about the culture that has acted upon them during their lifetime. Where we come from, our backgrounds and experiences, help determine how we will respond to a communication situation.

Most cultures and subcultures impinge upon our personal and private histories. Figure 2.1 graphically shows the relationship between culture, subculture, and our individual biographies.

The successful communicator must have some idea how culture will manifest itself during a communication situation. Most researchers in the area of intercultural communication believe that cultures and subcultures influence values

Figure 2.1
Spheres of Influence

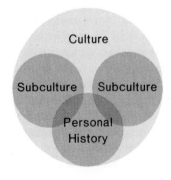

  Preliminary Considerations

and attitudes, patterns of thought, perception, language, and nonverbal behavior. Each of these areas is important enough to warrant further consideration.

The influence of cultural *attitudes* and *values* on communication should be quite apparent. A culture gives one a world view that is unique to that culture. Different cultures even have varying views regarding the roles of men and women, the relationship of individual and group, and the relationship of God and man. These and countless other examples demonstrate how our cultural backgrounds can affect our responses to a message.

The way we think, our *patterns of thought*, also shifts from culture to culture. Western thought patterns can appear rigid and structured. This Aristotelian mode of reasoning is based on logic and syllogism. The structures of Oriental thought can appear—to Western man—to depend on chance, fate, and occult sources for many conclusions.

Our *perception* of a communication act is often dominated by our culture. The judgment of beauty, for instance, is culturally based. In the United States thin women tend to represent the cultural stereotype of attractiveness. However, in much of Europe a full figure is more desirable than a slim one.

The *language* employed in communication is also a reflection of culture. Many subcultures evolve language codes that are part of their cultural experience. Blacks, for example, have an entire glossary of terms unique to their culture. "Jive" may mean a way of dancing to a person raised in the fifties, but to the black of today it has a very different meaning, i.e., "phony."

The *nonverbal* behaviors of a culture are often displayed during a communication encounter. Each culture, in obvious and in subtle ways, teaches its members various uses of and responses to such things as space, time, movement, eye contact, facial expression, and touch. As we attempt to communicate with a variety of people, coming from a host of cultures and subcultures, it is imperative that we know something about cultural variations that are apt to influence communication.

Individual Determinants

We are now ready to turn our attention to some of the individual factors that might help you understand something about the persons with whom you are going to be communicating. Some specific areas should reveal significant information regarding your audience's beliefs and attitudes.

1. *Discover the age of your listeners.* You know from past experience that you talk differently to a group of junior high school students than to a group of college students. Even what you talk about is influenced by the age differences. It is important for you to be sensitive to problems arising from age variations. Many times insight into age may also give insight into the past experiences of the audience. The depression, for example, may be a meaningful memory to an older person but only secondhand information to a younger individual. Countless experimental studies have revealed the effect age plays on interests, learning, opinion change, and on communication. Their findings reveal a number of interesting conclusions. For example, because older people have had a larger variety of experiences, they are more inclined to become entrenched in their opinions and hence much harder to

persuade. At the same time, studies suggest that younger persons are very susceptible to persuasion. Research also indicates that as we get older, social sensitivity and empathy increase.

Considerations of age also make it imperative for the speaker to review language similarities and differences. The meanings attributed to words such as *grass, stoned,* and *busted* are clearly related to age.

Admittedly, generalizations about different age groups are subject to many exceptions. Yet, by and large, a group of old persons will differ in attitudes and experiences from a group of young persons. This simple realization will greatly aid you in selecting materials to accomplish your purpose.

2. *Discover the sex of your listeners.* Are both males and females in the audience? The answer to this question may govern everything from your choice of subject to the examples you decide to place in your speech. The two sexes often live in different worlds. To explore the impact of sex roles on communication would be a never-ending task, for our particular gender propels us, in both subtle and manifest ways, to behave according to certain cultural patterns. A few examples will emphasize this idea. Women tend to learn faster than men. On certain topics women appear to be easier to persuade. Women are believed to be superior in verbal skills and more effective in developing empathy. The public speaker must be aware of these and other differences and try to ascertain their effect on the message.

Even though the speaker must be aware of differences in experiences imposed by our culture, he or she must also be aware of similarities. In recent years the behaviors and attitudes of women have undergone a major transformation. In areas of sexual relations, education, and employment, the sexes have grown closer together. They now share a number of common experiences in sports, language, occupations, and politics.

3. *Find the occupation of your listeners.* What people do for a living is a guide to their values, attitudes, and even their sense of humor. You know that a farmer may see things differently than a school teacher or a shopowner. Ask yourself, is the occupation of my audience relevant to my topic? The answer to this question applies to informative as well as to persuasive speeches. For occupation—what we are trained to do, and what we do most of the day—not only shapes our beliefs, but gives us various experiences. For example, a construction worker would most likely know about framing a house, while a college professor might have little experience with the terms and technology of building construction.

4. *Discover the intelligence and educational level of your listeners.* In order for communication to take place the audience must be able to understand what you say. You must be very careful not to overestimate or underestimate the intelligence of your listeners. In either case the cycle of communication can be broken if there is a lack of understanding. You should remember that formal education as well as education acquired through practical experience will help determine what your audience thinks about and how they react.

5. *Discover to what social, professional, and religious groups your listeners belong.* We see ourselves and others in terms of the roles we play. The groups

to which we belong contribute to the making of these roles. Group membership suggests, in a general way, types of people, their points of view, interests, and attitudes. It is apparent that such things as religious affiliation will influence our thinking on many topics. When you can learn the group membership of a large part of your audience, you have gained a valuable clue to listener attitudes and wants.

Data about group affiliations has important implications for the informative speech as well as the persuasive. A member of the Kennel Club might know more about the dangers of dog bites than does someone who belongs only to the Chess Club. Our general fund of knowledge seems to be *directly related* to how we spend our time. Whether we belong to the Reading Club, Ski Club, Church of Jesus Christ of Latter-Day Saints, Civil Liberties Union, National Organization of Women, or Girl Scouts, our affiliation with each of these groups tells other people something about us and what we deem important.

6. *Understand the influence of your listeners' geographical experiences.* Where they have been raised and where they live help determine what they believe and how they act. The small rural high school, with its 4-H programs and agricultural classes, offers experiences quite different from the situations faced by the student attending a large high school in the city. Interests and attitudes are partly shaped by these geographic experiences. For example, someone from an industrial section of the country, who earns a living working in a factory, might well have a view of conservation that is in conflict with the person from a principally rural section of the country.

There are even vocabulary shifts from one geographical region to another. Someone from a surfboard-riding area would most likely know the special meanings of words like *hang-ten, tubes,* and *soup,* while the person from a horse-riding region would have specific meanings for *bot eggs, tapaderos,* and *curb chain.*

Determining Audience Attitudes

Thus far we have been discussing how you as a speaker go about gathering information that will aid in understanding potential listeners. Once that information is collected and analyzed, you are in a position to determine how the audience will perceive you and your topic.

The Audience and the Speaker

Your relationship with each audience is a highly personal matter. There will be instances when every member of the audience knows you and perceives you as a friend. On other occasions you may find that the persons you are going to talk to know absolutely nothing about you. Each of these situations will produce a different audience attitude toward you. The importance of an audience's attitude toward a speaker will be developed in detail in chapter 9 when we discuss the concept of credibility. It is our thesis that not only must you assess what the audience's attitude is toward you, but more importantly, you must work toward having that attitude be a positive one. Creating that favorable attitude begins with an assessment of your relationship with the audience *before* you begin to talk to them. A question such as "What does the audience already know about me?" must be asked early in your preparation, for the answer will help you in areas ranging from the gathering of materials to the presenting of those materials.

The Audience and the Subject

Like the audience's attitude toward you, their knowledge of and attitudes toward your subject will influence every phase of your preparation and presentation. The arguments you employ, the language of those arguments, the content of your emotional appeals, and the ways in which you define new concepts are all touched by what the audience believes *before* you begin. Therefore, it is crucial that you use the information you have gathered from your analysis of your audience's cultural and personal background. The conclusions you reach will help answer questions regarding your listener's values, desires, beliefs, and knowledge level. For example, if you were going to talk about the successes of the United Nations to a group of Young Americans for Freedom (a rather conservative organization), you would have to adapt your material to appeal to their existing beliefs. You would know those beliefs only after you conducted your audience analysis.

Audience Analysis and "Me-ism"

We have stressed the fact that although your audience is made of separate individuals, you can, with a careful analysis, make some generalizations about what they are like, what they believe, and what they know. With the same scrupulous reflection, you can draw some conclusions regarding the type of general audience you will be facing. For example, there will be an impact on your entire speech if the audience is very formal. Likewise, if they are an informal group your language, delivery, and material will be influenced by this informality. And you know from your own experiences that you feel and speak differently to friends than you do to strangers.

In analyzing the type of audience you will be confronting, you should also ask yourself, "How interested is this audience in me and my subject?" You must always remember that as a speaker you are "invading" the life of another person. You are asking them to stop whatever they were doing or thinking and make you their most immediate concern. In this day of "me-ism," when our interests tend to be focused mainly on ourselves, you must determine the degree of this "me-ism" and work to overcome it. Personal concerns of the audience and audience apathy are two major problems facing all speakers. The first step in arresting audience apathy must come from your ability to identify the causes of that apathy. Therefore, trying to predict whether the audience will be neutral, friendly, apathetic, or hostile is one of your first responsibilities. Once these important decisions are made, you can be much more accurate in your use of humor, statistics, motive appeal, language, and other specific aspects of the speech.

Your Speaking Occasion

We have already established the importance of knowing your audience as a means of selecting, preparing, adapting, and adjusting your speech to accomplish your preconceived purpose. The speaking *occasion* also demands a careful analysis. Where you deliver your speech plays a prominent role in the entire communication process. A famous American humorist once observed that he could never speak in jest in a church.

A speaker's analysis of the occasion should involve the following considerations.

1. *What kind of occasion will it be?* The answer to this question affects the tone and purpose of the meeting, and hence the speech itself. Your initial concern should be to discover why the meeting is being held. Have the people gathered only to hear your speech or do they meet on a regular basis? You should also know whether the procedure will be ritualistic, parliamentary, formal, or informal. Finally, the location of the meeting and the time of day should be investigated. All of these factors will have an influence on your speech.

2. *What will the physical surroundings be?* The physical setting in which the speech is delivered often contributes considerably to the success or failure of the speaker's attempt to get a message across. The speaker should consider such factors as whether or not the speech is delivered indoors or outside, the acoustics of the room or hall, the presence or absence of a public address system, the seating arrangements, lighting arrangements, and any outside distractions and noises. All of these factors will govern, to some degree, the mood and attention span of the audience.

3. *What will precede and follow your speech?* Your message is never sent to passive, inactive minds. You must always remember, whether on or off the speaker's platform, that your listeners had a "state of mind" before you sent your first sound. They were thinking about something before you entered their lives and asked for attention—what they *were* doing is important. You should know whether or not your speech comes before or after dinner, whether other speakers will precede you, and other factors related to the mental state of the listeners.

Empathy

To be an effective communicator you must take into account the person or persons receiving the message. The speaker is but one half of the communication process; the audience is the other half. Being able to understand the audience is, in a real sense, being able to see things as the audience sees them. Once you are able to see and to feel as the audience does, you are in a position to put into words those ideas that will elicit maximum agreement and understanding.

All human communication demands that the sender of a message make predictions about how persons will respond to that message. All of us carry around in our minds images of other persons, and take these images into account whenever we speak. The successful communicator is one who is accurate in his or her predictions and fully understands the receiver. When you make accurate predictions, you have skill in what the psychologist calls *empathy*—the process of projecting ourselves into others' personalities. By placing yourself in the shoes of the receiver you are developing empathy. By analyzing your audience, finding their attitudes, desires, backgrounds, interests, and goals, you are constructing a picture of them that will enable you to make predictions. It is only by empathy—the sharing of another's personality—that you can hope to send meaningful and real messages.

To project yourself into another's personality demands that you have a picture or an image of the other person. *Who is he or she?* How do you gather the data to answer that question? Basically, you gather the data for the image of the other person in four closely related phases.

The first pieces of information that help form these images often come *before the communication encounter.* How often have you had someone tell you about Professor Jones before you met Jones? They tell you "he is a good guy, likes students, but is strict regarding attendance." This information, supplied before you ever communicate with Jones, helps you construct your image and, hence, helps you predict what message and behavior will be appropriate. In addition, before the actual communication act, you may find that the other person is a doctor, teacher, plumber, student, or bus driver. This information, once again pre-encounter, gives you possible data for your prediction.

Be cautious of the danger of responding to the pre-encounter image as if, in some way, it represented the entire person. Empathy can be hindered by responding to only part of the image.

The second source of information regarding the other person often comes quickly and before any words pass between the two parties. This *nonverbal (preverbal)* information comes in a variety of forms. For example, research suggests that some of our images and impressions come from our first eye-contact with another person. How many times have you looked someone in the eye, before a word was ever spoken, and felt you liked this person and knew something about him or her? The term *charisma* is often used to describe the feeling we have about another person—a feeling that is hard to isolate and explain.

We get other nonverbal information about a person before we start to exchange words. Our image of the other person is shaped by such nonverbal cues as dress, manner, and stature. In all instances we use this information to construct a profile of the person with whom we are to communicate.

The third body of information we gather comes from the *verbal messages* we get from other persons. What we hear others say gives us a great deal of insight into what they are like. If someone tells you "I always vote the straight Democratic ticket because the Republicans have never done a thing for the working person," you use this sentence to decide many other factors about the person who said it. What persons talk about and what they say about the subjects they select can offer us data for our image of them.

A fourth area of image building comes to us by means of what we might call *extraneous messages.* By extraneous we mean *information that is often apart from the person.* For example, do we not make judgments and generalizations about persons when we discover what cars they drive, what cigarettes they smoke (if any), and what restaurants they frequent? Even where persons live and the clubs they belong to offer us insight into their personalities. This extraneous data often offers us a more complete picture of our subjects.

Thus, we gather information about others in four ways, and we use this data as a means of constructing an image or profile of them. That image often tells us what these persons are like, and hence we can better empathize with them and better make predictions about how they will respond to us and our message.

Interference with Empathy	It will be useful for us to pause and look briefly at those factors that might interfere with our being able to see things from another individual's point of view.

It will be useful for us to pause and look briefly at those factors that might interfere with our being able to see things from another individual's point of view.

If you are thinking constantly about yourself, it is difficult to concentrate on cues given by other persons—cues that might offer insight into their personalities. A successful communicator cares about others, is aware of others, and is not preoccupied with thoughts about himself or herself. In short, constant *self-focus* hinders empathy.

Another interference is our common tendency *to note only some features of behavior* to the exclusion of others. We notice when someone does not smile and at once draw a conclusion about that person—a conclusion based on only one bit of information. Individuals are complex, and it is an error in communication to let one isolated act represent the entire person.

Although there are many other hindrances to empathy we will conclude by mentioning only one more, and it is perhaps the most common. We refer to our tendency to react to stereotyped notions about the meaning of physical features, race, religion, and nationality. In committing this error we assume that *all* people of the same group or class are automatically alike. We forget the uniqueness of the individual.

It is hard work to empathize. It demands a commitment on the part of both parties—a commitment that says you are willing to expend the energy to discover all that you can about the other person. Research in empathy indicates that high motivation (the commitment we talked about) will definitely help in understanding the other person's personality.

The Audience and Empathy

The audience also experiences a kind of empathy during the speaking situation. As you deliver your talk, the audience is feeling (sharing) the experiences along with you. For example, when you appear nervous and tense, the audience also feels uncomfortable and strained. When you manifest sincere enthusiasm, the audience will experience a similar sensation. You should therefore be aware of this rapport, and your appearance and actions should attempt to make the audience feel at ease.

Choosing the Title of the Speech

You may face a few instances when you are asked to furnish a title for your speech. On these occasions it will be helpful if your title is (a) brief, (b) appropriate, (c) provocative, and (d) suggests the purpose of your speech. A few examples might improve your ability to select titles that reflect all four criteria.

Recently one of our students gave a speech, entitled "Credit Cards: Bankruptcy Made Easy," in which she reviewed the growth of credit card buying and high interest rates in the United States. Her title stimulated interest in her talk prior to the actual presentation. Titles such as "The Abolishment of Student Body Government," or "Understanding and Loving Rattlesnakes" are other instances of titles that capture attention and steer the listener toward the content of the speech.

Summary

Communication normally takes place because the speaker wants to achieve some preconceived purpose. Thus the purpose must be clear in his or her mind. The public speaker will usually be preparing and giving speeches that fall into three general speech purposes—to *inform*, to *persuade*, and to *entertain*. In addition to selecting a general purpose, the speaker must formulate a specific purpose that describes the immediate and exact nature of the response wanted from the audience.

In deciding on a method of preparation and delivery, the speaker can use any one of the following procedures—(1) speaking from a manuscript, (2) speaking from memory, (3) impromptu speaking, and (4) extemporaneous speaking. The extemporaneous method is most recommended for the beginning speaker.

In order to adapt his or her purpose to a specific audience, the speaker should analyze the audience. Valuable insight into the listener's needs, wants, attitudes, and experiences can be gained by discovering the listener's age, sex, occupation, intelligence and education, and social, professional, and religious affiliations, and geographical experiences.

By implementing the material gathered through an analysis of the audience and the occasion, the speaker can use empathy—the projecting of oneself into the personalities of one's listeners. Knowing what the listeners are like enables the communicator "to speak their language."

Speakers may encounter situations that make it necessary for them to furnish titles for their speeches. In these cases it is important to remember that a good title is brief, appropriate, provocative, and one that suggests the purpose of the speech.

Suggested Readings

Clevenger, Theodore, Jr. *Audience Analysis*. Indianapolis: Bobbs-Merrill, 1966.

Dickens, Milton. *Speech: Dynamic Communication*. 3d ed. New York: Harcourt Brace Jovanovich, 1974. Chapter 11.

Hasling, John. *The Message, The Speaker, The Audience*. New York: McGraw-Hill, 1976. Chapter 4.

Hoehler, Jerry W.; Anatol, Karl W. E.; and Applbaum, Ronald L. *Public Communication*. New York: Macmillan Publishing, 1978. Chapter 9.

Myers, Gail E., and Myers, Michele Tolela. *Communicating When We Speak*. 2d ed. New York: McGraw-Hill, 1978. Chapter 6.

Thompson, Wayne. *Responsible and Effective Communication*. Boston: Houghton Mifflin, 1978. Chapter 3.

Sound and Action
Presenting the Message

In the previous chapter we discussed methods of speech delivery—memorization, manuscript, extemporaneous, and impromptu. And you will recall that in chapter 1 we noted some ways of controlling the feelings of apprehension we all experience during speech delivery. We noted in particular the value of thorough preparation, of acknowledging the fact that nervous tension is normal and even desirable, of remembering that the audience is your friend, and of giving your nervous energy a healthy outlet through useful movements and gestures.

Now we will focus on delivery from a third vantage point. We want to call your attention to some of the ways in which your nonverbal behavior during speech presentation sends out messages to the audience, and we want to suggest principles that may assist you in keeping your nonverbal messages consistent with your verbal messages. You may have heard the speech act divided into "what you say" and "how you say it." Effective speech delivery fuses the verbal and nonverbal elements so successfully that "how you say it" becomes an indistinguishable part of "what you say." Let us examine, then, two main groups of nonverbal elements—what the audience sees and what the audience hears.

Visual Dimensions of Presentation

Of those nonverbal communication elements perceived visually by the audience, the three with which we shall be most concerned are the speaker's general appearance, movements, and spatial relationship to the audience. An awareness of the role each plays in influencing listener reaction to the speaker's verbal message may enable you to make constructive use of it and avoid placing barriers in your path to communication effectiveness.

Your General Appearance

Your posture, apparel, and facial expression all send signals to the listener. We shall examine a few of the ways in which they exert an influence.

Posture

The influence of posture may be better understood if we visualize three speakers: one stands ramrod straight like a soldier at rigid attention; another merely slouches; and a third stands with feet placed comfortably apart, shoulders held straight (but not rigidly so). The "soldier" posture probably makes you suspect that the speaker is tense and anxious; the slouchy posture very likely suggests that the speaker is lacking in enthusiasm or energy; and the last posture may say to you, "That person is apparently comfortable, but also alert." But before we praise or condemn any of these postures we need to take into account the accompanying verbal message. The real test of a posture is its compatibility with the verbal message being uttered—for there is no single posture that is always right for all speakers on all occasions.

The foregoing postures have found the speaker in a standing position. We have all observed occasions when a speaker, at some point in the speech, sat on the edge of a desk or chair or perhaps sat on the apron of a stage. The seated position often communicates a feeling of informality and relaxation. Such things as the physical surroundings, the distance between speaker and audience, the social conventions operative in the communication situation, and, most importantly, the governing purpose of the communicative act will usually dictate whether the message—or any portion thereof—is delivered from a standing position, a seated position, or even a reclining position.

We shall have more to say of the postures just discussed when we turn our attention to the speaker's movements and how they are affected by the posture the speaker adopts.

Apparel and Grooming

As listeners we tend to make generalizations about speakers from the clothes they wear, the objects they keep on their person, and their grooming generally. Even before a word is spoken, the audience "sizes up" and tentatively labels the speaker. "He's wearing a business suit; guess he's an 'establishment' type." "She's wearing jeans and a flannel shirt; bet she's an outdoor type." "He has long hair and a bushy beard; probably a radical freak." "Look at the size of that diamond she's wearing! Bet her old man is loaded." Then the speaker commences talking and we reexamine the tentative label we have imposed. Perhaps we discover that the speaker's appearance has been deceiving. "Well, I'll be darned! She doesn't *look* like an engineer." "He's a college president? You've got to be kidding. He's wearing a T-shirt, denims, and tennis shoes."

We are not so much concerned with the validity of generalizations drawn by listeners on the basis of the speaker's apparel and grooming as we are with stressing the point that generalizations are *drawn*, and the speaker should be ready to accept the consequences.

It is impossible to define appropriate dress or appropriate grooming except in terms of the individual speaking situation. So it is most important for you to become familiar with the audience's standards and expectations. Your grooming and apparel, like your posture, should be compatible with your subject, your purpose, the audience, and the occasion.

Facial Expression and Gaze

One of the most revealing visual signals that the speaker sends comes from the face. From facial expression we form impressions of the speaker's attitude toward us, toward himself or herself, and toward the subject matter. It is possible that the expression may tell us "I like you people," "I'm really enthusiastic about my topic," "I believe what I'm saying," or it may tell us just the opposite. It may depict a wide range of emotions from fear to confidence, from joy to sadness. Tiny subtleties of expression we may not consciously be aware of are telling us that one speaker's animation is sincerely motivated, that another speaker's animation is feigned. It is probably no coincidence that the speaker who lacks facial expression generally lacks all animation, visual and vocal. If this lack of animation stems from apathy toward the ideas being expressed, the solution would seem to be to abandon the speech rather than to affect a display of animation. While the affected animation might gain attention, it would probably result in the listener being conscious of the affectation rather than the ideas of the speech. On the other hand, if the lack of animation results from inhibition rather than from apathy, then the answer lies essentially in placing oneself in the proper psychological attitude.

Our eyes are capable of sending innumerable messages. They tell others when our communication channels are open, when we wish to terminate or avoid communication. They say something of our emotional state, be it elation or depression, interest or boredom, trust or suspicion, love or hatred. The quality of interpersonal relationships is often signalled by the kind of eye contact taking place. It reveals information concerning status relationships, interest, motivation, anxiety, and a host of other factors that are in operation during communication.

Our eyes are equally important as receivers. We use eye contact when seeking the reactions of others to us and our messages. Seeing what is happening is an excellent way of measuring the success or failure of our speech.

Your Movements

In order to appreciate the role and importance of bodily action in communication, we should be aware of these two facts about the nature of movement: (1) movement conveys meaning, and (2) movement influences attention.

Movement and Meaning

To watch a television program with the audio turned down is to witness the power of movement to communicate meaning. We can see at times that no dialogue is taking place—that the meaning is being communicated primarily through actions. The hero flings his golf club to the ground over a missed putt; the heroine raises an amused eyebrow. No dialogue is necessary to complete the message. At other times the movement suggests only the speaker's attitude or emotional state. We need dialogue to complete the meaning. We know the speaker is angry, but we don't know what is causing the anger. So we turn up the sound to learn that the speaker's car is being repossessed. Or perhaps the speaker's movements are not directly related to the dialogue. Finally, the speaker's movements may actually transmit a meaning contradictory to the meaning being transmitted by the words. The seemingly jaded television announcer mouthing extravagant words of praise for a product is all too common a sight. We can only assume the announcer is going through the motions of enthusiasm for the actions tells us that he or she is pretending.

We should note that the absence of movement—the static state—is also a conveyor of meaning. Segments of the verbal message may actually be intensified in meaning by the suspension of bodily action. All too often, however, the static state results from psychological factors (the inhibiting influence of a strange situation, for example) or from the adoption of a bodily position that makes movement uncomfortable or impossible.

Movement and Attention	If you were to glance up from this page for a few moments, the chances are that your eyes would rove idly around the room, not resting on anything in particular, until there was movement of some sort. Perhaps a pet would wander into the room, or a scrap of paper would blow past your window. Instantly your eyes would fasten on the moving object and would linger there until some more powerful stimulus drew them away. *Movement draws attention.*

There are many applications of this factor of attention in various media of communication. A motion picture will attract our attention more quickly than a still picture. A still picture that *depicts action* will attract our attention more quickly than one that depicts a static situation. A flashing neon sign attracts us more quickly than a steadily glowing sign. The movement causes us to keep our eyes, and thus our attention, on the object.

Given the power to intensify listener attention through appropriate bodily action, we are unwise not to employ it. In fact, our natural impulse *is* to use it. Bodily movement during the communicative act is a natural, spontaneous response to our own uttered thoughts, the reactions of the listener, and the impact of the occasion. In most informal, unstructured communication situations we use movement freely, without inhibition. We are not even conscious of using it, because it accompanies so naturally our utterances. The public speaking situation, on the other hand, frequently imposes restraints that inhibit us from our natural impulse to move. We root ourselves in one spot (usually behind a lectern) and remain there for the duration of the speech. We grip the lectern or thrust our hands in our pockets or otherwise immobilize them so that they can not be used for meaningful, spontaneous gestures. Thus we are deprived of the use of an important means of reinforcing our verbal message and of successfully competing with the other stimuli that are fighting to gain the listener's attention.

Unfortunately there is no sure cure for the paralysis that often besets us in the formal, structured communication situation. Perhaps the adoption of a healthy mental attitude, a genuine desire to share ideas with others, is the best course to follow. The more we concentrate on our ideas and our listener's responses to those ideas, the less we will be concerned with the inhibiting formalities of the public speaking occasion.

Now let us add an important qualification to our observations about the power of movement to gain and hold attention. Movements, both graceful and awkward, appropriate and inappropriate, helpful and distracting, draw our attention. So movement can be an asset or a liability. It will be an asset only if it directs the listener's attention ultimately to the verbal message being communicated.

If the role of movement is to enhance or augment the verbal message, then its effect should be essentially subliminal. Once we begin to notice the communicator's actions instead of the verbal message, his or her purpose for communicating suffers.

Facilitating Movement	When circumstances suggest that meaningful bodily action will improve message transmission, the communicator should adopt a bodily position that encourages (or at least does not inhibit) easy, spontaneous action. What that position should be depends upon the kind and amount of movement called for by the particular

communication situation. If the occasion does not call for a formal "stand-up speech," the movements of the speaker are likely to be largely gestural in character. When speaker and listener are in very close proximity, changing facial expressions may be the only manifestations of movement. In such cases the speaker would do well to place himself or herself in a position that does not immobilize the muscles necessary for easy use of hands, arms, and facial expression.

Perhaps we can determine the characteristics of an appropriate stance for the "stand-up speech" if we reexamine the postures we discussed earlier. The "slouch" tends to inhibit movement of the entire body from one location to another within the speaking area because you must first return to a position of equilibrium before you can move easily to the right or left, toward the listener, or away from the listener. So you take the path of least resistance and remain in the "slouch."

The "soldier at attention" posture encourages movement, but movement of the wrong kind. It produces a nervous, rocking motion that can call so much attention to itself that it overrides the verbal message.

The last posture we discussed, the "alert" posture, probably provides the best starting point for meaningful movement. Many speakers find it easier to move from that posture when they feel it necessary. However, the best advice is to experiment with a variety of positions and make an honest appraisal of each.

Movement of the Entire Body

Movement of the entire body from one place to another within the confines of the communication situation is often motivated by a transition in ideas or by a desire to make an idea more emphatic. Lateral movements (to the speaker's left or right) frequently signal a change from one point in the message to the following point. Picture how such a lateral movement would readily accompany this statement: "Now, if you think that was a flimsy excuse, listen to the one I heard today."

A movement toward the listener is often associated with our desire to make an idea emphatic. "Now listen to this," says one person, *leaning toward* a listener in a conversation The same principle operates in a public speaking situation except that the movement may be more pronounced; instead of leaning toward the listeners, we may actually take a step or two toward them.

We have earlier observed that the wrong kind of movement can measurably reduce the effectiveness of the verbal message. The pencil tapper, the sleeve tugger, and the nose rubber come to mind. It is probably better to have no movement at all than to have such distracting movements. They are, after all, manifestations of nervous tension seeking release. The best way to avoid the buildup of this tension is to employ the meaningful movements we have discussed, thus affording the tension a constructive outlet.

Movement of the Hands and Arms

Probably you have attempted to communicate with another person in a situation where a high noise level made speech impossible. Perhaps you resorted to some kind of gestural exchange. Indeed, many persons are able to use gestures as substitutes for the spoken words. While we have no wish to propound a theory of communication based on gesture alone, we do wish to remind you of the power of gestures to heighten attention and to intensify the meaning conveyed by the spoken word.

"But it doesn't feel natural!" is a lament that every speech teacher hears when he or she suggests that a student try to employ gestural activity in a public speaking situation. Yet that same student in a conversation out in the hall, probably uses scores of gestures and is not aware of doing so. Why does the student "freeze up" in front of an audience? Why does the act of gesturing feel unnatural?

Most of us acquire a number of inhibitions when we have to appear before an audience. These inhibitions are simply the manifestation of a response to a strange situation. We become tense, as we do in any fearful situation. Those same hands that moved about so freely and effortlessly when we were conversing with a friend suddenly are bound by some invisible force. Our first impulse is to get them out of sight. So we thrust them into our pockets (where they will probably begin to jingle coins and keys), we lock them behind our backs, we hide them in our armpits, we clasp them together in front of us in the so-called figleaf position, or, if a lectern is handy, we grip it until our knuckles whiten. This may well be one reason why it does not feel natural to gesture at such times; we have placed our hands and ourselves in a position that inhibits free, spontaneous movement.

Just as we have to assume a stance that will not inhibit movement of the entire body from one point to another on the platform, we have to assume a starting position for the hands and arms that does not inhibit their movement. The best advice is to keep the hands and arms unencumbered. Then when we feel the subconscious urge to gesture, they can move naturally into action.

Limitations upon Use of Movement

Now that we have suggested ways in which bodily action can be used to reinforce the verbal elements of the message, we should make note of several limitations upon its use.

1. *Bodily action should be sincerely motivated.* To gesture effectively we must *feel* like gesturing. If we force ourselves to employ action when we do not feel like it, the listener can usually detect the artifice, equating this artificiality with insincerity. If we use planned actions, we run the risk of concentrating upon the actions rather than the ideas we are uttering. Conscious use of movements, gestures, and facial expressions should be reserved for practice sessions.
2. *Bodily action should not be overused.* Most of us habitually use certain actions for emphasis, but if we are not careful, we overwork those actions to the point that the listener begins to notice the actions rather than the ideas they are supposed to emphasize. By cultivating a greater variety of actions during practice sessions, we will be less likely to overwork any one spontaneous action.
3. *Bodily action should be appropriate to the occasion.* The same speech can often be delivered in several ways, depending upon the circumstances under which it is delivered. For example, if we are speaking in a large room where there is some distance between the speaker and the most remote section of

the audience, we will have to make actions more pronounced so that they can be clearly seen. If we have a small, intimate room, our actions will be subtler (and probably fewer in number). Careful analysis of the audience and occasion will reveal the extent to which use should be made of the visible aspects of delivery.

Your Spatial
Relationship to
the Audience

The physical distance between you and your listeners can affect the quality of the communication encounter. It affects you as a speaker in several ways. First, it has an impact on your use of movement, gesture, and facial expression. If these nonverbal elements are to serve you properly, they must be seen. Therefore, the greater the distance between you and your listener, the more exaggerated these visual factors must be. Second, it affects your use of voice. If there is no public address system available, you will probably have to talk louder and enunciate more distinctly as distance increases between you and your audience. Third, physical distance may affect your feeling of *mental* proximity to the audience. Some speakers are disturbed when a large space separates them from their listeners. In order to get close to the listener mentally, they have to get close physically as well. The listener may experience this same feeling. Distance may produce a feeling of estrangement from the speaker. Rapport can be affected by spatial relationships.

The most extensive studies of spatial cues have been conducted within the last fifteen years. Edward T. Hall, for example, attempted to develop a system for the classification of proxemic or spatial behavior. His schema, which should be of interest to the student of communication, is divided into various zones or proxemic distances.

Public distance—close phase—is that proxemic distance extending from twelve to twenty-five feet. It is the distance at which a person's voice is loud and clear. Public distance is, moreover, the distance at which many interactions are first initiated.

Social distance—far phase—is seven to twelve feet. This is the distance at which (1) business and social discourse of a more formal nature are conducted, (2) desks in offices are placed to hold off visitors, (3) fine details of the face and body cannot be perceived, and (4) the whole face and body of the person, with space around it, may be taken in without shifting the eyes.

Social distance—close phase—extends from four to seven feet. At this distance the eye can take in an ever-increasing amount of the person. Close-phase social distance is the proxemic distance at which most casual social gatherings take place and that people who work together employ when interacting.

Personal distance—far phase—is the proxemic distance between two individuals extending from two and one-half to four feet. It is the distance at which one is kept at arm's length. Far-phase personal distance is the distance just outside the range of easy touching; it is also the range at which the fine details of a person's face are clearly visible. Skin texture, the presence of prematurely gray hair, wrinkles, and other features of the face can easily be seen at this distance.

*Personal distance—close phase—*is the proxemic distance between one and one-half to two and one-half feet. It is the distance at which one can hold or grasp the other person and where visual feedback is very noticeable.

*Intimate distance—far phase—*is the proxemic distance from six to eighteen inches. Detailed features of the face are clearly visible. The voice at this distance is normally held at a very low level or even a whisper.

*Intimate distance—close phase—*is the proxemic distance in humans extending from maximum contact to six inches. It is the distance of love-making, wrestling, comforting, protecting, or the distance at which physical contact or the high possibility of physical involvement is uppermost in the awareness of both persons.

It is apparent that some of the distances just described may have greater application to interpersonal encounters than to public speaking situations. Nonetheless, the speaker is well advised to remember that distance has an influence on the outcome of communication of any kind. Spatial cues should be used in a manner consistent with the speaker's reason for communicating.

Aural Dimensions of Presentation

While part of the speaker's message may be conveyed by visual means, it is by sound—vocalized sound—that the linguistic elements of the message are carried. But the voice does more than simply render a word-symbol into audible form; it enables us to impart various shades of meaning to that spoken word. Moreover our voice, like our posture, movements, gestures, and facial expressions, tells things about us quite apart from the verbal message we are uttering. For these reasons we need to sharpen our awareness of the capabilities of the voice to help or hinder oral communication.

Voice and Word Meaning

Let us examine first how our vocal behavior affects the *sense* of what we utter. If we were to take the sentence, "The detective is the murderer," and shift the point of emphasis from one word to another, we could come up with a variety of meanings:

The DETECTIVE is the murderer (not someone else).

The detective IS the murderer (my hunch was right).

The detective is the MURDERER (not the protector of the innocent).

Or note how inflectional variations modify the meaning of the simple word "really."

"Really?" (Are you sure?)

"Really." (Absolutely certain.)

"Really!" (How dare you!)

These examples illustrate the importance of vocal behavior in adding dimension to the meaning of spoken words. The rate that we utter words, the degree of intensity we impart to each one, the variations in pitch we employ, the harshness or mellowness of the sound of each word—all add shades of meaning to the spoken word, just as punctuation marks, special type faces, and indentations modify the meaning of the written word.

Voice and Personality

Not only does the voice affect the meaning of the message, it affects the listener's impression of the speaker as a person. In fact, it may evoke a misleading impression of the speaker as a person. A thin, weak voice may hide a person of vigor and courage. A monotonous voice may hide a person with great inner enthusiasm. The great Greek orator, Demosthenes, undoubtedly realized that his speech impediment communicated a false impression of his true worth; so he labored hard to overcome the impediment. It should also be pointed out that a voice ringing with sincerity and enthusiasm may conceal the most unscrupulous sophist.

The listener must not be hasty in equating tone of voice with character and personality; the voice may be part of a mask hiding the real identity of the speaker. The speaker, in turn, must realize that he or she is judged not only by words spoken but by meanings that listeners attach to the sound of the voice that carries those words.

Voice and Attention

Earlier in this chapter we observed that movement is a factor of attention, and we noted how movement of the body as a whole, movement of the hands and arms, and movement of the facial muscles all serve to keep the audience attentive. This attention factor of movement or activity is applicable to vocal behavior as well. The voice that moves—or more accurately, the voice that is *varied*—holds attention. The speaker who fails to vary pitch, loudness, rate, or quality may have difficulty sustaining audience attention for any appreciable length of time unless the verbal message is especially compelling. Of course, vocal variations should always be properly motivated. It would be ludicrous, for example, to alter your rate of speaking just for the sake of gaining attention. That would only call attention to your use of the device. No delivery technique should call attention to itself; *it should direct attention to the message.*

Controllable Elements of Voice

If our vocal behavior fails to gain and hold attention, fails to enhance word meaning, or projects an inaccurate impression of personality, we tend to place the blame upon Nature. The popular lament is, "I just wasn't born with a good voice!" Undeniably, Nature does impose limitations upon us. Perhaps the vocal equipment we were born with is inferior to that of our neighbor. But it is in the *use* of the equipment that we are more apt to find the cause of success or failure. Much of our vocal effectiveness depends upon the way in which we control the loudness, pitch, quality, rate, distinctness, and correctness of the sounds we produce.

Loudness	The first requisite of vocal sound is that it be loud enough for comfortable hearing. Listeners may be willing to exert extra effort to hear a person with a weak voice, if that person has something compelling to say. Even so, it is likely that the sheer physical exertion of straining to hear the speaker will ultimately cause the listener to abandon further effort. If, on the other hand, a speaker talks at a painfully loud level, the listener will be more concerned with the discomfort of the sound than its meaning.

While attaining a comfortable volume should be our first concern, we must not overlook the need for *changes* in loudness level. It is by varying our loudness that we enhance word meaning and sustain attention. A speech delivered without variations in loudness is analogous to a symphony played without *crescendo* or *diminuendo.*

Changes in loudness are particularly helpful in giving emphasis to words or phrases. Uttering a word at an intensity level different from that used with the other words in a sentence will direct audience attention to its importance. While such emphasis may be attained by making the sound suddenly louder or softer, recent research suggests that a sudden change to a softer level is apt to be the more effective means of emphasis.

Pitch	The rate of vibration of the vocal folds determines the pitch of the voice. The slower the vibration, the lower the key. The faster the vibration, the higher the key. The length and thickness of your vocal cords will determine the extremes of pitch your voice is capable of producing. Persons with vocal folds of relatively great length and thickness, for example, will probably have bass voices. Whether our natural pitch range is classified as bass, tenor, or soprano, we have a great flexibility of pitch levels within that range. When we wish to produce a higher note, a series of muscles causes our vocal folds to stretch, much in the same manner as we might stretch a rubber band. A lower note is produced by relaxing these same muscles.

Changes in pitch level within our normal range provide us with one of the most effective means of gaining attention and imparting meaning to utterance. Yet, under the duress of a formal speaking situation, some persons may inhibit their natural tendency to vary the pitch level. The resultant effect, which we call monotony, robs their words of much meaning and exerts a deadening effect upon the listener's attention. There are other people whose voices are monotonous even in informal conversation. Very likely their monotone is the product of long conditioning. For example, a person raised in a family opposed to any display of emotion probably learned by example to inhibit animation in delivery, both in its visual aspects and its vocal aspects.

Quality	Quality is usually expressed in the terms *strident, rasping, aspirate, mellow, harsh, orotund,* and a variety of other descriptive labels. The speaker's vocal quality can be one of the most obvious signs of emotional attitude at the moment of speaking. The nervous speaker usually tenses throat muscles inadvertently, and the resulting voice quality is apt to be thin and strident. As the speaker relaxes, the throat cavity enlarges, and voice quality becomes much more pleasant. When we grow angry, our voice quality becomes harsh and aspirate; when

we grow nostalgic and indulge in reverie, the voice takes on an almost whispery quality.

If we truly *feel* the meaning of what we are saying, our voice quality will usually take on those characteristics that the audience associates with the sentiment we are expressing.

Rate

Intelligibility, meaning, and attention are all affected by the speaker's rate of utterance. If the rate is too fast, intelligibility may suffer. If the rate is slow when it should be fast or fast when it should be slow, meaning may suffer. Or if the rate is not correctly varied, attention may wane.

We measure rate in terms of the number of words uttered per minute. It is generally agreed that 125 to 150 words per minute constitutes a satisfactory rate for public speaking, but modifications must be made to adapt to room acoustics, audience reactions, the atmosphere of the occasion, and most importantly, to the material of the speech.

Two factors that influence our rate of speaking are *pause* and *duration* of *sound*. The pause can be one of our most effective "oral punctuation marks." It does for the spoken word what the comma, colon, parenthesis, and dash do for the written word. The misplaced pause, the vocalized pause, or the pause that signals a mental blank can mar a speech that is otherwise effective. *Duration* refers to the time consumed in uttering vowel and consonant sounds. The duration of vowel sounds in particular affects word meaning. To illustrate, utter the word *long,* holding the vowel sound but briefly; now, utter the word again, prolonging the vowel sound. The emotional coloration of words is thus modified by changes in duration.

The number of words uttered per minute is, then, dependent upon how much time is spent in pausing (or hesitating) as well as in actually producing the individual sounds of each word. If accused of talking too fast or too slow, try to ascertain whether the problem is faulty management of duration or of pause. It is not unusual for a person, when asked to slow down his or her rate of speaking, to maintain the usual duration while pausing more often or pausing for longer periods. The real culprit in such cases is often faulty management of duration rather than an excessive number of words per minute. Eighty words per minute may seem excessive if each word is given inadequate duration.

Variety of rate is as important as variety of pitch or loudness. The speaker who seems to be following a metronome in his or her rate of utterance can cloud meaning and diminish attention almost as quickly as a person with a monotone. Emphasis and mood changes can be effectively expressed by variations in rate. For example, when we wish to emphasize one particular statement of a paragraph, we tend to utter it more slowly than the sentences that precede or follow it. A mood of excitement is usually accompanied by an acceleration in rate; a mood of sobriety, with a slowing down in rate.

Distinctness

The clarity of the sounds we produce, though determined in part by our pitch, loudness, and rate, is determined principally by the way we manage the organs of articulation. Some sounds depend upon precise lip movements, others upon critical placement of the tongue, and still others upon full use of the jaw.

Lip laziness results in the poor enunciation of such consonants as *p, b, v,* and *f.* Tongue placement must be precise for clear production of consonants like *t, d, k,* and *g* as well as all of the vowel sounds. The importance of jaw action to clear enunciation can be seen if you try reciting the alphabet through clenched teeth.

In striving for greater precision, avoid going to the exteme of overpreciseness, which the audience interprets as a sign of affectation. Your speech teacher may offer suggestions for the improvement of your enunciation. If so, get in the habit of implementing these improvements in your everyday conversation; then the demands of other speaking situations will be much easier to fulfill.

Correctness

While enunciation has to do with the distinctness of a spoken word, pronunciation has to do with its correctness. It is possible to enunciate a word with the greatest clarity while grossly mispronouncing it. Faults of pronunciation are apt to be less easily forgiven by the listener than faults of enunciation, because they seem to reflect the speaker's intelligence rather than just his or her muscular dexterity.

One difficulty in determining acceptable pronunciation is the various dialect areas within the country. It is customary to view the continental United States as divided into three principal dialect areas: the Southern dialect area, embracing most of the territory south of the Mason-Dixon Line and east of the Mississippi; the Eastern dialect area, covering the Northeastern states, principally New England; and the General American dialect area, comprised of the rest of the country. Television and radio broadcasters have largely adopted the General American dialect because it has fewer distinctly regional characteristics. One way to understand the other two dialect areas is in terms of their departure from General American. Among the characteristics assigned to the Southern dialect is the prolongation of certain vowel sounds (sometimes referred to as the Southern drawl) and the softening of the hard *r* sound (*hard* is pronounced *haahd*). The Eastern dialect also softens the *r* sound, but it shortens rather than lengthens the duration of vowel sounds in many instances.

What we have then are regional standards of pronunciation. What might be regarded as acceptable in Atlanta might not be so in Duluth. Moreover, within each dialect area there are various subcultures that have their own standards of correctness. However, with the growing mobility of our society and the pervasiveness of mass communication, regional and cultural differences in pronunciation are becoming less evident. We do not wish to overemphasize the impact of dialect, but you should be aware of the fact that research findings indicate the possibility of a connection between a speaker's dialect and the audience's perception of his or her credibility.

The most practical method for discovering the prevailing standard of pronunciation is to listen to the educated speakers in your particular geographic and cultural area. For the pronunciation of little-used words, names of places, and foreign expressions, a good contemporary pronouncing dictionary is your most reliable guide.

Taking Stock of Needs

With these general guidelines for using bodily action and vocal variety in mind, take a careful inventory of your current delivery practices in various communication situations. Enlist the aid of friends who will offer candid views of your assets and liabilities in informal conversation, discussions, and conferences. Ask your speech instructor for an analysis of your needs in public speaking situations. Try to find answers to questions such as these: To what *degree* do I employ bodily action and effective vocal variety in each of the various communication situations? To an insufficient degree in public speaking, a sufficient degree in conversation? To a distracting degree in some cases? What is the *quality* of the action I do employ? Does it help or hinder the communication of my ideas? Is it meaningful action? Does it call attention to itself? If so, why? Does my posture communicate a positive impression? Does it combine ease with alertness? Are my movements and gestures graceful and decisive, or are they hesitant, tentative, lacking in vigor and enthusiasm? Do I have any annoying mannerisms that should be curbed? Does my use of my voice add to or detract from the communication situation? Securing answers to these and other pertinent questions will enable you to chart your course toward greater effectiveness in the use of visible and audible aspects of communication.

As you approach the task of improving your use of voice and body action in speaking, bear in mind these words from Dr. Hugh Blair, one of the great speech critics of the eighteenth century:

> If one has naturally any gross defect in his voice or gestures, he begins at the wrong end, if he attempts at reforming them only when he is to speak in public. He should begin with rectifying them in his private manner of speaking; and then carry to the public the right habit he has formed. For when a speaker is engaged in a public discourse, he should not be then employing his attention about his manner, or thinking of his tones and gestures. If he be so employed, study and affectation will appear. He ought to be then quite in earnest; wholly occupied with his subject and his sentiments; leaving nature, and previously formed habits, to prompt and suggest his manner of delivery.

Summary

For effective oral communication it is essential that verbal and nonverbal elements of the message work in harmony. The nonverbal elements of the message are visual and vocal. The visual constituents include the speaker's general appearance (posture, apparel, grooming, facial expression), movements, and spatial relationship to the audience. One's appearance should provide nonverbal cues that are compatible with the verbal message being uttered. Movements convey meaning and help sustain attention. The speaker should adopt a bodily position that does not inhibit spontaneous movement. Movement on the platform is generally motivated by a desire to make an idea emphatic or to suggest a transition from one idea to another. The speaker's action should be sincerely motivated, should be appropriate to the subject, to the audience, and to the occasion, and should not be overused. The amount of space between the speaker and hearer can affect the quality of the communication encounter. The speaker should employ spatial cues in a manner consistent with the speech purpose.

The voice does more than simply render a word symbol into audible form. It enables the speaker to impart various shades of meaning to the spoken word, it transmits an impression of the speaker as a person, and it acts as a factor of attention. The controllable elements of voice are pitch, loudness, rate, and quality. These elements should be varied in a manner consistent with the sense of the verbal element of the message. Faults in distinctness of vocal sounds (enunciation) are more readily forgiven than faults in the correctness of the sounds (pronunciation). Acceptability of pronunciation varies from region to region. You are advised to emulate the pronunciation of the best-educated speakers in your geographical area.

Suggested Readings

Bormann, Ernest G., and Bormann, Nancy C. *Speech Communication*. 2d ed. New York: Harper and Row, 1977. Chapters 4–5.

Brooks, William D. *Speech Communication*. 3d ed. Dubuque, IA: Wm. C. Brown Company Publishers, 1978. Chapter 12.

Ehninger, Douglas; Monroe, Alan H.; and Gronbeck, Bruce E. *Principles and Types of Speech Communication*. 8th ed. Glenview, IL: Scott, Foresman, 1978. Chapters 14, 15.

Knapp, Mark L. *Nonverbal Communication in Human Interaction*. 2d ed. New York: Holt, Rinehart and Winston, 1978.

Leathers, Dale G. *Nonverbal Communications Systems*. Boston: Allyn and Bacon, 1976.

Reid, Loren. *Speaking Well*. 3d ed. New York: McGraw-Hill, 1977. Chapters 12, 13.

Listening
Evaluation and Criticism

Know how to listen and
you will profit even
from those who talk
badly.

Plutarch

"Some persons don't listen very well."

"What did you say?"

This exchange might well serve as the keynote of this chapter. For although listening is an important human activity, most persons are not very proficient at it. The significance of listening might best be demonstrated by the fact that it plays such a vital and essential role in our individual lives and, indeed, in our civilization. Much of what we know about the past has come to us through listening. Small children learn much about their new world through listening, for it is their first means of acquiring information and ideas about their environment. As adults we use listening more than any other communication skill. The time we spend in listening far exceeds the time spent in reading, writing, or speaking. It has been estimated that we spend 40 to 50 percent of our total communication time engaged in listening. In fact, one of the authors of this text conducted a research project that concluded that we spend more than one-third of our waking hours listening. Stop in the middle of what you are doing a few times during the day, and you will soon discover that the statistics concerning listening are quite valid. We listen at home, on the job, at school, and at play.

Inherent in our definition and explanation of communication is the concept that speech is a two-way process. Speaking and listening are the two indispensable ingredients of communication; there can be no effective speech without someone to listen. If our discussion of oral communication is to have real meaning, then, we must give a proper share of attention to listening.

Listening, as part of the communication process, has taken on added importance with the onset of the "era of communication." Not only are we having to listen more, but we are confronted with a larger variety of individuals making specific demands on our actions and thoughts. Some of these individuals rely on the supposition that we are poor listeners. The cult leader wants our minds, the politician wants our votes, and the huckster wants our money. Listening is extremely important in a time when mass media seek to determine our tastes and run our lives.

But what kind of listeners are we? There is sufficient evidence to support the generalization that people, as a whole, are poor listeners. Two separate studies concluded that a large percentage of those tested could not locate a central idea after listening to exposition that had been designed for clarity and simplicity. Other results point to the generalization that listeners are able to comprehend only a small percentage of what they hear. Perhaps the best proof for the assertion that people are poor listeners can be found by some serious introspection on the part of each of us. Many of the most common communication breakdowns can indeed be assigned to faulty listening. Too many of us are conditioned to believe that if we do not understand something, it is the fault of the speaker.

Research into the listening habits of students reveals some alarming results. Ask yourself how you rank in the six common weaknesses uncovered by researchers.

1. Persons tend to stop listening when the material is uninteresting. The findings show that most of us pay attention only to that material we like.
2. Persons tend to be influenced more by the dramatic elements of a message than by the logical elements.
3. Most persons have a short listening span.
4. Most listeners have a difficult time separating the essential from the nonessential.
5. Listeners are influenced more by the speaker's voice than by the reasoning of the message.
6. Persons tend to believe what they hear in broadcast speeches. Their assumption seems to be that if speakers are on radio or television, they must be important and their ideas therefore merit belief.

Substituting good listening habits for the common faults just mentioned can produce important benefits. Sharpened awareness is good protection against the devices and techniques of the unethical and sophistic speaker. Furthermore, good listening enables you to add to your storehouse of information, to update and revise your collection of facts, skills, attitudes, and beliefs. It adds depth and dimension to even the simplest daily experiences. You will find yourself noticing and appreciating things of which you had previously been unaware. Finally, good listening helps to improve your speaking. By listening carefully to the speeches of others, you will be able to select those characteristics of content and delivery that ought to be emulated and those that should be avoided.

You will discover that most of the time spent in speech class is spent listening to student speeches and to remarks of the instructor. In fact, you will probably listen to over one hundred speeches in your class, while you deliver only five or six. Take full advantage of this listening time to sharpen your perception, and you will be a better speaker as well as a better listener for the experience.

Purposes and Levels of Listening

The purposes for listening are as diversified as the reasons for speaking. Yet there are basically only two major purposes for listening—social and informational.

Social listening is often used when our purpose is either therapeutic or for enjoyment. By therapeutic we mean those countless communication contacts when we share feelings and build and maintain supporting relationships. For example, imagine that a close friend has just smashed his new car and tells you how frustrated and upset he is. In this circumstance there is really nothing you can do, yet your friend feels better because you have listened and offered moral support.

The enjoyable aspects of listening are rather obvious. We listen to music, watch television, go to movies and plays, and engage in a great deal of social conversation.

Although most listening involves *information*, there are many occasions when that information has some specialized purpose. We may need it so that we can perform a specific act. For example, we listen in order to learn how to saddle a horse. The information we are listening to may also be used as part of our decision-making processes—listening to a political speaker asking for our vote.

Not only does listening serve both social and informational purposes, it operates on different levels and at varying degrees of efficiency. For example, we listen to the "Information" operator offering us a telephone number that we promptly forget as soon as we have dialed it. We have listened only to the degree that will permit short-lived recall of the requested number. On the other hand, a friend tells us how to treat a rattlesnake bite shortly before we embark on a rock-climbing trip and we understand and recall that information for some time thereafter. Then again we listen to other communication partners and come away with little or no recall or understanding of their messages. It would appear, then, that the listening level to which we should all aspire is the one that best enables us to *understand* and *remember* what we hear. Because this is a book about improvement, we are concerned with helping you reach that ideal level of listening efficiency.

Barriers to Effective Listening

Listening is a complex activity. It consists of two component activities—the physical operation of a sense organ and an accompanying mental process. Some authorities distinguish *hearing* from *listening*, maintaining that when we hear, we perceive sounds only, but when we listen, hearing is accompanied by a deliberate and purposeful act of the mind. To listen means to get meaning from that which is heard. This distinction cautions us that attention to a speaker's voice is no guarantee of efficient listening. There are many other reasons why our listening behavior is often impeded. Some of these barriers are worth examining in detail, for they can keep us from participating in an enjoyable and enlightening experience.

Physical Conditions As a Barrier

As a listener you will experience some physical barriers over which you have no control and others over which you have some measure of control. Distracting sounds, poor acoustics, and uncomfortable seating arrangements are usually distractions that you cannot manipulate, although there are times when you can move your seat or close a window. The most effective device for surmounting most physical barriers is *concentration,* the core of all good listening.

The real danger of a physical barrier is that the listener may use the barrier (distraction) as an excuse for tuning the speaker out. We all know from experience that we can yield to any distraction quite easily, and thus make this distraction the main focus of our attention. The conscientious listener and the sincere speaker are aware of the problems caused by physical barriers, and both work diligently to overcome these obstructions to listening.

A Casual Attitude As a Barrier

Too often we approach the communication situation without the right frame of mind. We all tend to believe that because we hear noises and sounds, we are listening. One can hear and yet not listen. Because hearing is relatively easy, we assume that listening can also be somewhat casual and something we can do without much concentration and effort. Yet, it is this very attitude that forms one of the major barriers to listening.

This casual attitude toward listening develops in a very subtle way and over a long period of time. All day long we move in and out of listening situations that have different purposes. We listen to music or talk to friends and then quickly go to our history class. Without even realizing it, we slide from situations that demand very little concentration to informational encounters that call for higher levels of emotional commitment. While a casual listening attitude is permissible in a pleasurable encounter, it represents a serious barrier when one is attempting to listen for information.

Speaking-Thinking Rate As a Barrier

It is estimated that we speak an average of 125 to 150 words per minute. Our mind, however, is able to cope with approximately 400 words per minute. This means that the mind has a great deal of idle time. This excess time forms one of the major barriers to proficient listening. In most instances the time is spent wandering away from the task of critical and careful listening. It is during this free time that many listeners surrender to external distractions. The listening-thinking gap is often used for mental excursions ranging from daydreaming to thinking about the speaker's hairstyle. It would be far more beneficial to both sender and receiver if this time were spent analyzing the message.

Status and Role As a Barrier

Your impression of a person's status will determine, to a large degree, what you learn from that person and what influence he or she will have over your attitudes. From your own experience you have seen how your regard for the speaker influences what you actually hear. Status relationships between speaker and listener, as well as the various roles they both play, frequently determine the success or failure of the communication act.

We also know that when we respect someone, we tend to listen more attentively. Unfortunately, we may become overly concerned with the speaker as a person and neglect to think critically about what is being said. This barrier applies both to speakers for whom we have a high regard as well as to those for whom we have a lower regard. The good listener must recognize prestige, role, and status as factors present in all communication and must not let them prevent maximum comprehension and evaluation of what is being said.

Poor Listening Habits As a Barrier

Like so much of human behavior, listening tends to follow consistent patterns. Most of us fall into listening patterns that become so habitual we fail to fully realize we are creating a listening barrier. Although all of the barriers discussed in this section can become habitualized, Nichols and Stevens have suggested the six most common bad habits. At the risk of some duplication, they are listed here.

1. *Faking attention.* Perhaps most of us have learned to fake attention so as not to appear discourteous. Or maybe we wanted a teacher to think we were interested and learning. The danger of such fakery is that it may become habitual. It is easy for us to fall into the habit of faking listening and forget to sincerely pay attention.
2. *Listening only for facts.* Many times we listen only for facts and forget to locate main ideas. Try to listen for ideas first and then facts that support or explain the ideas.
3. *Avoiding difficult material.* Most of us feel comfortable with what we know and avoid what is unfamiliar or difficult. We turn off those listening situations requiring too much energy. Such avoidance becomes a habitualized pattern—whenever the material becomes slightly difficult, such a listener will drift away mentally, if not physically.
4. *Avoiding the uninteresting.* We often make the mistake of equating "interesting" with "valuable" and, hence, stop listening too soon.
5. *Criticizing delivery.* We often become overly concerned with *how* someone says something and forget to listen to *what* he or she says. A speaker is rejected and not listened to because of delivery rather than ideas.
6. *Yielding to distractions.* We have already discussed how physical conditions can be a barrier to listening. But there are mental and semantic distractions as well. *Mental* distractions occur when we talk silently to our favorite companion—ourselves. When our daydreams and fantasies take over and we forget about the speaker, we have a mental distraction. Ask yourself how many times a day you are supposed to be listening but, instead, find yourself planning tomorrow or evaluating what you did yesterday.

    We also frequently yield to *semantic* distractions. Persons often have different meanings for the same word, and if these differences are too great, a semantic distraction can occur. For example, if the speaker and listener were from different generations and cultures, a phrase such as "My, what a foxy chick" could cause a semantic distraction. What usually happens is that the listener must stop and think about specific meanings while the speaker continues his or her presentation.

Lack of Common Experiences As a Barrier

A barrier in listening can occur when speaker and listener are far apart in their backgrounds and in their current living environments. It is difficult to understand what is being said if you have not experienced, either directly or indirectly, the concepts being discussed. A college graduate, born and raised in a large eastern city, may well have a difficult time understanding and experiencing the messages and ideas of a farmer who has always lived in a small rural community. A true meeting of the minds is hampered when speaker and listener have lived in two separate worlds.

Preconceived Attitudes As a Barrier

When we listen we also make abundant use of our prejudices and our personal beliefs. These attitudes are usually deep-seated, developed over a long period of time, and it is not always easy to create a posture of open-mindedness. A Democrat listening to a Republican speaker will be less likely to give the speaker a fair hearing because of preconceived attitudes about the characteristics of Republicanism. To break the barrier of preconceived attitudes we must try to exert some command over our emotions and initial responses. We must try to hold judgment until we have *listened*—completely and objectively—to what is said.

Constant Self-Focus As a Barrier

We have talked about being overly concerned with self in connection with a number of the other barriers; yet this particular problem is important enough to warrant special consideration. There are usually three reasons for allowing personal concerns to dominate listening behavior. First, listening is often obstructed when we adopt the "I must defend my position" attitude. In these instances we stop listening and engage ourselves in mental debate. If someone says to us, "Gun laws in this country are too rigid," and to ourselves we say, "What is he talking about? Last year there were over ten thousand people killed with hand guns," then clearly a barrier to continued listening has arisen.

Second, many of us adopt the "I already know what you have to say" attitude. This barrier begins to form when we say to ourselves, "Oh no, not another speech on drug addiction." We would suggest that the person who assumes this position may be missing a great deal of life. Think of what a narrow view we have when we are so dogmatic as to believe we know all there is to know on any subject. Much of what we have learned has been acquired by listening, and we would be foolish to ever stop listening.

Our last self-focus barrier finds us wondering, "How am I coming through?" In such a situation our concern is not with the listening, but rather with what we are going to say and how we appear. We can all grant that most people are slightly egocentric and vain; however, when this preoccupation with self dominates our thoughts, we have trouble deciding where to focus our attention. Listening is suspended when we pause to ask ourselves, "I wonder if she thought my remark was clever?"

It is important to remember that these barriers can destroy the critical link between speaker and listener. In communication we receive word-symbols representing someone else's message, and we attempt to extract from them the meaning intended by the sender. In speaking we cannot go back and relisten as we can go back and reread; so the word-symbol relationship must be free from barriers whenever possible.

Improving Your Listening

Listening is a communication skill that can be improved with serious practice and training. If you genuinely desire to improve, your speech class offers an excellent arena for that improvement. You will have an opportunity to listen to a variety of speakers discussing a wide range of topics. You might begin your efforts at improvement by having your listening behavior reflect some of the suggestions listed below.

An analysis of your current listening habits may provide the motivation you need to improve your listening in the future. In a sense we are voicing the maxim "know thyself." When we talk about beginning your improvement with introspection, we mean both your outward and inward listening characteristics. Let us explain. By outward characteristics we are referring to how others perceive you as a listener. Your posture, eye contact, and the like will influence the kind of messages persons send you. Speaking and listening are interrelated as part of the activity we call communication. Therefore, how people relate to you correlates with how you listen, or at least *appear* to listen, to them. Hence, we suggest you try to identify just how you present yourself to others. Do you appear interested, enthusiastic, sincere, bored? The answers to these and other such questions will help you understand your role as a listener.

The second listening characteristic relates to what is going on in your head. We have already mentioned the importance of being objective, and now we are asking you to take this objectivity one step further by trying to recognize the prejudices and biases that you carry around inside you. If you have a negative attitude toward homosexuals, and a member of the Gay Students Union speaks to you, this prejudice will influence how you listen. However, by identifying these internal states, and by being able to assess their influence on how you listen, you might be able to listen more objectively and receive some positive rewards from the exchange.

**Be Motivated to
Listen**

Probably the most important step you can take in becoming a better listener is to resolve that *you will listen* more efficiently. This simple commitment will give you a sound new attitude about listening, and improvement will be noticeable at once. What we suggest is quite transparent—*want to listen.*

Efficient listening begins with motivation. Researchers in the area of listening have concluded that if you are motivated to listen, you will be a more alert and active receiver. The material will be more meaningful if you believe it affects you personally. What prompts you to listen might be something as pragmatic as making a sale if you listen carefully to what your customer is saying or as abstract as listening because you owe it to the speaker. In either case, if you are motivated, you will discover that you cannot be easily distracted.

Although motivation, in itself, is not enough to overcome all problems in listening, it is requisite to becoming a good listener. In short, to be a good listener you should bring the following attitudes to the listening situation: (1) want to listen, (2) find a personal reason for listening, and (3) be willing to do your part in the listening situation.

**Be Prepared to
Listen**

Think about listening even before the speaker sends the first message by keeping yourself informed on topics that you may have occasion to judge and evaluate.

For specific listening experiences prepare yourself in four ways:

1. Learn all you can about the subject, speaker, and situation. This knowledge, much like an audience analysis, will help you understand and appraise what the speaker will say. It will also aid you in comprehending and overcoming the problems of word-symbol relationships.

2. Minimize physical barriers by placing yourself in a position where you can easily see and hear the speaker.
3. Eliminate all distractions in your environment that might call attention away from the speaker. For example, leave the school newspaper outside the classroom; it might later become a distraction.
4. Be ready to take notes when appropriate. Having to stop and look for paper and pencil during the talk may force you to miss key points.

Be Objective

You can improve your listening immeasurably by maintaining an objective attitude as you listen to what is being discussed. You should approach a communication situation with an open mind and a spirit of inquiry.

Attend critically to each of the speaker's words, but do not make judgments until points are fully developed. Be alert for items that are implausible and misleading; but be aware of the larger principle the speaker is developing. Let the speaker explain and summarize all the main points before you draw conclusions.

We cease to be objective listeners when we allow our emotions and our prejudices to control our understanding. As we listen to speakers who profess views alien to our own, we sometimes fail to hear them out because our feelings are so deeply involved. Our natural tendency is to start composing a rebuttal of the opposing ideas and thinking of further arguments. Our emotions are getting in the way of what is actually being said. Admittedly, it is difficult to control our emotions and our preconceived attitudes, but conscious effort to declare a truce with bias will aid our overall comprehension of what is being expressed.

Be Alert to All Clues

It is important to listen for the speaker's *main* ideas. This must be a conscious and diligent search, for we cannot expect every speaker to underline the main point or stop and say, "What follows is my central thesis."

Be watchful for all specific clues to meaning contained in the elements of the speaking situation. The setting, the staging of the event, and the program notes can give insight to what will be said. The speaker's inflection, rate, emphasis, voice quality, and bodily actions can often offer clues to the meaning of what is being said and what the speaker feels is most important.

Clues naturally abound in the content and arrangement of the material. The vigilant listener makes note of the speaker's use of partitions, enumerations, transitions, topic sentences, and internal and final summaries. Clues common to writing, such as boldface type, italics, and quotation marks, are replaced with clues of voice, body, material, and arrangement.

Make Use of Thinking-Speaking Time Difference

As noted earlier, we normally think at a pace about three times faster than our speaking pace. As good listeners we can use this time to think about what the speaker is saying. We can ask ourselves, "How does this item relate to the speaker's main purpose? How does this main point support that purpose?" As alert listeners we can make this time gap work for us instead of against us. By concentrating on what is being said, instead of worrying or mentally arguing with the speaker, we can put the time difference to efficient use. This extra time can also be used to take notes when the situation warrants. Finally, the free time can always be used to summarize mentally and review what the speaker has said.

Avoid the "Mystery of Words" Fallacy

A good listener is always aware that words being used by the speaker may not accurately represent what the speaker thinks or feels. The person talking is using words to represent an idea or a feeling; the word is not the idea or feeling but an abstract symbol standing for what the speaker really means. As a trained listener, try to go beyond the words you hear. Be concerned with the speaker's motives and purposes. Finding out *why* someone is talking can often yield information far more valuable than that gained from the words themselves.

Empathy provides another way of avoiding the "mystery of words" fallacy. If you can see the problem (issue) the way the speaker sees it, the chances of reaching a mutual frame of reference will be greatly enhanced. In essence, you must ask yourself if the words used by the speaker represent his or her *true* feelings and ideas.

Use Feedback

Making abundant use of feedback is another way we gain more from communication encounters. As listeners we can use the opportunity feedback affords us to talk back to the sender of the message. In its most undisguised form this feedback can be as simple as telling the speaker you do not understand. This form of feedback lets you hear the message again, either repeated in the same words or explained in a different manner.

There are a number of ideas for the listener to keep in mind when using feedback. First, the speaker must perceive the feedback you are sending. Requests for clarification are lost if they are not received. Second, the feedback must not be ambiguous. It does not aid a speaker if he or she must stop and try to decide what emotion your facial expression is trying to convey. Are you smiling to say you understand what is being talked about, or is the grin you wear a reflection of sarcasm? Third, the feedback you give the speaker should directly relate to what is going on. It is of little benefit to either party if response is delayed to the point when it is no longer germane.

Practice Listening

Proficiency in any skill is the result of a great deal of conscientious effort. You should therefore practice listening. The poor listener avoids difficult listening situations and evades dull material. A case in point might be a college lecture on a highly abstract concept that defies the application of interest devices by even the most skillful speaker. In such cases the listener has to work along with the speaker at gaining meaning. It is a great temptation to stop listening when listening requires effort. Because of this the weak listener never improves. Force yourself to practice; make yourself listen to music, speeches, and conversations that seem to hold no *obvious* interest value.

Listening to Speeches

The act of receiving oral language involves three steps: (1) recall or deduction of meanings from each spoken word-symbol, (2) comprehension of ideas presented by different combinations of these word-symbols, and (3) use of the ideas presented to build understanding by adding to, modifying, or rejecting previous learning. We must perceive, comprehend, and finally use or reject what the speaker says.

We are constantly besieged with requests to vote, give, buy, feel, and think in one way or another. A poor listener is easy prey for the sophist, huckster, shyster, and propagandist. Our major defenses against those who choose to influence and control our behavior are critical thinking and cautious evaluation. Both of these skills can be learned, and your speech class, by allowing you an opportunity to hear over a hundred speeches, is an excellent place to cultivate your listening ability.

As a listener you have a responsibility to listen attentively if you are to judge and evaluate, and possibly accept or reject what is being said. Ethical responsibility in the speech act is not borne by the speaker alone. The listener as well as the speaker shares in the moral issues of the speech act. We might say that a listener's first obligation is to offer full attention to the speaker. Admittedly this is much easier to write about than to carry out. Each communication act is rife with distractions, but these must be overcome if we are to fairly analyze what we hear.

Once you have paid attention, you are better able to locate the techniques and devices of the unethical speaker. You will also be able to make valid decisions on what is being proposed.

As a responsible listener you must be alert to the ethical character of those who address you. It is useful to be aware of the propaganda devices that are daily employed. The Institute of Propaganda Analysis has defined the following forms as a partial list of the most common techniques.

1. *Name-calling.* This device attempts to give a person or an idea a bad label. It is used to make us reject and condemn the idea or person without examining the evidence. For example, you may have heard something like: "This clearly shows that Ms. Smith, by her immoral actions, is un-American and disloyal to the principles of our great country"; "The proposal recommended by the school board is undemocratic, dishonest, and riddled with graft and corruption"; or, "Senator Jones should not be elected to the U.S. Senate because he is a 'radical liberal.' "

   Name-calling has played an immense and powerful role in the history of our civilization. Bad names have ruined reputations, caused wars, and sent people to prison. Be wary of the individual who uses name-calling instead of concrete evidence and logical reasoning.

2. *Glittering generality.* In this case a "virtue word" is used to make the hearer accept and approve the thing or idea without examining the evidence. We believe in, fight for, live by "virtue words" about which we have deep-seated feelings. Such words are *Christianity, freedom, right, democracy, motherhood,* and *liberty.* If a proposition is "for the good of the people," or "will maintain the Constitution," the speaker suggests it cannot be bad.

3. *Testimonial.* This technique consists of having some respected person say that a given idea, program, product, or individual is good or bad without furnishing any basis for the value judgment. In many instances the "expert" is not even competent to evaluate the issue under discussion. Be on the watch

for phrases such as, "My doctor said," or "The President said," for these, in many instances, may be an indication that the speaker is appealing to you through testimonial. Remember the issue, not just the person.

4. *Plain Folks.* This method is used by the speaker attempting to convince an audience that he or she and the ideas presented are good and honest because they are "of the people," the "plain folks." This is often the technique of military dictatorships. How often have we heard new regimes say, "We have overthrown the government because it was cruel to the poor and simple peasants." In our own country we hear politicians say they want the vote "of the common person." Speakers even use the jargon of a particular group to demonstrate they are the "plain folks."

5. *Card Stacking.* This method involves the selection and use of facts or falsehoods, illustrations or distractions, and logical or illogical statements in order to give the best or the worst possible case for an idea, program, person, or product. The sender selects only those items that support his or her position, regardless of the distortion they may produce. Listing a few of the accomplishments of one's administration while leaving out all of the failures is an example of this technique. A speaker, of course, may not always have to offer all sides of a question: therefore the listener must be alert.

6. *Bandwagon.* This device implies that since many others have accepted a given proposal, the listener should do likewise. "Jump on the bandwagon," "Be on the winning side," "Everyone is doing it,"—all are examples of the bandwagon technique.

7. *Half-truths.* An unethical speaker will often tell only part of a fact or story knowing full well that the entire piece of evidence would harm his or her cause. A speaker who says, "Hunters need hand guns so they can continue to hunt," is leaving out some important facts regarding the relationship between cheap handguns ("Saturday night specials") and murders. There are many speakers who deliberately leave out important and basic evidence when presenting their arguments.

8. *Labeling.* The roots of this device are often found in negative stereotypes. Speakers employ labeling to generalize about an entire class of people or events. For example, to say "that hippie," or "those Jews" is to infer that all persons in that category carry a negative connotation. We know, of course, that such evaluation and labeling is negative by implication and does not allow for individual differences.

These techniques can on occasion be used legitimately, but their unethical use should not be condoned.

Speech Criticism Through communication we influence other persons. In most instances this influence alters another person's behavior toward predetermined goals. Because of the impact we have on each other, it behooves us as listeners to question much of what we hear. Being critical does not mean that we offer blanket rejections to all we encounter. Instead, criticism enables us to question, evaluate, and eventually make logical judgments concerning the messages with which we are confronted.

We are all speech critics, for we are asked to listen to and evaluate oral discourse all day long. Criticism, like speaking and listening, can have various levels of proficiency. Becoming knowledgeable about speech criticism is a responsibility that should be assumed by all educated citizens. Decision-making is part of the democratic process, and sound decisions are more likely to be reached if the citizenry possesses the skills necessary for the intelligent evaluation of a variety of viewpoints.

Wilson and Arnold maintain that the critic may examine a speech from three general orientations—*pragmatic, ethical,* or *artistic.* The critic with a pragmatic orientation is primarily concerned with the effect of the speech. Granting that the speaker has a specific purpose for engaging in communication, the pragmatic critic asks questions concerning the success of the speech. Did the speaker get results? Was the specific purpose accomplished?

The ethically oriented critic focuses on the speaker's motives. Did the speaker deal with important and timely issues in an honest and sincere manner? The critic's conclusions are often quite subjective because it is difficult for all members of a culture to agree on ethical standards. Yet the ethical analysis is important because it forces us to look at moral and philosophical issues vital to us and our society.

The critic with an artistic orientation is concerned with the speaker's skill in employing the ingredients of successful speech-making. What rhetorical methods were used? How practiced and creative was the speaker in the use of these methods?

As you would suspect, in most instances a speech critic applies all three points of view to oral discourse. Once the general questions have been asked, the critic moves to a series of specific questions. Let us examine a few of the items about which specific questions need to be asked as a means of establishing guidelines for you to follow.

The first issue facing any critic concerns the speaker's purpose. All communication induces changes on the part of the listener. In discussing these changes we should remember that *each person*, by the response he or she makes, is the most accurate gauge of the speaker's purpose. One person may well laugh at material that brings a companion to the brink of sorrow. This is why any analysis of purpose must begin with the assumption that speech purpose is the domain of the *creator* of the message. Therefore, the listener asks this important question: "What does the speaker want from the audience?" Many critics find it useful to answer this question by placing the speaker's intent under one of the General Ends of Speech (informing, persuading, entertaining). Others use the setting of the speech to analyze the speaker's purpose (courtroom speeches, ceremonial speeches, and so forth).

The critical listener who analyzes speech purposes in more detail must investigate the speaker's specific purpose. You will recall that this is the specific response being sought by the speaker ("By the end of my speech I want my audience to. . . .").

The critical listener distinguishes the issue from the person. We can sometimes become so impressed with a speaker's personality, voice, and image that we neglect to evaluate what he or she says. The critical listener separates what the speaker says from what the speaker is.

The critical listener is aware of the problems inherent in language. Words are symbols standing for things— they are not the things themselves. The critical listener recognizes loaded words and ambiguous words and learns to be careful of words such as *un-American, freedom, liberalism, socialism, or extremism.* One word may have many uses, and the critical listener tries to interpret the speaker's meaning in light of this variety of uses.

The critical listener applies the tests of evidence and reasoning. He or she is familiar with the propaganda techniques we have discussed and is able to isolate half-truth, name-calling, and other devices.

The critical listener detects the substitution of generalities for specifics—of glibness for sincerity. He or she demands dates, names, numbers, and places. The speaker who omits key information is often the same person who relies on innuendos and who exaggerates some points out of proportion to their importance while understating other more fundamental points.

The critical listener applies the tests of evidence and reasoning (to be discussed in chapter 5) to the material presented by the speaker. He or she is concerned with the validity and reliability of illustrations, examples, statistics, testimony, and analogies. By checking the authenticity of the facts presented and the probability that the facts mean what they are said to mean, the critical listener is able to make more accurate judgments.

Finally, the critical listener questions the relevance of the material offered by the speaker. He or she knows that material may meet all the tests of reliability and validity and yet be irrelevant to the point under discussion. "So what?" or "What is the point?" are the critical listener's inevitable questions.

Evaluating Speeches

At the end of most classroom speeches you will have an opportunity to present an informal critique, either oral or written. As you evaluate the speeches of others, try to implement the broad principles discussed by your instructor and by this text. The following items are designed to guide your assignments in speech evaluation.

1. *Did the speaker have a worthwhile purpose?* Whenever we speak we are occupying both the life and the time of another individual. Therefore, all listeners have a right to ask whether or not the purpose of the speech justified the amount of time they gave it (or were asked to give it). Was the purpose clear or were the speaker and the audience part of an ambiguous encounter? Aimless ramblings, touching on topics from pets to pollution, serve no real purpose and only contribute to confusion.

2. *Closely related to the first question is the speaker's level of commitment.* Has the speaker made an attempt to be objective and fair to himself or herself, to the audience, and to the subject? Did the speaker seem to care about communicating, or was he or she simply going through the motions of fulfilling an assignment? For example, did the speaker appear to have practiced the speech?

3. *Did the speaker know the subject?* Listeners have a right to ask that the sender of any message be prepared. Specifically, we can inquire as to the amount of research manifest in the speech. We have all listened to speakers who sounded as if they had prepared their remarks as they walked from their chair to the rostrum. This may be appropriate for an impromptu speech, but it should not be tolerated when the topic calls for in-depth analysis and research.

4. *Was there evidence that the speaker had analyzed the audience?* Were such factors as the audience's age, sex, education, and attitudes taken into consideration? Did the speaker indicate that the speech was being directed at the classroom audience or at some hypothetical audience?

5. *Was the speech structurally sound?* Did the subdivisions, both major and minor, relate to and support the main ideas? Were the transitions between ideas clear?

6. *Did the speaker use language meaningfully?* Did he or she employ words and phrases that were clear and adequately defined? Were imagery and word pictures used effectively? Did he or she avoid clichés, slang, poor grammar? Was the speaker's usage appropriate to the audience, the occasion, the subject?

7. *Did the speaker use factors of attention and interest in both the content and delivery of the speech?* Too many of us are guilty of assuming that all we have to do is talk and the audience will listen. The folly of this view is made evident when as listeners we are asked to consider a speech that not only lacks interest, but also is presented by someone who makes no attempt at arousing and focusing our attention.

8. *Did the speaker's illustrations, examples, statistics, testimony, and analogies meet the tests of evidence?* Was enough evidence employed to support each point?

9. *How effectively did the speaker employ visual aspects of delivery?* Did he or she maintain good eye-contact? Did he or she have good posture? Were gestures and movements skillfully executed? Were animated facial expressions used?

10. *How effectively did the speaker employ his or her voice?* Was there sufficient variety of rate, pitch, volume? Was enunciation clear and pronunciation correct?

11. *Was the speaker a credible spokesperson on the subject?* Did words, actions, and dress contribute to the speech's believability? Or did the speaker behave in ways that detracted from his or her credibility?

12. *What was the total impression left by the speech?* As listeners, we should evaluate the main idea as well as the subpoints. At the end of the speech we should ask ourselves, "What is the overall effect of the speech?"

These are by no means the only categories for evaluation. Doubtless you will discover others as you gain experience in listening to various types of speeches.

Three important suggestions are worth noting before we conclude this section. First, speech evaluation, in the classroom or out, should include much more than negative critical comments. We should point out praiseworthy qualities so that the speaker will be aware of those things he or she is doing well. For example, praise should be offered if the speaker employs concrete evidence for all of the assertions in a speech.

Second, our evaluations should tender suggestions for improvement. Constructive criticism allows both the speaker and the listener to learn from the communication experience. For example, how helpful it would be if you could tell certain members of your class that their speaking would be improved if they provided transitions as they moved from main point to main point.

Our final bit of advice: Listen carefully to your classmates as they evaluate other speeches and speakers. You may find that your own speaking profits from remarks directed to other speakers. For instance, if a speaker is told that he talks too fast, you may pause and reflect on your own rate of speech.

Listener Responsibility

Communication is a two-way process—speaker and listener are interrelated and need each other for a variety of reasons. To be effective listeners we must do more than listen; we must assume some of the responsibility for the total communication act. Not only should we evaluate what we have gained from the speaker but also we should be aware of what we have *given* the speaker. Did we make the speaker feel comfortable? Did we encourage or discourage communication?

We all know from personal experience that we not only feel better about ourselves and other persons, but we communicate more effectively when we are receiving positive feedback from our listeners. Ask yourself how much incentive you would have to continue speaking if the persons before you were frowning or reading newspapers. In short, our behavior, as listeners, affects the speaker.

A listener response that adds to the communication encounter may be a brief comment or action conveying to the sender the idea that the receiver is interested, attentive, and wishes the sender to continue. It is made quietly and briefly so as not to interfere with the sender's train of thought. We are, of course, talking about the receiver's role—the giving of information back to the sender so that the sender may know something of his or her effectiveness and that someone is listening and caring.

There are a number of specific actions the listener may take that will aid the speaker in communicating. Some of the acts listed below apply to platform speaking, while others are useful in discussion, interviewing, or everyday conversation.

1. *Eye contact* establishes rapport between sender and receiver and also encourages communication. Research indicates that we seem to look at people more when we feel comfortable around them. This bit of information should be used by the communicator who is sincere in his or her effort.
2. *Nodding the head slightly* also tells the speaker that you (the listener) are part of the communication process.

3. An act as simple as *smiling* can offer warmth and support to the speaker. It may be just what he or she needs to get over the nervous feeling that often confronts speakers.
4. *Casual remarks* such as "I see," "uh-huh," and "is that so" involve the listener with the speaker.
5. *Asking relevant questions* helps the speaker in two ways. First, your question may enable the speaker to clarify a point of confusion that might be troubling other members of the audience. Second, by asking your question you are demonstrating your interest both in the speaker and in the topic. This kind of positive feedback will greatly aid the speaker.
6. There will be times when you can help the speaker by *remaining silent*. Too often we contaminate a communication encounter by talking.

The important thing to remember is that *listening also means helping and aiding the speaker*. Creating an atmosphere that will bring out the best in the speaker should be a goal of every listener. It is to the advantage of both parties that the communication act be a pleasurable one.

The suggestions above should not be carried out in an artificial or deceptive manner. Remember, faking attention is a poor listening habit. Actions that offer support should be genuine and sincere.

Speaker Responsibility

The sender initiates the communication act in order to have an influence over the subsequent behavior of other people. The sender has the need and the desire to communicate. As speakers, then, we must constantly strive to meet our communication responsibilities. We must see to it that the listener is attentive to what we are saying. In this way we can better meet our specific communication needs.

Here are some of the more common techniques the sender can use to encourage more effective listening.

Try to Empathize

It is important that you speak *to* your listeners. To do this you must understand them—understand how they will react to you and your message. This is best accomplished by trying to hear your ideas and words as the listeners will. For example, if you have not thought about your listeners, you might well talk on a subject that holds little or no interest for them. By employing empathy, you will be able to view the content as the listeners will and will not be asking them to listen to material that is inappropriate and uninteresting.

Adjust Your Delivery

In chapter 3 we talked about how the speaker's voice and body can aid the listener in understanding the verbal message. Always make sure you can be heard. It is very frustrating for a listener to strain in order to know what is being said. Moreover, delivery should be animated enough to arouse and maintain interest.

Use Feedback	We told the listener to use feedback to improve his or her listening, and now we suggest that the same principle applies to the speaker. As senders we should be sensitive to what our messages are doing to the people who receive them. Are they paying attention? Do they look interested? Do they look confused? Are they seeking more information? These are but a few of the questions feedback may answer. Once we secure this information, via feedback, we are in a better position to make the necessary adjustments. If we sense apathy, we can try to arouse attention and point the material directly to the needs of the audience.
Be Clear	It is very difficult to listen to a speech that rambles aimlessly. As speakers, we can meet part of our responsibilities by being well organized. We will have much more to say about clarity and organization later in the book, but for now, remember that it is unfair of us to ask a listener to make sense of our disconnected and disjointed wanderings.
Be Interesting	The obvious implications of this point hardly warrant discussion. If material lacks interest for us, it is difficult to listen. Hence, as speakers we must strive to have our content lively, stimulating, and relevant.

Summary	Listening is one of our most important communication skills. Effective listening is an active process that demands conscientious effort on the part of the listener. Virtually everyone can improve his or her listening ability by simply becoming aware of some of the problems of listening and their remedies.
	The listener who is sincere about improvement should be alert to the major barriers to effective listening: physical conditions, casual attitude, speaking-thinking rate, status and role, poor listening habits, lack of common experience, preconceived attitudes, and constant self-focus.
	Listening can be improved if we are motivated, prepared, objective, and alert to all the communication cues (verbal and nonverbal) contained within the speaking situation. In addition, making use of spare time, avoiding the "mystery of words" fallacy, using feedback, and practicing can also be useful for improving listening behavior.
	Speech criticism and evaluation were also explored in this chapter. We recommended that the listener question much of what he or she hears, and whenever possible offer constructive criticism to the speaker.
	Finally, we pointed out that both the listener and the speaker have certain communication responsibilities built into each encounter. The listener should create a positive psychological environment by adopting a listening attitude and posture that will encourage the speaker to reach his or her full potential—the listener should try to put the speaker at ease. The speaker can meet some of his or her obligations by (1) trying to empathize with the listener, (2) making adjustments to the delivery, (3) using feedback, (4) being sure that the message is clear and well organized, and (5) seeing that content is interesting—lively, stimulating, and relevant.

Suggested Readings

Barker, Larry L. *Listening Behavior.* Englewood Cliffs, NJ: Prentice-Hall, 1971.

Black, Edwin. *Rhetorical Criticism.* University of Wisconsin Press, 1968.

Cathcart, Robert. *Post Communication.* New York: Bobbs-Merrill, 1966.

Dominick, Barbara A. *The Art of Listening.* Springfield, IL: Charles C Thomas, 1958.

Duker, Sam. *Listening: Readings, Vol. 2.* Metuchen, NJ: Scarecrow Press, 1971.

Nichols, Ralph G., and Stevens, Leonard A. *Are You Listening?* New York: McGraw-Hill, 1957.

Walter, Otis M., and Scott, Robert L. *Thinking and Speaking.* 4th ed. New York: Macmillan Publishing, 1979. Chapter 9.

Weaver, Carl H. *Human Listening.* New York: Bobbs-Merrill, 1972.

Wilson, John F., and Arnold, Carroll C. *Public Speaking As a Liberal Art.* 4th ed. Boston: Allyn and Bacon, 1978. Chapter 11.

Zelko, Harold P., and Dance, Frank E. *Business and Professional Speech Communciation.* 2d ed. New York: Holt, Rinehart and Winston, 1978. Chapter 7.

Your Ideas

Part 2

Evidence
The Foundation of Your Ideas

To reason correctly from false principle is the perfection of sophistry.

Emmons

We begin this chapter with an obvious yet often overlooked axiom of human behavior—*your attitudes and beliefs are highly personal and private, residing inside you, and they may not be the same attitudes and beliefs held by other persons.* Just because you believe capital punishment should be abolished, does not automatically mean other persons share that same opinion. Something in *your life,* an experience, an article, a speaker, has given you the data and the rationale that enabled you to reach the personal view you now hold. But another individual, with different experiences, might well have internalized different personal beliefs. What is important for our analysis is not that attitudes and beliefs are personal, but that these pre-dispositions were brought about by material that was, at one time, external to you. Someone, by what they did or said, contributed to your belief. Because communication involves the sending and receiving of messages, you have not only been the recipient of material that helped form your attitudes, but you have also sent messages that influenced other people—shaped their attitudes and beliefs. What we seek to do now is simply build on this point by offering some suggestions that will enable you to become more effective on those occasions when you know in advance that you would like to change or alter another person's attitude.

As members of a society that uses communication to share experiences, thoughts, and feelings, we are constantly telling others about our ideas and beliefs. When we have an idea we wish to share with another party, we endeavor to express that idea clearly and effectively so the listener will "see what we are talking about." If we desire to change someone's mind, we also strive to clarify, amplify, and defend our position. It is, indeed, an exhilarating sensation to know that what we asserted is interesting, understandable, and believable because we explained, illustrated, and demonstrated its merits and usefulness.

What is true with respect to explaining and supporting your ideas in everyday conversation is just as true in public speaking, but more demanding. Just as the builder uses certain materials to construct a house, so you, as a speaker, have to supply the materials for developing main ideas, and primary and secondary headings. We all know that stating a point does not necessarily render it believable or true. There may be assertions that listeners will accept at face value because the assertions are consistent with their existing beliefs and prejudices. But more frequently listeners require that assertions be backed up with proof. For example, a speaker on a local college campus recently advocated that the football team be disbanded on the grounds that it was a financial burden to the

79

student body. In large part because this charge was merely asserted, and not supported with proof, the speaker's plea was not heeded. The efficient communicator seeks to support his or her observations and positions and does not depend on chance or fate to win a point. The communicator furnishes the listener with the materials that prove the assertion to be credible and reliable.

Verbal Support

Among the things we say about a particular subject, some are incidental while others are fundamental. The incidental are often used to get and hold attention, while the fundamental are vital to the accomplishment of our purpose. Therefore, one of our basic tasks as speakers is to study our subjects until we recognize those elements in them that are essential to accomplishing our purpose. Those essential components, which help render our ideas understandable and believable, are called *forms of support*. The word "support" furnishes an accurate description of their function, for the materials selected offer sustenance for the central theme of the speech. They enable you to say to the listener, "Driving at fifty-five miles an hour is an excellent law, and here is why." The "whys" (which are your forms of support) enable you to offer reasons that might make your opinions believable and acceptable to another person.

Let us consider some of the forms of support available when we find it necessary and beneficial to clarify or prove an important and fundamental assertion.

Illustration (Example)

From the earliest days of the history of the human race, the storyteller has commanded and held attention. Use of the narrative as a device for proving, clarifying, and maintaining interest has been discussed by writers from Aristotle to the present. The very fact that a story or an example holds our attention renders it an excellent tool in many communication situations.

An illustration is the narration of a happening or incident that amplifies, proves, or clarifies the point under consideration. It is, in a sense, the speaker saying to the audience, "Here is an example of what I mean." In addition, it often aids memory by making the important features more noteworthy.

The illustration usually takes one of three forms—*the detailed factual illustration, the undeveloped factual illustration (specific instance), and the hypothetical illustration.* Some overlapping may occur as the speaker limits or extends the details.

The detailed, factual illustration usually takes the form of a narrative (story) that answers the questions who? what? where? when? and how? Because of the detail in the story, and because the story is true, the illustration can be both vivid and meaningful to the audience. The knowledge that something actually occurred is a source of interest. Notice how interest is stirred when we hear someone say, "Let me tell you of a case that actually happened." Trying to convince an audience that LSD is dangerous, a student speaker used this detailed, factual illustration:

A friend of mine had heard so much about lysergic acid diethylamide, more commonly called LSD, that he decided to try some. He and a few friends went to the home of his girlfriend. He took the LSD and waited for the "trip." He had one! He had a vision of police. On his "trip" the police were always after him. Wherever he went the police were there. They were always trying to catch him, but in his vision they never could reach him. When he came "down" (off his "trip") he had paranoia tendency toward the police. He had the feeling for weeks after that the police were trying to catch him. It became so bad that he had to leave school and go to a hospital for treatment. For my friend LSD was indeed dangerous and a very bad "trip."

Factual illustrations are also useful for *clarifying* as well as *proving* a point. For example, a speaker wanted to convince his listeners that federal Head Start programs were beneficial to the young people who took part in the programs. By the following illustrations he was able to explain what he meant while offering support for his contention:

A few years ago the small town where I lived instituted a Head Start program—a program whereby the Federal government pays for preschool children, many from underpriviledged homes, to attend classes and engage in activities that enable them to receive specialized instruction in reading. Carlos, one youngster who took part in the program, is now in the second grade and reading at a third-grade level. His teacher believes he is doing so well because he was able to learn some essential reading skills before he was thrust into a crowded classroom. For Carlos, Head Start made a major difference.

Still another speaker used a factual illustration to establish the premise that teaching by television is often more effective than traditional methods. She told, in detail, of the success of a college anthropology class taught by television, and how students in this class learned more than students enrolled in classes taught in the usual manner.

Because it is limited to one example, the illustration often serves as the springboard for the presentation of additional and more specific examples. For instance, in the following example, notice how the speaker is able to use his factual illustration as an introduction to additional evidence on the topic of "The Importance of Recycling."

The other day while I was enjoying a walk along the beach I noticed a number of shiny objects floating in the water. At first I thought they were fish so I decided to walk closer and have a better look. Much to my surprise, my nose and eyes soon told me that what I was smelling and seeing was not fish, but tin cans, plastic trash bags, and garbage sacks. I was seeing the negative effects of what is called ocean dumping—a waste disposal system that I have since discovered is bringing harmful results to those areas that have tried to dispose of their trash in this manner. The problem, however, seems to be that incineration and sanitary landfill methods also present serious problems.

In using the detailed, factual illustration, you will find it worthwhile to keep a few criteria in mind. First, see to it that your example relates directly to your point. It is often a temptation to use an illustration simply because it is a good story. If the audience has a difficult time seeing the connection between your assertion and your illustration, confusion will result. Second, use sufficient detail, clothed in image-evoking language, so that your illustration holds the interest of the audience. Third, be accurate. Avoid making your narrative a mixture of fact and fiction. Fourth, use the factors of attention discussed in chapter 8 as a means of making your illustrations appealing to the audience.

The undeveloped factual illustration is an example that omits much of the detail and development that characterize the extended factual illustration. Several such brief, condensed examples may be advanced by the speaker as a means of indicating the widespread nature of the situation or suggesting the frequency of an occurrence. Since it is short and takes little time to present, it allows the speaker an opportunity to present a great deal of proof material in a minimum amount of time. For instance, if you are asserting that college graduates are having problems locating teaching positions, you might establish your point by stating, "John Timmons, a friend of mine who majored in education, could not find a teaching position after he graduated from college. Graduates from San Francisco State College and from UCLA are also reporting a great deal of difficulty in locating teaching jobs."

Still another example of this form of evidence might appear in a talk about the value of the honor system. The case could be aided by saying: "The University of Indiana has found the honor system successful; Purdue University and the University of California at Davis have also reported satisfactory results from the honor system." By using actual people, places, events, and things, the speaker makes the material both meaningful and persuasive.

Some examples may require only a few words, like the name of a town or a person, while others may call for a sentence or two. In any case, using undeveloped illustrations adds strength and understanding to an idea. They provide excellent proof and are often most effective when they directly follow a detailed factual illustration. For example, a student who wanted to prove that a recent automobile strike had adversely affected the workers supported the position by relating the true story of a worker and his family. The speaker then bolstered the case by citing a number of undeveloped factual illustrations involving other workers.

The hypothetical illustration is a detailed fictional illustration that seeks to let the audience see "what could be" or what they might "suppose." It is most often used as a method of depicting future events or of making the future seem graphically clear. In a speech dealing with a proposal to raise school taxes, you might offer a hypothetical illustration of how the proposal would affect the audience. Or, you might offer a detailed illustration to convince the listeners that high school dropouts have a difficult time securing employment—as in the following:

Suppose a friend of yours in high school decides that he has had enough school. He is doing poorly in math and English and feels there is no real need to finish the semester. On Saturday he asks the owner of a local market to give him a job. The market owner can pay only eighty dollars a week. But your friend, having never made that much money, decides to take the job instead of reporting back to school on Monday.

After about two weeks on the job he is dismissed. Business is off at the store and the owner can't afford any extra help. Your friend then goes from store to store and from factory to factory looking for some sort of employment. But he soon discovers that employers are not interested in hiring someone without at least a high school education. Your friend, in essence, is unable to find work because he left school.

Depicting the future with the illustration can place the listener in a situation that affects him or her personally and emotionally. A statement such as "What happens if you reject this plan?" affords the speaker an opportunity to place the listener in the center of a hypothetical picture. The following example, from a speech on cigarettes and lung cancer, shows how the listener may see himself or herself as the central figure in the illustration.

Let us assume for a moment that you are a smoker, and as a smoker you might find yourself in the following situation. You wake up one night and find that your chest hurts more than usual. At breakfast you also seem to be coughing more and are having difficulty catching your breath. You decide it is just a cold, so you put off going to the doctor. As the day goes on, the pain and the cough get worse, so you make an appointment to see the doctor. As part of your examination the doctor takes an X ray of your lungs, an X ray that reveals grave damage to your lungs. The doctor tells you what you already know—that if you had not smoked this might never have happened.

In using the hypothetical illustration you should keep a few key points in mind. First, you can select any story you want when you use a hypothetical illustration, but you should never present an imaginary story as being true-to-fact. Employing phrases such as "imagine a situation such as this," or "suppose you discover," will allow the listener to separate fact from fiction. Second, if the hypothetical illustration is going to be effective, it should be reasonable and capable of happening. An illustration that is an obvious exaggeration might offend the careful listener. Third, always remember that an imaginary story proves very little. As a student of communication you should try to locate a factual example if you are trying to prove a point, and rely on the hypothetical illustration if you are trying to clarify a point or arouse emotions. Fourth, in using the hypothetical example, like the factual, make certain that it is appropriate and related directly to the point in question. The story must not be in the speech for its own sake, but for the purpose of supporting or clarifying an idea.

Testing Examples and Illustrations

If you are to be confronted with examples, both as speaker and as listener, you must be sure the examples meet certain requirements. When you employ an example or an illustration, you may be asking the listener to draw a conclusion from the specific illustration. For instance, someone might try to condemn all

New York drivers because of a bad experience while driving on Broadway. In drawing the generalization from the specific example, the speaker is suggesting that the example supports the assertion. Therefore, the following precautions should be observed whenever you use or listen to examples and illustrations that are presented as a justification for a specific hypothesis.

1. *Are there enough examples to justify the generalization?* There can be, of course, no absolute measure of "enough" in applying this test. The answer depends on many factors, but largely upon the phenomena being discussed. If the conclusion drawn is controversial and primarily a value judgment, a listener should expect more than one or two illustrations. Someone telling you a friend was beaten and robbed in downtown Burbank would not be in a position to establish the premise that Burbank streets are dangerous with that single example.

2. *Is the example or illustration a typical case?* Often people try to change our beliefs and opinions by offering as proof an example that is, under closer examination, an isolated case. It would be unfair, for example, to judge the entire membership of a fraternity by the bad experience of one person.

3. *Is the example clearly relevant to the idea?* When we talked about critical listening in chapter 4, we suggested that the careful listener learns to ask "So what?" of certain information. Checking the relevancy of examples is merely an extension of that idea. If you were talking about the dangers of night driving and cited only an illustration of someone whose brakes failed, you would be guilty of offering an irrelevant case.

4. *Is there other evidence to support the conclusion being made by the generalization?* This test should be applied to any evidence, whether it is presented in the form of an illustration, statistic, testimony, or analogy. Before you are satisfied that the example proves the specific point, you should ask for other facts and authoritative opinions that might suggest the falsity or validity of the generalization. Suppose, for example, that you are urging reforms in college registration procedures and have offered a single illustration to substantiate the need for reforms. Your position will be enhanced if you offer additional support—such as citing remarks of the dean of admissions that add believability to your thesis.

Statistics

Statistics are examples. Instead of talking about one or two cases or instances, we attempt to measure and define them quantitatively. Statistics are facts or occurrences represented numerically; they compare or show proportions as a means of helping a speaker develop and prove a point. Used in this way statistics help compress, summarize, and simplify facts that relate to the issue in question. Statistics are simply generalizations derived from comparisons of individual instances.

Statistics, like illustrations, may be brief or quite detailed. The mere statement, "Medical authorities estimate that there are approximately thirty thousand hemophiliacs of all types in the United States," would be an example of the use of statistics. There are also occasions when statistics take a much longer form. Discussing the fact that waste disposal is a serious problem, a speaker used the following statistics to show just what people are trying to discard:

> In one year we needed to find a place to dump 2 million tons of major appliances, 22 million tons of food, 10 million tons of newspapers, 3 million tons of plates, towels, and napkins, and 52 million tons of bottles and containers.

You should not assume that because statistics are numbers they are automatically uninteresting. A well-trained speaker can make them appealing. Talking in opposition to the Resources Planning act, the speaker in the following example offered statistics in an interesting manner:

> Now obviously, America needs her Wilderness. But she already has quite a bit! Some 14.7 million acres to be exact. An area bigger than New Hampshire, Connecticut, Massachusetts, and Rhode Island combined. But how much is enough? Today, for example, an additional 350 million acres are either being proposed for Wilderness designation or study, or may eventually qualify for study. That's an area three and a half times the size of California.

Statistics often enable a speaker to make quite striking comparisons. Notice how a speaker, who is opposing the fifty-five miles-per-hour speed limit, uses comparisons to make his point:

> According to the calculations of most economists, the fifty-five mph limit causes enough of a traffic slowdown to waste about $6 billion worth of travel time per year. The National Highway Traffic Safety Administration says we save about four thousand five hundred lives per year because of the fifty-five mph limit. Hence, it costs about $1.5 million per life saved. Is this a bargain, or are there other social policies that might save more lives for less money? Well, it has been estimated that placing a smoke detector in every home in the U.S. would save about as many lives in total as the fifty-five mph limit, and would cost only fifty to eighty thousand dollars per life saved; or more kidney-dialysis machines could save lives for only about two thousand dollars per life saved; and there are even a number of highway improvements that can be made, through reducing roadside hazards, that cost only about twenty thousand to one hundred thousand dollars per life saved. At a cost of $1.3 million per saved life, the fifty-five mph limit is hardly a bargain.

Statistics are a strong form of proof and should be gathered and presented in the most effective manner possible. The following few rules may increase your effectiveness.

1. *Whenever possible, present your statistics as round numbers, especially when several are offered.* It is much easier to remember the population of a city if we hear "one and a half million," instead of "1,512,653." There

are, of course, instances where exactness is essential. The purpose for which the statistics are used should be the main factor in making your selection.

2. *Give specific and complete source citations for your statistics.* Saying "these statistics prove that" or "quoting from a reliable source" does not tell your audience where you located your information. If the material is controversial, it is useful to cite the magazine or book, specific pages, and the date. In most cases, however, the date and the name of the magazine will be sufficient—for example, "According to the June 14, 1979, issue of *Time* magazine." Documentation adds to the credibility and acceptability of your arguments.

3. *Avoid presenting too many statistics at one time.* A speech crammed with numbers can create confusion and boredom. Imagine a speaker who says:

> Let us look at what happened in 1978. On January 14 the profits for IMT went up 3%, a rise of 1% over 1975. This is a dollar increase of $2,474,743.32. When compared to April of 1976, which had a 4% increase, we can see a net gain of over $3,499,812.79.

4. *Make certain that your statistics directly relate to the point you are making.* The relationship between your statistics and your assertion would be hard to discern if you were to say, "Last year the sale of riding horses increased by 100%, so we can see that most people are tired of paying for gasoline."

Testing Statistics

Statistics can have a telling effect on an audience as they listen to the comprehensiveness inherent in most statistical data. Used with factual examples, comprehensiveness is combined with concreteness. Unfortunately, however, statistics are highly liable to error and abuse. The conscientious speaker, as well as the critical and careful listener, must be willing to apply certain criteria to the statistics he or she confronts.

1. *Are the units being compared actually comparable?* It may be said that city X has twenty-five more crimes than does city Y, but if city X counts all crime and city Y counts only crimes against people and not those against property, the statistics are unreliable. In addition, city X may have a population of one-hundred thousand, while city Y has only thirty-five thousand residents. In both of these cases the units compared are not comparable.

2. *Do the statistics cover a sufficient number of cases?* A statement that fifty percent of the voters polled favored Proposition II would be quite misleading if only ten people out of forty-thousand were asked their opinion.

3. *Do the statistics cover a sufficient period of time?* There are two considerations in applying this test. First, if one is going to talk about the high cost of foreign aid, current statistics must be given. The foreign aid bill changes each year, and what was valid five years ago is likely to be outdated today. Use current references whenever possible. Second, if you wish to draw conclusions from your data, you must be sure that the period covered is not exceptional. The flow of mail in December, unemployment figures in summer and winter, earnings of some companies during war time, and traffic after a football game are obviously exceptional cases.

4. *Are the statistics presented in a logical form?* Often a speaker will jump from percentages to raw scores without any explanation. When talking about the political makeup of New York City a speaker noted:

> City census figures show 15% of New Yorkers are Negro, 8% Puerto Rican, 11% Italian, 4% Irish. There are an estimated one million eight hundred thousand Jews, three million four hundred thousand Roman Catholics, and one million seven hundred thousand Protestants. And there are 3½ times as many registered Democrats as Republicans.

Notice that the speaker offers three different sets of numbers in one passage, and each set is presented in a manner different from the other sets.

5. *Were the gatherers of the statistics strongly interested in the outcome?* Whenever you gather and analyze evidence it is crucial that you examine the bias and attitudes found within the special groups that originally compiled the data. For example, if you were considering the cost of living and union membership in states with the "Right to Work Law," you might find different results as you approached the Bureau of Labor Statistics, the AFL-CIO, the Democratic National Committee, and the National Association of Manufacturers. In these instances the speaker should consider as many different sources as possible and try to locate a neutral source.

Testimony

In the complex world we live in it is impossible to be an authority on all topics. We have become increasingly dependent upon expert testimony of others as a way of helping us find the relevant facts of an issue or a concept. The public speaker must also, on many occasions, turn to an expert. Testimony of an authority, as a form of support for a specific point, is often the most important type of evidence a speaker can use. It can show that the opinions of persons of authority, or experts in the field, corroborate the speaker's own views. For example, if you were trying to convince an audience that periodic chest X rays could save lives, you might quote the testimony of the surgeon general of the United States: "Our office has long held the belief that systematic and regular chest X rays could help save the lives of many cancer and TB victims." A speaker giving a talk to convince an audience that the ex-convict has a difficult time reentering society used expert testimony in the following manner:

> Lester N. Smith, who served as Head Warden of Sing Sing prison for eleven years, indicated the scope of the problem faced by the ex-convict when he stated that society rejects the convict right down the line. It is hard for him to locate a job, almost impossible to own a home, and difficult to lead a normal life. The labor unions often bar him and big companies fear him. In a very real sense, he finds most roads back to a normal life filled with social and economic blocs.

In both the examples presented, the persons quoted have, because of their positions and expertise, known a great deal about the topic under discussion. In the next two instances—one on Angel Dust and the other on Welfare—notice how the persons cited are echoing the speaker's view while adding to their own credibility as experts:

> Dr. David Tompkins, who is the founder and medical director of the Haight Ashbury Free Medical Clinic, offered the following commentary on Angel Dust (often called PCP). "It's the most dangerous drug I've seen. And I've been in this business full-time for twelve years and have seen every imaginable drug."

> As one of the Commissioners of Welfare in Erie County, May Edgar is well aware of the problems faced by most welfare workers. In a recent article in *Newsweek* magazine she noted, "Welfare workers do not have time to know their cases or to acquire the necessary skills in rendering services to people and preventing them from becoming permanently dependent on public aid."

Your use of testimony can be made more effective by observing some simple guidelines.

1. *Cite complete sources when using testimony.* Let the listeners know where you found your evidence, whether it be magazine, book, newspaper, television program, or personal interview. You increase your personal credibility as well as the believability of your sources when you say "In the Sunday, November 17 issue of the *New York Times,* Chief Justic Burger noted. . . ."

2. *Select those experts who will carry considerable weight with your audience.* You should in all circumstances establish the person's credibility and explain to your audience why he or she is an expert. That is, make it clear to your listeners that this particular person should be respected. The audience's acceptance of the person will go a long way toward proving your point.

   There is a common tendency for many speakers to equate expert testimony with testimonial. Steve Martin may be a good comedian, but that does not qualify him as an expert on tooth decay.

3. *Do not try to memorize your quotations.* By reading your quotations directly you can assure accuracy and also avoid forgetting. Reading small portions of your speech, such as some of your evidence, will offer your audience a change of pace. Furthermore, the act of reading a particular quotation will enhance its credibility. A small card will not detract from your speech if you handle the card correctly.

4. *The testimony should be relevant to the point being discussed.* Speakers often cite an authority to prove a position, but on closer examination discover that the expert is talking about another problem. Imagine how ineffective it would be if you were talking about mental health and quoted this testimony: "There are a great many people in hospitals today who would not be there if they were not rushing to keep an appointment."

   On some occasions you might find it helpful to explain the relevance of a piece of testimony in your own words. You could say, "Police Chief Jones is telling us that. . . ."

5. *Whenever possible use brief quotations.* Long quotations are often quite difficult to follow and may hinder the audience's concentration. Even when paraphrasing you should aim at brevity.
6. *Attend carefully to the means of introducing quotations.* Lead-ins such as "In a speech last week the Secretary of State noted" and "So we see, as Professor Jones pointed out, overpopulation and food shortage present serious problems" will help hold the audience's attention at the same time they tell the source of the quotation and when it originated.
7. *Indicate the beginning and the end of any quotation so that the audience will be able to distinguish your opinions from those of the expert you are quoting.* However, avoid the all-too-common practice of "quote" and "unquote." A change of voice, a pause, a move, or a certain phrase can better indicate the beginning and the end of a quotation.

Testing Testimony

In using and listening to testimony, remember that an expert's opinion may not be based on concrete and comprehensive data. There are some safeguards we should observe whenever expert testimony is used.

1. *Is the authority quoted recognized as an expert in his or her field?* A common error today is to judge persons as experts in many areas because they happen to be particularly qualified in one field. A college professor may teach eighteenth-century English literature, but this does not qualify him or her as an expert in economic affairs. The person's training, background, and degrees are one indication, but common sense and critical judgment are additional tests of expert testimony and qualification.
2. *Is the person an unbiased observer?* Objectivity is essential if we are to respect and believe the testimony of the expert. The chairman of the Republican National Committee would hardly be qualified to give an objective account of a Democratic president's term in office.
3. *Is the reference to authority specific?* Quotations such as "according to an eminent authority" or "an expert in the field concluded" are vague and misleading. The audience should know exactly who is being quoted.
4. *When and where was the opinion expressed?* Statistics, theories, and findings are soon outdated. What an expert said in 1969 may not accurately express his or her views today. In addition, the place a statement is made may well influence what is said. The secretary of labor might well state one view at the Teamster's convention and expound another position, on the same theme, before the Chamber of Commerce.

Analogy or Comparison

We often ask someone to compare one idea or item with another. In trying to make our ideas clear, interesting, and impelling, we suggest that item A "resembles," "is similar to," or "is not as good as" item B. By using comparison we try to support our main thesis and explain our principal ideas.

Comparison frequently takes the form of *analogy*. In an analogy, similarities are pointed out in regard to persons, ideas, experiences, projects, institutions, or data, and conclusions are drawn on the basis of those similarities. The main function of analogy is to point out the similarities between what is already known and what is not. Using this technique as support or proof, you should show the listener that what he or she already believes or knows is similar to what you are trying to prove or explain. For example, if you are suggesting that it is dangerous to drive while intoxicated, you might offer the following analogy:

> We all know that driving a car at high speed during a foggy night is dangerous because of our impaired vision [known]. The same can be said of those who try to drive after consuming alcoholic beverages, for their vision is also obscured, and their life is in peril [unknown].

If arguing that compulsory arbitration is beneficial to the United States, a speaker could use an analogy in the following manner: "Compulsory arbitration of labor disputes has been very successful in New Zealand, which is a democratic country. Such arbitration might also work in the United States."

Analogies are divided into two types: *figurative* and *literal*. The *figurative* compares things of different classes, such as the United States Banking System with the human circulatory system, or an airplane with a bird. To say that writing a term paper is like learning to swim, because both have certain basic rules that are difficult at first and get easier with time, would be an example of a figurative analogy. This type of analogy is generally vivid, full of imagery, but has limited value as proof, since the dissimilarities of things in different classes are usually obvious and can be readily attacked—often to the disadvantage of the creator of the analogy.

Much more useful and valid is the *literal* analogy, whereby you compare items, ideas, institutions, persons, projects, data, or experiences of the same class. You might point out similarities between one instructor and another, one political creed and another, or one city and another. On the basis of the similarities, you build a theorem. You reason that if two or more things of the same class contain identical or nearly identical characteristics, certain conclusions that are true in one case may also be true in the other(s). For example, Winston Churchill employed a literal analogy when he compared the turning point of the Civil War with what he believed to be the turning point in World War II. Another example can be found in the speaker trying to persuade an audience that the United Nations Charter should be obeyed by all member nations:

> We Americans take a great deal of pride in the Constitution and the Bill of Rights. We know that our country would not be as great and as strong as it is if we were to discontinue our obedience and allegiance to the laws and regulations contained in these documents. The same can be said of the United Nations Charter. For just as each of us, as individuals, must comply with the Constitution and its provisions, so must the members of the United Nations comply with its laws and rules. If the individual nations do not observe and obey the laws of the Charter of the United Nations, it will not be an effective instrument for world peace.

The comparison and similarities are obvious—we are aware of the concepts behind the Constitution [known] the speaker suggests that the same concepts are inherent to the United Nations Charter [unknown]. In summary, you believe and understand one; therefore, you should believe and understand the other, for they are basically the same.

Testing Analogy

When selecting and using analogies, either figurative or literal, it is essential that your analogies meet certain requirements.

1. *Is the analogy clearly relevant to the idea?* To argue that since Sue and Mary both belong to the same social organization they must therefore think the same way politically is irrelevant use of analogy. The similarity of their organization may be interesting, but it is certainly not relevant.

2. *Do the points of likeness outweigh the points of difference?* If the differences of the *essential* features being compared outweigh the similarities, one can hardly establish a logical connection. If we compare a supermarket to a high school in order to make the point that each must keep its customers, we have overlooked some fundamental differences existing in the two cases.

3. *Is the premise (generalization) upon which the analogy is based accurate?* Saying "just as a ship sinks without a captain, so will our club be destroyed without a president" is an example of a false circumstance being used as a basis for the generalization, for a ship does not necessarily sink without a captain. The premise for the entire analogy and conclusion is therefore inaccurate and invalid.

4. *Is the analogy appropriate to the audience?* It is important for the audience to observe clearly the likenesses and the essential characteristics of the analogy. If one-half of the comparison confuses your listeners, you may find that your analogy has hindered rather than aided your speech. It would probably be confusing to a group of high school freshmen if you were to say, "The workings of the rotary engine are much like those of the epiglottis."

5. *Is the analogy upheld by other forms of support?* Analogies alone are seldom sufficient to prove a point. You should examine other types of evidence to see if the relationship between the known and the unknown can be verified.

Other Forms of Support

At the beginning of this chapter we noted that the forms of support occasionally overlap—that a factual illustration might well contain statistics. Certain other forms of support are closely related to the six already discussed. Many of these are further extensions and refinements of those just mentioned. For example, the *anecdote*, in which real-life characters are usually featured, the *fable*, in which animal characters speak and act as if they were humans, and the *parable*, a fictitious story from which a moral or religious lesson may be drawn—all are forms of the illustration. In addition, *long quotations*, at times, may be listed as a type of testimony.

Other devices for developing, amplifying, and clarifying, such as explanation, definition, restatement, repetition, and description, will be discussed in detail in chapter 8 when we examine the principles of informing. There are also many situations in which a speaker will use a combination of these devices. For example, you may have occasion to cite an expert who is, in turn, citing statistics or using analogy. The important concept for the student of communication to remember is that any of the techniques discussed in this book should be used if they will aid in securing the response desired. The various classifications suggested throughout the volume are a guide for specific occasions; the real communication situation must determine your final selection.

Visual Support

The importance and use of visual aids will be discussed specifically when we examine the speech to inform. However, visual aids are also useful as a means of supporting and proving an idea, principle, or concept. By *seeing* what is talked about, the listener brings still another of his or her senses into play. In trying to convince the judge that the stop sign was blocked from view by a large tree, the lawyer brought forth a photograph. On seeing the picture the judge ruled the defendant could not have seen the sign from his car. The old adage "seeing is believing" is made real by a specific chart, model, demonstration, or exhibit. In addition, statistics that are often detailed and confusing can be clarified and reinforced by a graph or table highlighting the main features.

The best advice for both the novice and the professional speaker using visual aids is to *practice!* By practicing with your visual aid, you will discover its strengths and weaknesses before the actual speaking situation occurs. In addition, the conscientious student should try to answer the following questions: (1) Can the audience see the important details contained within the visual aid? Are they large enough and clear enough? (2) Will the visual aid distract the audience? When and how shall I display it? (3) Does my visual aid directly support the point under consideration?

Finding Material

Clarence Darrow, one of the most famous trial lawyers of all time, noted, "Anybody who speaks should spend a thousand days on trying to get ideas and knowledge to every one day they spend on the way to tell it." While much of the information for our speeches comes from our personal experiences, we must remember that support and clarification are important, and that they take hard work.

Once you have selected your topic and decided your purpose, the serious task of deciding what you want to say begins. In making decisions concerning your material, you must begin by carefully thinking about the audience and your objectives. By placing the topic in its proper perspective, you will be better able to determine what you know about the central issues and what you must find out.

Experience and Observation

One of the best ways to gather material for speeches is to be alert to what goes on around you. If you go through life wearing blinders and not taking full advantage of all your senses, you are apt to miss much of the detail and information that life can offer. Plato wrote, "Knowledge is but to remember." To have the experiences and observations to remember, you must develop a philosophy of awareness. Being aware of the world around you is as simple as listening to speeches, listening to news programs, taking part in conversations, and keeping both eyes wide open as you move from environment to environment.

If being aware and alert is part of your daily philosophy, you can call forth personal experiences and firsthand observations for your speeches. These personal examples are often more vivid and lively than examples you merely read about. Therefore, as we suggested earlier, start your speech preparation by discovering your own ideas, beliefs, and feelings on the subject. *Examine your memory.*

You should be cautioned, however, about depending solely on the conclusions reached from observations. We all know that our perception of any happening is colored by our background and earlier experiences. This lack of objective perceptiveness can often influence what we *really* see and hear. Therefore, make effective and abundant use of observations and experiences, but always remember you are dealing with a statistic of one. More proof may be needed for a valid generalization.

Interviews

The experiences and observations of other persons, who might be in a better position to know more about the subject than you, are often excellent sources of information. The interview has several advantages. First, it enables you to ask specific questions that are directly related to your topic. This face-to-face situation lets you acquire quick responses to your questions. Second, the interview allows you a certain degree of selectivity. Instead of simply talking to someone who knows a little about the topic, you can gather data by going directly to an expert—someone with firsthand information.

As a college student you are in a position to make extensive use of interviews. Most professors are experts in specific fields and can offer you valuable assistance. To illustrate, if you were going to give a speech dealing with the problems of interracial marriages, you might gain useful information and new ideas from interviews with professors of sociology, psychology, religion, and marriage and family relations. In addition, you might seek an appointment with some of the campus clergy. In all of these instances you are increasing your background on the topic.

An interview of any kind requires forethought—arranging for the meeting, preparing an agenda, and thinking out the means of securing frank responses. The interviewer should also be on time, explain his or her purpose, take careful notes, and be careful not to misquote the person when the material is used.

Printed Material

Donald C. Bryant and Karl R. Wallace, in their text on oral communication, note, "The library is to the speechmaker what the laboratory is to the scientist. It is a place of search and research." Reading in books, magazines, periodicals, newspapers, and documents constitutes the largest single source of information at the disposal of any speaker.

Before recommending places to look for printed material, let us offer advice for all researchers.

1. *Read with a definite purpose.* We wrote earlier in this section that your preparation begins after you have decided on your specific purpose and reviewed your personal fund of information. With those two tasks behind you, it is much easier to seek only material that is relevant. You will also be able to be more selective and avoid going in many errant directions.

2. *Read more than you think you will use.* Most beginning students feel compelled to read only enough to get by. You will discover, however, that the most effective speakers have a grasp of the topic that goes beyond the material given in the speech.
3. *Be critical.* Examine many sources and opinions on the same topic. In this way you will be able to determine the validity of your ideas as well as the authenticity of what you read.
4. *Take complete and accurate notes on what you read.* It is important, for ethical as well as practical reasons, for you to keep a record of exactly where your material comes from. For example, if your material is from a magazine, you should have the name of the author, title of the article, name of the magazine, volume, date, and page. This material is cited in your speech and shown in your outline and bibliography. You should also use quotation marks when quoting directly. Plagiarism must be avoided at all times.
5. *Know your library.* Although similarities exist, no two libraries are alike. Discover what catalog system your library uses, what reference books it has, its physical facilities, its special collections, its regulations, and its hours. Feel free to ask questions of those who work in the library. Timidity may cost you access to valuable information.

Indexes

The library card catalog, with its subject, title, and author index, is a superb starting point for your research. In this file you will find a complete listing of books found in your library. The *Reader's Guide to Periodical Literature,* published each month, is a cumulative index of articles published in more than a hundred selected periodicals. Articles are listed alphabetically according to author, title, and subject. Two newspapers, the *New York Times* and the *London Times,* are also indexed.

In addition to the common indexes cited above, the diligent student might have occasion to consult the *Bulletin of Public Affairs Information Service* and the *International Index.* The activity of the United States Senate and the House of Representatives is completely indexed in the *Congressional Record.* Some learned information can be secured by investigating the *Agricultural Index, Applied Science and Technology Index, Educational Index, Psychological Index, Psychological Abstracts, Social Science Abstracts,* and *The Monthly Catalog—United States Government Publications.*

Reference Books

Most of us are familiar with the practice of starting our research by turning to the encyclopedia. However, the task of investigation must not stop there; the sincere communicator makes use of other reference materials.

The World Almanac, The Statesman's Year Book, Information Please Almanac, Statistical Abstract of the United States, and *Commerce Reports—* all furnish facts and figures that the speaker may find useful.

Literary references can be found in such books as *Bartlett's Familiar Quotations, Oxford Dictionary of Quotations,* and *The Home Book of Quotations.*

For information about people, it is always beneficial to look at biographical guides. A few of the more useful guides are *Current Biography, Dictionary of*

American Biography, Who's Who, Who's Who in America, Webster's Biographical Dictionary, and *International Who's Who.*

Newspapers

Information on almost any topic can be secured from newspapers. While books normally take years to be written and published, newspapers are an excellent source of current happenings and information. Some of the leading newspapers are the *New York Times, Christian Science Monitor, Washington (D.C.) Post,* and the *Los Angeles Times.* Two highly regarded foreign newspapers are the *London Times* and the *Manchester Guardian.* Students with speech topics limited to regional problems and issues will find it helpful to consult local newspapers.

Magazines and Pamphlets

There are hundreds of magazines available in the United States, and it would be impossible to list all of them. However, several current publications contain articles on a wide range of subjects: *Time, Newsweek, United States News and World Report, Business Week, Fortune, New Republic, Forbes, Reporter, Nation, Atlantic Monthly, Commonweal, Harper's Magazine, Current History, National Geographic, Foreign Affairs, Yale Review,* and *Vital Speeches of the Day.*

Most libraries have a large collection of pamphlets that are hard to catalog and index because of their size and subject. These pamphlets, which are printed and circulated by various groups and organizations, such as the American Medical Association and the Automobile Club, cover a wide range of topics. Normally this material can be secured from the library's vertical file or by asking the librarian the location of the college's pamphlet collection. *The Vertical File Service Catalog* also lists pamphlets published and distributed by various organizations and agencies.

Academic Journals

In addition to the countless magazines written for the general public there are hundreds of very specialized journals written for specific audiences. Whether the topic be education, political science, sociology, speech, home economics, or engineering, there are academic publications available. Ask any library assistant to help you locate the specific journal related to the field you are investigating.

Recording Your Material

As you do your research you will discover that it is impossible to remember all you have heard and read. It is also difficult to be accurate when you are trying to keep facts, figures, and quotations in your head. Therefore, recording your information for further use is a vital step in speech preparation.

Seeing that the information is *usable* should be one of your primary concerns when recording your data. Hence you should try to develop a research and recording style with which you feel comfortable. Even though this choice is a personal matter, let us suggest some guidelines that will aid you in making the most efficient use of your research.

1. *Most speakers find that using index cards, either 4" × 6" or 3" × 5", helps them with both their organization and retrieval of data.* Because each

card contains only one piece of information, they can be shuffled into a variety of stacks that may parallel main points and sub-points. The individual entries, when viewed in total, will also reveal those areas where additional research is needed.

2. *It is essential that the material be recorded in an accurate manner and a usable form.* This means that the complete reference should be shown on the card so that you can cite the source in your speech. Listed below is one method of recording bibliographical citations:

Books: Toffler, Alvin. *Future Shock.* New York: Random House, Inc., 1970.

Burgoon, Michael, and Michael Ruffner. *Human Communication.* New York: Holt, Rinehart and Winston, 1978.

Periodicals: Atkins, Charles K. "Effects of Drug Commercials on Young Viewers," *Journal of Communication,* Autumn 1978, Vol. 28, #4, pp. 71–79.

"In Pennsylvania: Trying to Make Football Injury-Free," *Newsweek*, November 20, 1978, pp. 8–9.

3. *See that all your cards are as complete as possible.* Do not fear writing more than you might be able to use. Being generous with your note-taking could save a trip to the library at midnight as you try to track down the rest of the reference.

4. *Your research cards should not only include the correct citations and quoted material, but should also contain your personal evaluations of the material.* Notes to yourself will come in handy as you begin to piece the speech into the organizational scheme you eventually select. In short, each card should include (a) the complete citation, (b) the quoted material, and (c) your personal comments.

When to Use the Forms of Support

Determining when the various forms of support are needed is no easy task. Every audience, occasion, and topic has special demands that make each communication encounter a unique and dynamic experience. There are, however, basic questions to ask when you are deciding where support should be used.

1. *Are you making a statement that will be accepted as true simply because you assert it?* For example, if you want to convince an audience that educational benefits for veterans should be increased, you must do more than say, "The meager grants now awarded under the GI Bill are so small that many veterans cannot attend college." Any intelligent listener would most likely respond by saying, "What do you mean?" or "How do you know this is true?" You should use forms of support when you are making a statement that needs substantiation as a means of establishing its authenticity, believability, and plausibility.

2. *How much substantiation is needed?* There is no simple formula for deciding how much support any assertion will require. In most instances you will have to depend on your own good judgment and common sense. View the

assertion or statement from the perspective of your audience. If you were a listener, would you need and demand proof for the opinions being expressed? One audience might accept the contention that a college education is useful; a skeptical audience would demand support.

3. *Are you making a statement that requires no further clarification?* As we have pointed out, the forms of support are often used for clarification as well as for proof. Now we ask, "Is my idea clear?" If the answer is no, support is needed. If we were to say, "There is often a stigma attached to persons who have been mentally ill," we run the risk of our audience not knowing what we mean. However, we could clarify our point by an illustration about someone who has been stigmatized because of confinement in an institution.

Detecting Fallacies

Thus far in this chapter we have stressed three closely related principles: good speakers include sufficient evidence to support their positions; they test their evidence to see that it is valid and reliable; and they do serious research and investigation to supplement their ideas. However, simply locating and employing evidence and material are not enough, for the use the speaker makes of this material is as important as the material itself. The speaker's reasoning must be clear and free from fallacies—being cognizant of the more common fallacies, you will be able to avoid their use in your utterances. In addition, as a listener you might be able to use this knowledge about fallacies as part of your defense against the sophistry of others.

Since communication concerns sending and receiving messages, the thorough student must be alert to mistaken arguments, faulty reasoning, and irrelevant evidence. The examination of evidence, reasoning, and ideas for weaknesses is a search for fallacies. Over one hundred years ago Richard Whately, a noted logician, classified as a fallacy "any unsound mode of arguing which appears to demand our conviction, and to be decisive of the question in hand, when in fairness it is not."

Logicians, social psychologists, and rhetoricians make repeated attempts to classify types of fallacies, but a satisfactory hard-and-fast division of them has not been found. Not only is there a problem of classification and division, but there is the question of what to include and what to exclude. Discussions of fallacies often contain lists with as many as fifty-one specific kinds of fallacies. In the course of talking about propaganda and listening, we have mentioned some of the more common types of errors in reasoning and evidence. What is included now is a partial list of fallacies with which the student of communication should be familiar.

Hasty Generalization

Snap judgments, jumping to conclusions, or generalizations based on insufficient evidence or experience are all examples of the hasty generalization fallacy. In this fallacy the speaker draws a universal conclusion from evidence warranting only a restricted conclusion.

This fallacy is common in daily life. Most of us can recall instances in which travelers have experienced one or two unpleasant situations and then reached conclusions concerning the honesty and character of all the people in that particular city. Or the example of the person who will not take Professor Smith for history because he knows two students who received D's from Smith. Another example is the speaker who concluded that all supporters of the Peace and Freedom Party were Communists. The speaker stated, "Eric Foresman supported Peace and Freedom and he is a Communist; Scott Allen supported them and he, too, is a Communist. So, you see that all supporters of Peace and Freedom are Communists."

We mentioned some ways to guard against this fallacy earlier in this chapter when we looked at ways of testing the example and the illustration. It might be wise to return to that section and notice how you can use some of those same techniques to detect the generalization that is irrelevant and based on an isolated case.

Begging the Question

The fallacy of begging the question is committed by assuming at the onset of the argument the very point that is to be established in the conclusion. That is, the speaker assumes the truth or falsity of a statement without proof. If someone making a speech were to state, "the widespread cheating among our students is bad and should therefore be abolished," he or she would be begging the question. In this example the speaker is taking for granted that cheating exists, when the statement cannot justify such a conclusion.

Begging the question normally appears in the form of "arguing in a circle." When one proposition is used to prove another proposition, we are engaging in this fallacy. Arguing in a circle usually appears in the following form: "Medical Plan X is best because the experts say so. How do we know who the experts are? They are the persons who prefer Medical Plan X." In this case, begging the question is illustrated by taking as a premise what is true only if the conclusion has been granted to be correct.

Non Sequitur

In a broad sense, any argument that fails to establish its conclusion may be said to be *non sequitur,* for the meaning of the term is simply, "It does not follow." More specifically, the fallacy of *non sequitur* means that a conclusion is drawn from premises that provide no adequate logical ground for it, or that have no relevant connection with it. "Jones is a good husband and a fine father, so he ought to be elected mayor." It is quite obvious in this example that a logical cause-effect relationship cannot be made. Still other statements point out how speakers reach false conclusions as they try to establish cause-effect connections. "Since only a few people have the ability to handle the complex problems of industry, the wealth and power of this country rightfully belongs in the hands of the rich." "The child is unhappy, beautiful, and a college freshman; she must therefore come from an average American family."

One of the most common and insidious forms of this fallacy, is *post hoc, ergo propter hoc,* or "after this, therefore because of this." This fallacy assumes that because one occurrence *precedes another in time,* the one is the *cause* of the other. Superstitions belong here. If you walk under a ladder on your way to class and receive an "A" that same day, and then conclude that walking under a ladder gives "A's," you are guilty of *post hoc, ergo propter hoc*. Recently a speaker noted, "Since minority groups have been given more educational opportunity we have had an increase in the crime rate throughout the United States. I would conclude, therefore, that the growth in crime is directly related to education." Here again it is just not sufficient to say there is a connection simply because one thing followed the other. In short, because two things happen in sequence does not mean that they are logically or causally connected.

Nonrational and Irrelevant Evidence

The use of nonrational and irrelevant material is one of the greatest causes for errors in reasoning. Many of these problems were discussed in chapter 4 when we mentioned the techniques and devices employed by the propagandist. However, these fallacies are so prevalent that they warrant further examination. The most common types of nonrational evidence are (1) appeals to the emotions and prejudices, (2) appeals to tradition and authority, and (3) appeals to personalities rather than issues.

Appealing to the emotions and prejudices of the audience, called *argumentum ad populum,* is a common technique of the speaker who prefers to deal with the passions of the audience rather than the salient issues of the topic. Instead of presenting empirical evidence and logical argument, the *ad populum* speaker attempts to win support with phrases such as, "Jewish parasites," "slaughtered women and children," "un-American traitor," "Catholic demagogue," and "friend of the Communists." Fortunately, appeals to passions and prejudices become less successful as we become more educated. Yet we must be alert at all times to separate the essential from the nonessential.

A second fallacy, *argumentum ad vercundiam,* shows itself when the speaker offers proof for his or her position by making an appeal to authority, to a "name," or to an institution. If the authority is legitimately connected to the subject, we have a valid use of expert opinion. The fallacy occurs if the appeal is made to justify an authority out of his domain or an unreliable authority. For example, "George Washington, the father of our country, warned us against the danger of foreign alliances. Therefore, we should withdraw from the North Atlantic Treaty Organization." It is agreed that Washington was an influential figure during the early history of the United States, but the needs of modern foreign affairs are quite different from the needs expressed in Washington's era. The best defense against the *ad vercundiam* fallacy is the use of the tests of authority discussed earlier in the chapter.

In the *argumentum ad hominem* fallacy the speaker attacks someone's character instead of dealing with the relevant issues at hand. That is, the arguments are transferred from principles to personalities. A speaker is engaging in an *ad hominem* argument when he or she states, "The city's new highway program should be vetoed. The highway commissioner is a notorious troublemaker and a former lobbyist." Another case is the speaker who notes, "How can the Rockefellers help the poor? They have never been cold or hungry." Notice that in both these instances the merits of the issue are disregarded while attention is focused upon the source. The best defense against this approach is to demand that the person speaking, whether yourself or someone else, stay on the topic and include only material that is obviously relevant.

Summary

In this chapter we were concerned with four factors of communication that directly affect one another—evidence, testing evidence, locating material, and detecting fallacies.

The forms of support treated in this chapter represent the fundamental devices used in most types of public discourse and in most private communication situations. These forms are the detailed factual illustration, the undeveloped illustration (specific instance), the hypothetical illustration, statistics, testimony, analogy, and visual aids.

Evidence must meet certain standards if it is to be clear, persuasive, and effective. In his book *Argumentation and Debate,* Austin J. Freeley sets forth an excellent summary for testing evidence. His interpretation, in addition to the specific tests discussed in this chapter, should always be considered in using forms of support.

(1) Is there sufficient evidence? (2) Is the evidence clear? (3) Is the evidence consistent with other known evidence? (4) Can the evidence be verified? (5) Does the evidence come from a competent source? (6) Does the evidence come from an unprejudiced source? (7) Does the evidence come from a reliable source? (8) Is the evidence relevant to the problem? (9) Is the evidence statistically sound? (10) Is it the most recent evidence?

In the search for material, the speaker can use personal experiences and observations, conduct interviews, consult indexes, and use newspapers, pamphlets, magazines, and academic journals.

One must, in addition to finding evidence, use the forms of support in a sound and logical manner. In thinking straight, the speaker, as well as the listener, should be alert to certain fallacies. The most common errors in reasoning and using evidence are hasty generalization, begging the question, *non sequitur*, and irrational and irrelevant evidence.

Suggested Readings

Aldrich, Ella Virginia. *Using Books and Libraries.* 5th ed. Englewood Cliffs, NJ: Prentice-Hall, 1967.

Bettinghaus, Erwin P. *The Nature of Proof.* 2d ed. New York: Bobbs-Merrill, 1972.

Capp, Glenn R., and Capp, Richard G. *Basic Oral Communication.* 2d ed. Englewood Cliffs, NJ: Prentice-Hall, 1976. Chapters 7, 8.

Kelley, Win. *Breaking the Barriers in Public Speaking.* Dubuque, IA: Kendall/Hunt Publishing, 1978. Chapter 4.

Monroe, Alan H.; Ehninger, Douglas; and Gronbeck, Bruce E. *Principles and Types of Speech Communication.* 8th ed. Glenview, IL: Scott, Foresman, 1978. Chapters 10, 11.

Newman, Robert P., and Newman, Dele R. *Evidence.* Boston: Houghton Mifflin, 1969.

Phillips, Gerald M., and Zolten, J. Jerome. *Structuring Speech.* Indianapolis: Bobbs-Merrill, 1976. Chapter 6.

Your Ideas

Organization
Assembling Your Ideas

In the preceding chapter we were concerned with collecting the ideas and data that might go into a speech. Let us assume, then, that we have before us a mass of collected speech materials. Obviously it will not magically form itself into a speech. Our immediate task is to analyze the materials on hand and to sort them, placing each piece of evidence into its proper pile with other related pieces of evidence. This process of analysis will enable us to find "what it all adds up to." Once this is done we are ready for the process of reassembly, or synthesis, of the sorted materials to communicate our predetermined purpose. This process of putting it all together with a beginning, a middle, and an end is the central concern of this chapter.

The organizational process benefits speakers in several ways. It helps them detect weaknesses in the fabric of their logic and inadequacies in the amount and quality of their evidence. It enables them to juxtapose ideas in a variety of ways and thus determine the sequence best fitted to their audience and to the accomplishment of their purpose. Clear organization helps them to retain ideas with greater ease during the pressure of message presentation. Finally, speakers benefit in most cases from the added credibility attached to their well-organized ideas.

But it is ultimately for the listener's benefit that we attend to organizational strategies. Our message must be understood at the moment of encounter, because the listener, unlike the reader, cannot arrest the message and study it at leisure. Clear organization facilitates understanding and encourages the listener to remain attentive.

While there are a variety of approaches to assembling the message, we shall concentrate upon the method that involves formulating a core statement that expresses the central idea of the message, phrasing main points to support the core statement (and subpoints to support the main points, if needed), and choosing appropriate patterns to show relationships among the points. We shall discuss the devising of an overall speech plan, the mechanics of outlining, and the formulation of the introduction and the conclusion.

Our approach presumes the traditional three-fold division of the message into introduction, body, and conclusion. While not all messages require this formal division, it is workable in the majority of cases.

The Core Statement

The simplest form of speech has two essential ingredients: (1) a statement or point that requires clarification, amplification, or proof and (2) the materials that clarify, amplify, or prove the statement. A complex speech is simply a combination of such units revolving around an even more general statement. The most general statement of the speech we shall call the *core statement*; the less general statements we shall call the *main points*; the least general statements we shall call *subpoints*. We may visualize the levels of generality as follows (materials are hypothetical):

Core Statement:	Jazz music is becoming more popular.
Main Point:	I. It is evident in the increasing sales of jazz records.
Subpoint:	A. U.S. sales are rising.
Support:	1. *Billboard* reports a 27% increase in sales in New York City alone.
Support:	2. Record distributors on both coasts report a two-month backlog of orders.
Subpoint:	B. International sales are rising.
Support:	1. London stores report stacks of jazz records are selling-out overnight.
Support:	2. Continental distributors say French and Italian markets are at an all-time high.
Main Point:	II. It is evident in the increasing number of jazz concerts being scheduled.
	(and so on)

The core statement is called by some authors the *subject sentence,* the *theme sentence,* the *thesis,* or the *proposition.* Whatever the label used, it signifies the element that gives unity to everything in the speech. Lest our calling the core statement "the most general statement of the speech" be misleading, we should stress that its wording should be so precise that it will not invite the listener to expect more than will be covered in the ensuing development.

The core statement sometimes is phrased as a value judgment, such as "Walking is the safest exercise for most adults." It may take the form of a statement of alleged fact, such as "Many famous people have suffered from epilepsy." It may be worded as a policy position, such as "Section 5 of the County Charter should be rewritten." It may suggest the steps in a process: "Decorating a concrete surface involves etching the surface, priming the surface, and painting the surface." It may suggest the parts of a whole: "The principal parts of a sailboat rudder are the tiller, the head, and the blade." Or it may suggest the characteristics that distinguish the subject from other closely related subjects, as in a definition of stage fright: "Stage fright is a form of communication apprehension specific to a given public communication encounter."

Ideally, formulation of the core statement will take place at the end of your investigation or analysis of the subject. With the results of your research before you, you will be in a position to ask yourself, "What does all this add up to?" Your answer to that question should provide a core statement. Then you will be ready to reassemble the subject for your hearer—to organize your speech.

The principal benefit derived from formulating the core statement at the outset of the organizational process is that it will provide you with an immediate test of the relevance of any material you expect to introduce in the speech. If any main point, subpoint, or supporting material does not clearly relate to the core sentence, then it should be discarded as irrelevant. *Thus the core statement helps insure the unity of the speech.*

It is entirely possible that the core statement may not be spoken during the speech, but it should be implicit in the way in which the speech unfolds. If it is spoken during the speech, it may occur in the opening statement of the introduction, at the start of the body or development of the speech, or at the end of the speech. Whether it should be spoken and when it should be spoken cannot be prescribed by rule. Your careful analysis of the audience should afford a clue. Remember, one of its functions is to keep you from introducing materials that are irrelevant and hence confusing to the listener.

Formulating Main Points and Subpoints

Since the core statement is the most general statement of the speech, we must ask: What less-general statements does it suggest? These less-general statements, as we have noted earlier, constitute the main points of the body of the speech.

Selection and phrasing of the main points should be undertaken with the following guidelines in mind: (1) each main point must grow out of the core statement; (2) each main point must be clearly distinguishable from the other main points; (3) collectively, the main points should develop the core statement completely. Let us examine more fully these three guidelines in operation.

1. *Kinship to the core statement.* If a statement is to be labeled a main point, it must contribute toward proving, explaining, or illustrating the core statement. In an argumentative speech, one quick test of relevance is to place such connectives as *because* and *for* between the core statement and the alleged main point. For example:

Core Statement: Aerosol spray cans are dangerous, *because*

      I. They can explode if stored indiscriminately.
      II. They can cause serious injury if the release valve is accidentally pointed toward the user.
      III. Some cans contain propellants that are allegedly capable of depleting the Earth's ozone layer.

In an expository speech you can test relevance by using *for example, as follows, namely,* and *in that.*

Core Statement: Badminton is similar to Ping Pong, *for example*

      I. Both require a playing area divided by a net.
      II. Both require hitting an object over the net.
      III. They require a similar scoring system.

Can you detect which of the following main points does not meet the test of relevance?

Core Statement: The microwave oven has a variety of uses.

> I. It can defrost frozen foods quickly.
> II. It can roast large cuts of meat.
> III. It can bake pies and cakes.
> IV. It takes up little space.

2. *Distinguishability from other main points.* While the main points of a speech have a common kinship to the core statement, they should not overlap one another. Which of the following main points seem to be covering the same ground?

Core Statement: Capital punishment should be abolished.

> I. It is not effective.
> II. It does not accomplish anything.
> III. It is not morally defensible.
> IV. It does not have popular support.

Points I and II appear to overlap while III and IV are apparently dealing with separate issues. In essence, then, there are only three main points.

Unless this characteristic of distinguishability is observed in the selection and phrasing of main points, the listener is likely to become confused.

3. *Collective completeness of main points.* We have not discovered all of the main points of a speech if there is a facet of the core statement that has not been developed. For example: We do not usually consider a family complete unless all the children and both parents are present. And as another example: The mainland visitor to Hawaii often makes the mistake of alluding to matters "back in the States"—a person who makes a generalization about the United States without taking Hawaii into account is quickly corrected.

Determining all of the essential constituents is seldom easy. The salesperson who wants to convince a customer that a particular automobile is the best one to buy has to determine the essential constituents of "best," not from a personal vantage point, but from the predicted vantage point of the customer. To a customer the "best" car might be the most stylish, or the most economical to operate, or the most powerful. So it is necessary for you to look at your core statement from the vantage point of the listener and ask, "What points will the speaker have to cover before winning my agreement?" or "What points will the speaker have to clarify before I understand fully?"

Although our discussion in this section has centered around the selection and phrasing of main points, all of the principles brought out are equally applicable to the selection and phrasing of subpoints, since the subpoint bears the same relationship to the main point as the main point bears to the core statement.

Patterns of Relationship

Psychologists tell us that things perceived in isolation usually lack meaning; we must see them in relationship to other things to give them meaning. All of us employ habitual patterns of organizing our perceptions into meaningful relationships. Some things we perceive within a temporal frame; others in terms of spatial placement; still others in terms of logical parts, components, or divisions. We have patterns for perceiving relationships that are argumentative in character, others that are nonargumentative. The number of possible patterns of organization is probably incalculable, but we wish to call your attention to some that have proved particularly serviceable to speakers over the years.

Time Relationships

Certain subjects lend themselves ideally to development in a time sequence. For example, if we wished to discuss the development of home entertainment equipment, we might start with the equipment of some years past and move forward in time to the equipment of today; or move in reverse from the present to the past. Our main points might appear as follows:

Core Statement: In the last three decades there have been dramatic developments in home entertainment equipment.

     I. The fifties saw the popularization of black-and-white TV and stereo sound equipment.
    II. The sixties saw the advent of color TV and miniaturized audio components.
    III. The seventies saw the development of video games and video cassette recorders.

The step-by-step method used in describing a process or in offering instructions is a kind of time pattern. In discussing what happens to a letter from the time it is mailed until it is received, we might arrange our points accordingly:

Core Statement: Mail handling involves collection, sorting, and distribution.

     I. The first step is mail collection.
    II. The second step is primary sorting.
    III. The third step is final sorting.
    IV. The fourth step is primary distribution.
    V. The fifth step is final distribution.

Instructions in changing a tire might include these steps: (1) laying out the proper tools, (2) jacking up the car, (3) removing the flat tire, (4) putting on the spare tire, and (5) letting down the jack.

Keep the number of main points in a time pattern as few as possible— ideally, between three and five—so they can be easily retained by the speaker and easily followed by the hearer. This necessitates placing a number of chronological details under such general groupings as "The first era was . . . .," "The first decade was characterized by . . . .," or "The ancient Greeks were the first to systematize the study of public speaking."

Spatial Relationships	The ways in which a series of items relate to one another in space affords us an effective organizational device. In describing a building, we might arrange the details from basement to attic, from north wing to south wing, from entrance to exit, from front to rear. For example:

Core Statement: The proposed shopping mart will have three principal departments.

    I. The ground floor will house wearing apparel.

    II. The second floor will house major appliances.

    III. The third floor will house home furnishings.

The layout of a college campus might be visualized by employing the spatial pattern:

Core Statement: Each quadrant of the campus serves a special purpose.

    I. The northwest quadrant contains all student housing.

    II. The northeast quadrant contains the principal classroom buildings.

    III. The southeast quadrant contains the library and student union building.

    IV. The southwest quadrant contains the athletic plant.

Other topics can best be discussed in terms of geographical distribution. In discussing petroleum reserves, we might arrange materials as follows:

Core Statement: Oil reserves are widely distributed around the globe.

    I. There are reserves in the Middle East.

    II. There are reserves in the Arctic.

    III. There are reserves in Mexico and Venezuela.

It is possible to combine a spatial pattern with a time pattern in discussing certain topics.

Core Statement: The Brazilian "killer bee" is spreading northward at a steady rate.

    I. It was introduced into Brazil shortly after the close of World War II.

    II. It has now reached Central America.

    III. Scientists predict it will invade the southern United States by 1985.

Topical Relationships	The constituent parts of certain subjects show relationships that are neither temporal nor spatial in character. Instead, the relationships form natural divisions, such as component parts, qualities, features, functions, roles, levels of hierarchy, to name but a fraction of the variations possible. A few examples may illustrate the wide array of speech subjects that can be treated topically.

Core Statement:	The good leader combines four basic qualities.

     I. He or she is intelligent.
    II. He or she is decisive.
   III. He or she is emotionally mature.
   IV. He or she is compassionate.

Core Statement:	Governmental reforms are badly needed.

     I. The executive branch has too much power.
    II. The legislative branch has too little power.
   III. The judicial branch does not use its power.

Core Statement:	Shoppers for a used car should have knowledge of certain factors.

     I. They should know what cars to avoid.
    II. They should know where to shop.
   III. They should know how to inspect the car.

Core Statement:	Trouble is most likely to occur in a gasoline engine in one of three systems.

     I. It may occur in the electrical system.
    II. It may occur in the fuel system.
   III. It may occur in the drive train.

The foregoing patterns of time, space, and topical relationship are particularly useful in presenting non-argumentative thought relationships. Speeches of exposition, description, and narration provide many opportunities for the employment of these patterns. Moreover, it is possible that a variety of these patterns can be employed within a single speech. The main points, for example, might follow a topical pattern, the subheads developing a given main point might follow a spatial pattern, the subheads developing another main point might use the time pattern.

Strategies of Arrangement

We have discussed some of the ways main points may relate to one another and to the core statement. Now let us see how they may be put together to facilitate the speaker's purpose. In determining your plan of organization you will want to take into account certain predictions you have made about your listeners-to-be as a result of your audience analysis—their probable level of acquaintance with the topic, their probable attitude toward your specific purpose, their probable attitude toward you as a spokesperson on the topic. There is obviously no one plan of organization suitable for all topics and purposes, but a number of useful designs have gained popularity over the years. A brief examination of some of these strategies of arrangement may suggest the range of choices available to you.

Problem-Solution Sequence	A very popular pattern for recommending the adoption of a policy, the problem-solution sequence (1) presents a problem area, (2) announces a proposed solution to the problem, and (3) defends the proposed solution. If you wished to advocate conversion to solar energy, you might arrange your points as follows:

Core Statement: The United States should convert to solar energy.

(Problem)

    I. Present energy sources are unsatisfactory.
        A. They are in diminishing supply.
            (support)
        B. They are costly.
            (support)
        C. They are hazardous to the environment.
            (support)

(Solution)

    II. Solar energy represents a solution to our energy problems.
        A. It is inexhaustible in supply.
            (support)
        B. It is inexpensive.
            (support)
        C. It presents no hazard to our environment.
            (support)

(Defense)

    III. Conversion to solar energy is feasible.
        A. It is technically feasible.
            (support)
        B. It is economically feasible.
            (support)

(Defense)

    IV. Disadvantages of conversion are minor.
        A. Workers in affected industries such as coal and petroleum could be absorbed into other industries.
            (support)
        B. The physical facilities affected could be converted to other uses.
            (support)

(Defense)

    V. Conversion to solar energy is the best solution to adopt.
        A. It does not have the limitations of geothermal energy.
            (support)
        B. It does not present the dangers of nuclear energy.
            (support)

Note that both main heads and subheads are arranged topically. The main heads involve the topics of problem, solution, and defense of solution. The subheads involve several groups of topics. In I and II the subheads use the topics of cost, supply, and safety. In III they use the topics of engineering feasibility and financial feasibility. In IV the subheads are displaced workers and obsolete facilities. And in V the subheads are limitations and dangers.

The Motivated Sequence	Professor Alan H. Monroe in his *Principles and Types of Speech Communication* popularized the division of speeches into a series of steps that he labeled "The Motivated Sequence." When applied to persuasive speeches, this format involves the following steps: (1) The *Attention* step, wherein the speaker secures initial audience attention; (2) The *Need* step, wherein the audience is made aware of the existence of a problem; (3) The *Satisfaction* step, wherein a solution to that problem is explained and defended; (4) The *Visualization* step, wherein the speaker envisions what the future will be like if the recommended solution is put into practice (or not put into practice); and (5) The *Action* step, wherein the audience is given directions for implementing the solution. Note the similarity between the problem-solution sequence described earlier and the Need and Satisfaction steps of the Motivated Sequence.

When the Motivated Sequence is applied to informational speeches the Visualization and Action steps may be omitted. The Attention step of the informational speech, like the persuasive speech, is designed to capture the listener's attention. The Need step is aimed at making the audience feel a need for the information to be presented. And, of course, the Satisfaction step provides the needed information.

The applications of the Motivated Sequence extend beyond public speaking. Witness, for example, a typical commercial message on television.

Attention:	Closeup of a gasoline pump dial spinning madly. Harried driver looks on aghast.
Need:	Voice asks, "Own a gas guzzler?"
Satisfaction:	Voice replies, "Why not trade it in on our new SUB-COMPACT?" There follows verbal and visual account of salient features of the car.
Visualization:	Driver, no longer harried, waves to service station attendant as he drives by without stopping. Attendant looks forlornly at idle gas pump.
Action:	Voice says, "Come to 2320 Mesa Boulevard today. We're open till nine."

Level-of-Acceptability Sequence

When there is apt to be strong listener resistance to the point of view held by the speaker, a favorite organizational strategy is to start with ideas known to be acceptable to the listener and then work gradually toward less acceptable ideas until the least acceptable idea is reached. This movement from most acceptable to least acceptable is often signalled by the speaker's early use of the "common ground" technique. An example of this form of strategy is seen in the following abbreviated outline:

I. Americans are suffering from inflation.
II. Americans want steps taken to fight inflation.
III. Effective steps require the participation of all Americans.
IV. The most effective step Americans can take is to hold the line on wages.

Core Statement:	There should be a moratorium on all wage increases in the coming year.

The first point represents the area of "common ground." Presumably, the audience will accept this idea without challenge. The second point may possibly require some demonstration, although it, too, might fall within the area of "common ground." The third point may be more difficult to establish, particularly if there is a prevailing attitude among the listeners of "let the other guy do it." The fourth point would most likely meet the greatest resistance. But if the speaker succeeds in establishing these points in order, the Core Statement is more likely to be heard with favor than if it were announced at the outset.

The Extended Illustration

This speech design is applicable to both informative and persuasive speeches. A speaker who wishes to explain the duties of a police officer, for example, might build the speech around a typical day in the life of a real or hypothetical officer. By translating the facts into narrative form the speaker uses an effective ingredient for keeping audience interest high.

A persuasive speech designed to elicit contributions to the multiple sclerosis fund might be translated into a narrative involving a person who contracts multiple sclerosis and the ensuing struggle for recovery.

Other Sequences

The placement of ideas in order of increasing difficulty is as old as the history of teaching. Instruction frequently follows the sequence *from the simplest idea to the most complex.* For example, multicellular speech structure can be better comprehended if one begins by comprehending the simplest form of speech, the single cell, and then moves in increasing complexity toward the most sophisticated forms.

Another application of placement in order of increasing difficulty is movement *from familiar ideas to unfamiliar ideas.* It has become virtually axiomatic that explanation is the process of relating the unknown to the known. *Extended comparisons or analogies* likewise epitomize this expository design.

Outlining the Message

The speech outline is the tool for arraying constituent parts of the message into the most orderly and dynamic sequence. Outlining is the process of synthesis rendered into tangible form so the speaker can see the interrelationship of the parts, their proportions, the adequacy of their development, and how well they function in the aggregate.

The speaker making optimum use of outlining first assembles a master outline (sometimes called a *brief*) designed to promote the thorough understanding of a subject in all its ramifications. Such an outline contains far more material than ever reaches the presentation stage. It serves as the warehouse from which to draw materials for the presentation outline. The presentation outline is drafted with the listener in mind; thus it is much more selective than the master outline.

Although experienced speakers may employ an abbreviated form of outlining that features the use of key words or key phrases, beginning speakers profit more from use of the complete-sentence outline. It is especially important in outlining argumentative discourses that the complete-sentence form be used, since logical relationships cannot be clearly expressed through the use of key words or phrases. You will discover, too, that the extra effort involved in constructing a complete-sentence outline pays off in greater ease of retention of ideas during presentation.

The following principles should be observed in the preparation of outlines:

1. *Assign only one idea or statement to each unit of the outline.* Note the difference in clarity between *a* and *b.*

   (a)

   I. Since it applies more easily and costs less, latex-base paint is preferable to oil-base paint; in addition, it dries faster and it is not as messy.

   (b)

   I. Latex-base paint is preferable to oil-base paint. (for)
       A. It applies more easily.
       B. It dries faster.
       C. It is not as messy.
       D. It costs less.

2. *Do not allow points to overlap.* The following example represents an infraction of this rule.

   I. Animals are in danger of contracting the disease.
       A. Wild animals are in danger.
       B. Domesticated animals are in danger.
       C. Pets are in danger.

   The inclusion of C throws the pattern into confusion since pets could be either wild or domesticated animals.

3. *Maintain consistent levels of importance among coordinate points.* Units that are labeled as main points, for example, should share common elements. The intrusion of a unit of greater or lesser magnitude will destroy the consistency of the pattern. For example:

   I. The senator's political base is statewide.
       A. Dade County supports him.
       B. Warren County supports him.
       C. Statler County supports him.
       D. New residents support him.

   The inclusion of D breaks the consistency of the pattern and introduces an annoying element of disproportion.

4. *Maintain clear levels of subordination.* Through proper use of symbols and indentation, the hierarchy of points is indicated. Compare the examples that follow.

(a)

I. Advantages of natural gas are
   A. Convenience
   B. Efficiency
   C. Safety
   D. Sources of Gas
      1. In the Southwest
      2. In the East
      3. In the Midwest

(b)

I. Advantages of natural gas are
   A. Convenience
   B. Efficiency
   C. Safety
II. Sources of natural gas are
   A. In the Southwest
   B. In the East
   C. In the Midwest

5. *Use a consistent set of symbols and indentations to indicate relationships among main headings and subheadings.* The usual system is:

I. Main heading —————————————————————
  A. Subheading —————————————————————
     1. ——————————————————————
       a. ——————————————————————
         (1) ——————————————————————
         (2) ——————————————————————
       b. ——————————————————————
     2. ——————————————————————
  B. ——————————————————————
II. ——————————————————————

Note that main headings are consistently designated by roman numerals, that subheadings that explain, illustrate, or prove the main headings to which they are immediately subordinated are designated by capital letters, that the level subordinate to the subheadings is designated by Arabic numerals, and so on down the scale of importance.

An outline for an entire speech would probably be divided into four parts: introduction, core statement, body, and conclusion. In some speech classes the instructor might require a title for the speech, a statement of general and specific purposes, and a bibliography of sources consulted. The following is an outline of a fictional informational speech:

The Landscaper's Dream

Introduction

I. Over five million words concerning lawn care are printed in U.S. newspapers every week.
II. Today I want to tell you of a new grass that may revolutionize the weekend habits of the American homeowner.

Core Statement: New Hybrid R50 is an ideal grass for western homeowners.

Body

I. It is attractive.
   A. It has a rich green color.
      1. Photo A shows a plot of R50 in early spring.
      2. Photo B shows the same plot in late summer.
   B. It has a carpetlike texture.
      1. Photo C shows a cross section of a piece of R50 sod.
      2. Photo D shows R50 used in a putting green.
II. It is inexpensive.
   A. The initial cost is low.
      1. Seed cost is lower than that of *Dichondra*.
      2. Turf prices are about the same as the cheapest Bermuda grass.
   B. Maintenance cost is low.
      1. It requires only a light application of all-purpose lawn food in the early spring.
      2. At the height of the growing season it requires mowing only twice a month.
III. It is tough.
   A. It resists weather extremes.
      1. It tolerates extreme heat.
         (a) It flourishes in a test plot in Death Valley.
         (b) Landscapers have planted it on the shores of Lake Havasu in Arizona.
      2. It tolerates moderate cold.
         (a) It does well in the Sierra foothills.
         (b) It flourishes in the Southern California mountain areas.
   B. It resists the usual enemies of grass.
      1. It resists lawn moths.
      2. It resists fungus.

Conclusion

I. R50 is not yet available for you hapless lawn mower jockeys, but it should be in plentiful supply within five years.
II. Meanwhile, you'd better wear glasses if you're planning to read all five million words printed about lawn care every week.

Beginning and Ending the Speech

Our focus thus far has been upon ways and means of structuring those ideas intended to develop the central idea, or Core Statement, of the speech. A perusal of the outline of "The Landscaper's Dream" shows that the development of the Core Statement takes place in the body of the speech. But what of the materials that precede and follow the body of any speech? How does one devise an appropriate introduction and conclusion? This final section of the chapter will answer these questions.

Preparing the Introduction

The introduction to any speech should accomplish two basic purposes: (1) it should get the attention of the audience and (2) it should prepare the audience for what is to follow. Unless the first purpose is achieved, all of the speaker's efforts are for naught. Unless the second purpose is achieved, the speaker risks failure in accomplishing the desired goal.

Gaining Attention

What percentage of the introduction should be devoted to getting the audience's attention? The answer must be, unfortunately, "It all depends." Perhaps the audience is waiting expectantly for the speaker. The mere act of the speaker appearing on the platform may gain attention. On the other hand, the speech may face the stiffest sort of competition for the audience's attention. Perhaps the audience is more concerned with the discomfort of sitting in a hot, stuffy room. Perhaps members of the audience are engaged in animated conversation. Perhaps the speaker faces the kind of captive audience found in required speech classes!

While it would be impossible to catalog all the ways of opening a speech in an attention-compelling fashion, the following devices are among the most commonly employed. No one device can be regarded as universally applicable. Your choice will ultimately be governed by your subject, purpose, and audience.

Quotation

A thought-provoking or curiosity-arousing quotation can be an effective device for opening many speeches. For example, if you wished to discuss reasons why your listeners should try to cultivate better listening habits, you might use this opening:

> "Nature has given man one tongue and two ears, that we may hear twice as much as we speak." This contemporary-sounding observation was offered by the great Stoic philosopher Epictetus nineteen centuries ago.

A speaker who discussed the relative longevity of men and women opened a speech with this quotation:

> "The stronger sex is actually the weaker sex because of the weakness of the stronger sex for the weaker sex." This humorous observation noted in the evening newspaper just yesterday has more truth to it than appears at first glance.

The important criteria to use in selecting a quotation for an opening are *relevance, provocativeness,* and *good taste.* A quotation cited simply to gain attention and nothing more is apt to create ill will when it becomes obvious to the listener that the device bears no connection to the speaker's subject. The quotation that is not provocative simply fails in its task of eliciting audience attention. Finally, the quotation that is in poor taste will certainly get the audience's attention, but it is apt to be the kind of attention that militates against the accomplishment of the speaker's purpose.

Illustration or Story

Among the most familiar devices for opening speeches are stories or illustrations. When properly handled they can be the most effective openings of all, because interesting narratives cause the listener to attend effortlessly. On the other hand, tired stories that the audience has heard innumerable times can turn off audience attention. Before using this familiar opening device the speaker should make certain (1) that the story or illustration is fresh (old stories told from a new slant are as fresh as brand-new stories), (2) that it is pertinent to the main theme of the speech, (3) that it can be effectively related by the speaker (any limitations as a storyteller should be considered), and (4) that it be in good taste. This last quality cannot be stressed too much, especially if the story is a humorous one. The speaker must be extremely thorough in audience analysis to ferret out any information that would signal issues of taste. As a general rule it is wise to avoid stories that derive their humor from ridicule of religion or racial origin. Self-directed ridicule is perhaps the safest form of humor to employ in the story or illustration. (See our treatment of illustrations in the preceding chapter for additional guidelines.)

Reference to a Recent Event

While sitting in the waiting room at your dentist's office, have you ever discovered that the only magazine remaining in the rack is a two-year-old copy of a weekly news magazine? Even if you had not read it when it was published, you are not very curious to read it now because it is "old hat." You are concerned with what is current.

Whenever possible the wise speaker will try to associate the theme of the speech with something recent. For example, a speaker wishing to explain the laser principle might allude to a recent news broadcast reporting the use of laser-beam eye surgery on a celebrity. Someone wishing to discuss measures for tax reform might first refer to a news clipping reporting the number of millionaires who escaped payment of income taxes by using loopholes in existing tax laws. This association of your theme with a recent happening gives a freshness and immediacy to your ideas that makes an audience interested in listening further.

Rhetorical Question

We are all familiar with the interest value of suspense in drama. Even when we know the hero is going to emerge triumphant in the final scene, we can not help but feel anxiety for his welfare as he meets obstacle after obstacle along the way. Of course, when the final outcome is unpredictable, the suspense can become even more extreme.

The speaker would do well to emulate the playwright in employing suspense as a factor of interest. Starting the speech with a rhetorical question is one application of suspense to speaking. A skillfully phrased question that puts the audience in a state of expectancy for an answer can be a very effective means of gaining attention. But let us call attention to that important qualification—*that puts the audience in a state of expectancy for an answer.*

Without this qualification, the rhetorical question is ineffectual as an attention device. Of course, what puts an audience in a state of expectancy will differ from audience to audience. A group of entering freshmen would have their attention piqued by hearing the dean of admissions use this rhetorical question at an orientation meeting, "How many of you will be here next year to start your sophomore year?"

The question, "Where can you buy a first edition of Campbell's *A Philosophy of Rhetoric* for twenty-nine cents?" would probably evoke this reaction from a group of chemistry majors: "I don't know and I don't care to know!" To an audience of graduate students of rhetoric or to a group of dedicated bibliophiles it might well have an electrifying effect. Here again you can see the importance of knowing your audience before you plan your strategy.

Startling Statement

An audience that is apathetic toward the speaker's topic can often be made attentive by a statement that startles or shocks them. This is particularly true of speeches on familiar themes, such as requests for contributions to charitable organizations, to cancer drives, to heart funds, or speeches exhorting hearers to exercise their right to vote, or urging them to wear seat belts. The startling statement in such cases might be a direct reference to a person or persons in the audience. For example, a speaker might begin: "I'm sure that all of you are just as sad as I am that these three gentlemen sitting in the front row are going to have to undergo a lengthy hospitalization that will cause them to use up all their savings, sell their homes, and most of their belongings." Such a statement would certainly get the attention of the "three gentlemen" and would probably arouse the curiosity of the other members of the audience. To be effective, the startling statement, like all attention devices, should be relevant to the topic and should rest upon a thorough understanding of your audience. It is easy to see that indiscriminate use of the startling statement could have a self-defeating effect.

Promise of Reward

A statement promising reward for careful listening can, like the rhetorical question, generate suspense. Thus it can serve as an effective opening device for speeches on a wide variety of topics.

Here are examples from classroom speeches that have generated suspense: "That next five minutes may be the most important five minutes of your life," said the speaker prior to giving instructions on administering aid to someone choking on a food particle. "If you follow the suggestions I'm about to cite, you'll be two-hundred dollars richer by the end of this semester," was the preface to a speech on deceptive food packaging. Another speaker provoked attention by needling the listeners as follows, "Whether you realize it or not, you are a major contributor to air pollution because of some common faults in your driving habits."

Reference to the Subject	The use of a simple reference to the subject as a means of gaining attention should be reserved for those subjects in which your audience is already interested, so that the mere mention of the subject will provoke a high level of interest. If your topic does not possess an inherent interest value for your audience, avoid this type of opening. To illustrate, we can guess that an audience will be inherently interested in gossipy information about famous public figures. Therefore, we can, with impunity, open with, "Today I'd like to share with you some little-known facts about the after-hours behavior of one of our highest ranking government officials." We can also guess that an audience will not be inherently interested in an explanation of some esoteric subject. Thus, "Today I'd like to talk about residual disjunctive enthymemes" will probably produce a yawn from the listener.

If your topic has a high curiosity potential or if it is a topic that people are talking excitedly about before your speech, a simple reference to the subject may be your quickest way to achieve audience attention. If your topic does not have these built-in guarantees of audience interest, you had better choose another attention device.

Reference to the Occasion	This device may be very useful on relatively formal speech occasions, such as a banquet, a graduation ceremony, a dedication, a special lecture—in any case where the *occasion* is the dominant factor. In the average speech class, however, such a formal opening would seem stuffy and affected, unless it happened to be the first day or the last day of the class.
Preparing Your Audience for the Speech	This function of the introduction may be accomplished in a wide variety of ways. What constitutes adequate audience preparation can never be universally prescribed. However, we can describe some of the things commonly done; your topic, purpose, and analysis of the audience will dictate which of these will be applicable in your case.
Justifying the Topic	When your listeners have not gathered for the express purpose of hearing you talk about a given topic, you need to offer them a reason for listening. "So you're going to talk about petroleum distillates. What's in it for us?" may well be the kind of reaction the audience experiences upon the announcement of your topic. Well, what *is* in it for them? How do petroleum distillates affect their lives? Will your treatment of the subject benefit them in some tangible way? Will it help them be healthier, be more productive? Will it benefit them in intangible ways? Will it satisfy their sense of curiosity? Will it satisfy their need for emotional expression?

In speeches to inform, the justification of the topic answers the question, "Why do I need this information?" In the speech to persuade it answers such questions as "How does this issue affect me?" "Why should I be concerned about this problem and its solution?"

Sometimes the device used for gaining attention can also serve to justify the topic. For example, a rhetorical question may provoke attention and instill a need for information.

Remember that justification of the topic is not always needed. In many cases the audience will arrive already motivated. For instance, it would be unnecessary to spend time justifying a discussion of proposed pay raises before an audience of college professors who would be the recipients of the salary increase.

Delimiting the Topic

You may find it necessary to draw the boundaries of your discussion when approaching certain topics. To say "I'm going to discuss marijuana" is to lead the audience to anticipate a number of possibilities. Will you discuss the structure of the marijuana plant, where marijuana is grown, how marijuana is processed, how marijuana affects the user, the legalization of the sale of marijuana, who uses marijuana, the effects of marijuana versus the effects of alcohol? In such cases it may be well for you to point out not only what you are going to include but also what you are going to exclude from the discussion. By providing listeners with the boundaries of your discussion, you enable them to adjust their expectations accordingly. It helps them clear their minds of issues that are beside the point of your speech. Furthermore, it gives the audience a certain kind of security to know just how far you intend to go. It will then not be so impatient for those beautiful words, "And in conclusion. . . ."

To be sure, there are occasions when it is unwise to indicate the boundaries of your discussion, especially if the creation of a feeling of suspense is essential to the accomplishment of your purpose. (But be sure this is not a rationalization resulting from confusion in your own mind about the boundaries of your discussion.)

Presenting Your Speaking Credentials

If your authority to speak on a subject is not known to your listeners, it may be necessary for you to establish it in the speech. Normally, this would be done for you by the person introducing you to the audience, but if the introducer is derelict in this duty (or if there is no introducer at all), the task falls upon you.

Why should your credentials be made known? Audiences place greater credibility in the remarks of speakers they consider to be expert. Furthermore, they tend to listen more attentively to the expert. One of the authors of this text recalls a classroom speech dealing with an incident of presidential "jawboning" of the members of Congress. After the speech a member of the class asked the student speaker where he had obtained his information. He replied, "My father is a member of the House of Representatives." This heretofore undisclosed bit of information about one of their fellow classmates had an electrifying effect upon the students. Suddenly the speaker's remarks had a new significance, and the class sentiment was "I wish he'd give the speech over again."

What are your credentials? Obviously you cannot always be an expert in the sense of being directly involved. But that does not mean you cannot speak with authority on a subject. Through reading and research you can so familiarize yourself with a subject that you are an expert in comparison with your listeners. Perhaps your authority derives from close association with those who are, in fact, experts.

How shall you make your credentials known? This can usually be accomplished without creating the impression of immodesty. Here are a few examples:

"I'd like to share with you some facts about radiation poisoning that I learned in a class in radiological medicine last semester."

"As a 'Navy brat' I've had more 'hometowns' than I can remember right offhand. But my favorite hometown has always been San Diego. Today I'd like to discuss just what it is that makes San Diego unique."

"In doing a term paper for American history last semester, I became interested in Benedict Arnold's role in the American Revolution. Just how serious were his misdeeds? Was the war effort really hampered? I shall attempt to give you my answers to these questions today."

Defining Terms

If the subject you are discussing involves special terminology, jargon, or technical vocabulary, offer definitions early in the speech. Perhaps you will set aside a portion of the introduction to define all terms to be used, or perhaps you will define each term when it first appears in the speech.

*Providing
Background
Information*

Occasionally a full appreciation or understanding of a subject cannot be gained unless one is familiar with certain background details. The background materials are often in the form of historical details. To discuss a great event without indicating the historical context in which it occurred is to deny the listener an important dimension for understanding the event.

Other background details may be physical in nature. For example, to have the audience sense the grandeur of the Lincoln Memorial, one has to put it in physical context. An architect's genius cannot be fully appreciated by simply examining the building he or she has designed. One has to see how the building integrates with its physical environment.

*Establishing
Common Ground*

Not infrequently we are forced to take an unpopular stand on a controversial issue. If we wish to win audience support for our position, we must pave the way carefully. One of the measures used is the establishment of a common ground of belief between speaker and listener. In essence, this means that you will take pains to stress areas of agreement before turning to those issues on which you and your audience hold divergent viewpoints. It is even conceivable that this act of establishing a common ground may occupy the major share of your speech.

**Preparing the
Conclusion**

"Well, I guess that's about all. Are there any questions?" This is an all-too-common ending to speeches. Judge for yourself whether it accomplishes the usual functions of a speech conclusion: (1) Does it redirect the audience's attention to the central point of the speech? (2) Does it usher the listener into the frame of mind that should be dominant at the end? (3) Does it leave the listener with a sense of completeness?

We would hazard the guess that the average speech student gives less thought to preparing the conclusion than to any other facet of speech preparation.

Yet the conclusion can be the most critical part of the speech. An ineffectual ending can undermine all that has been accomplished by the speaker in the preceding portions of the speech.

Let us examine, then, some of the possible methods of ending a speech effectively.

Summary

A brief recapitulation of the main points of the speech is a common device used in concluding. It is particularly valuable in instructional speeches, because it reinforces the instructions that the speaker wishes the audience to recall. For example, in concluding a speech on the fundamentals of tennis a speaker would use the summary in the following manner: "Today, having learned some of the elementary techniques of tennis, try to remember (1) that you should always keep your eye on the ball, (2) that you should keep your arm firm, and (3) that your swing should follow through." In persuasive speeches the summary can serve to remind the listener that sound reasons have been advanced for the belief the speaker wishes them to hold or for the action he or she wishes them to take.

Usually the summary is employed in conjunction with other concluding devices, since by itself it may not accomplish all the purposes of a conclusion that we have discussed.

Quotation

Just as the quotation can be effectively employed as a means of gaining attention at the beginning of a speech, it can be employed to end the speech on a graceful, stimulating note. Sometimes it is possible to use two quotations from the same person, one for a beginning and one for an ending. Or perhaps a repetition of the same quotation used in the opening will be fitting at the end. Whatever the quotation chosen, it should meet the tests of relevance, good taste, and impact.

A good example of the effective use of a quotation can be seen in Martin Luther King's famous "I Have a Dream" speech:

> From every mountainside, let freedom ring, and when this happens . . . when we allow freedom to ring, when we let it ring from every village and every hamlet, from every state and every city, we will be able to speed up that day when all of God's children, black men and white men, Jews and Gentiles, Protestants and Catholics, will be able to join hands and sing in the words of the old Negro spiritual, "Free at last! Thank God Almighty, we are free at last!"

Illustration or Story

Like the quotation, the illustration or story can be used effectively at both extremities of the speech. It is particularly useful as a method of making visual for the listener the import of what you have been discussing in the body of the speech. It distills the essence of your message and presents it in a form that makes it memorable to the listener.

If the prevailing mood of your speech has been one of unrelieved seriousness, an illustration or story in a light vein may provide the touch needed to leave the audience in the right frame of mind.

Speeches designed to stimulate the audience to greater efforts or stronger devotion to some cause or ideal lend themselves well to this kind of ending. Occasionally an informative speech can employ this ending as well if the speaker wishes the audience to seek information in addition to that just presented in the body of the speech. In any case, the challenge should be worded in such a way as to encourage a spirit of optimism in the audience's attempt to meet the challenge. If the challenge seems impossible to fulfill, a negative attitude is generated that runs counter to the speaker's intentions.

A classic example of the use of challenge is the often-quoted conclusion of John F. Kennedy's Inaugural Address:

> And so, my fellow Americans: Ask not what your country can do for you—ask what you can do for your country.
>
> My fellow citizens of the world: Ask not what America will do for you, but what together we can do for the freedom of man.
>
> Finally, whether you are citizens of America or citizens of the world, ask of us here the same high standards of strength and sacrifice which we ask of you. With a good conscience our only sure reward, with history the final judge of our deeds, let us go forth to lead the land we love, asking His blessing and His help, but knowing that here on earth God's work must truly be our own.

Declaration of Intent

Speeches intended to induce action can be concluded effectively when the speaker sets an example for the audience by declaring what he or she personally plans to do. Patrick Henry's famous closing remarks in his "Liberty or Death" speech is the first example that comes to mind. A less familiar example can be seen in a speech delivered by Daniel Webster in the U.S. Senate when he and Calhoun were debating the nature of the Constitution:

> I am ready to perform my own appropriate part, whenever and wherever the occasion may call on me, and to take my chance among those upon whom blows may fall first and fall thickest. I shall exert every faculty I possess in aiding to prevent the Constitution from being nullified, destroyed, or impaired; and even should I see it fall, I will still, with a voice feeble, perhaps, but earnest as ever issued from human lips, and with fidelity and zeal which nothing shall extinguish, call on the People to come to its rescue.

Summary

The process of assembling the speech usually begins with the formulation of a core statement embodying the central idea of the speech. Growing out of the core statement are the main points, subpoints, and supporting materials. Coordinate points should (1) relate to the core statement, (2) relate to one another yet be separable from one another, and (3) collectively develop the statement under which they stand. Coordinate points should be meaningfully grouped. Among the patterns of grouping are chronological arrangement, spatial arrangement, and topical arrangement. Once grouped, they should be put into a sequence that will most effectively support the core statement. Overall strategies of arrangement include the Problem-Solution Sequence, the Motivated Sequence, the Level-of-Acceptability Sequence, the Extended Illustration, and various designs suitable to either exposition or persuasion.

The outline is the tool for arranging constituent parts of the message into orderly sequence. Good outline form features the use of a consistent set of symbols to show proper subordination of ideas. Each unit of the outline should contain only one idea; points should not be allowed to overlap; coordinate points should be consistent.

After the body of the speech is designed, the speaker formulates an introduction and a conclusion. An introduction serves to gain attention and prepare the audience for what is to follow. Among the methods of gaining attention are quotation, illustration or story, reference to a recent event, rhetorical question, startling statement, promise of reward, reference to the subject, and reference to the occasion. Preparing the audience for what is to follow may involve justifying the topic, delimiting the topic, presenting your speaking credentials, defining terms, providing background information, and establishing a common ground.

The conclusion serves to redirect the audience's attention to the core statement, to usher the audience into the frame of mind consistent with the speaker's purpose, and to give the listener a sense of completeness. Some methods of concluding are summary, quotation, illustration or story, challenge, and declaration of intent.

Suggested Readings

Brooks, William D. *Speech Communication.* 3d ed. Dubuque, IA: Wm. C. Brown Company Publishers, 1978. Chapter 12.

Monroe, Alan H.; Ehninger, Douglas; and Gronbeck, Bruce E. *Principles and Types of Speech Communication.* 8th ed. Glenview, IL: Scott, Foresman, 1978. Chapters 9, 10, 11, 12.

Reid, Loren. *Speaking Well.* 3d ed. New York: McGraw-Hill, 1977. Chapters 10, 11.

Scheidel, Thomas M. *Speech Communication and Human Interaction.* 2d ed. Glenview, IL: Scott, Foresman, 1976. Chapter 13.

Zannes, Estelle, and Goldhaber, Gerald. *Stand up and Speak out.* Reading, MA: Addison-Wesley Publishing, 1978. Chapter 6.

Language
The Medium of Your Ideas

One of our greatest human needs is the need to share our impressions, opinions, beliefs, emotions, and knowledge with others. If we are suddenly deprived of a means of sharing, our world is thrown into confusion. Those clues to self-identity gained from "bouncing our ideas off" other persons are lost. Our very survival is imperiled. So the agency for sharing—language—is of paramount importance. Yet we often underestimate its importance and impact. Consider these questions: During your waking hours what are some of the ways you use language? What do you ask words to do for you? If you reflect for a moment on these questions, you will probably discover that you ask words (1) to tell someone how you feel ("The killing of baby seals to make fur coats is criminal!"); (2) to explain a process to a friend ("Carol, changing the oil in your car is really quite simple."); (3) to influence our environment ("We must see to it that handguns are no longer available in the United States."); (4) to gather information ("John, what do you know about solar heat?"); and (5) to have others offer us comfort ("I received a traffic ticket yesterday and I'm sure upset."). In all these instances, and countless others, we have asked words to help us share our internal states.

This ability to manipulate words is one of our unique features. Unlike other animals, humans use a sophisticated coding system (word-symbols) as the main means of communication. Through millions of years of evolution we have developed both the physical and social tools necessary for language to function. Because we can hear, speak, and reason, we are able to use word-symbols as one way of sharing our experiences with others. We can have sounds, or marks on a paper, stand for (represent) objects, things, ideas, and feelings. As a society we have decided that when the word *dog* is spoken or written it stands for "a domesticated, carnivorous mammal." A word as abstract and general as *love* is a man-made symbol representing something else (often deep affection we have for another person).

Words are a kind of shorthand. They are substitutes for the real thing. We tinker with them and manipulate them so that we can have some degree of influence over the environments in which we find ourselves. Realizing these facts about language and its influence, the student of speech communication should ask two questions: Do my verbal accounts give the listener a true picture of reality? Does my word selection really convey to others the impressions I want to make? The answers to these two questions will serve as the basis for this chapter. We will examine those principles and techniques of language usage that will help your material come closer to reality (the life-facts), and we will also examine those principles and techniques that will enable others to see and feel what you are trying to share.

At the outset, be mindful of the obvious fact that language generated to be heard is somewhat different from language produced to be read. Language in speech-making should possess slightly different characteristics than language to be read. A review of desirable characteristics might help you begin the process of developing a new attitude toward the role of language in oral communication.

Oral communication should contain more personal pronouns. Personal pronouns are used because the speaker is face-to-face with the audience, and this *live* presence makes interaction more informal than television (which is one-way) or reading. The parties engaging in oral communication are occupying the same environment and will therefore find it easier and more comfortable to use pronouns such as "we," "ours," "yours," and "I." Notice the conversational differences in the following sentences: "*One* must realize that unemployment affects the entire country," and "*We* must realize that unemployment affects all of *us*."

Oral communication requires more varied types of sentences. The period and the comma are not available when we speak. We have to use pauses and phrases as kinds of punctuation. Therefore, we often find it convenient to speak in sentences that would appear awkward if they were written. We even use more fragmented sentences in oral communication.

Oral communication should contain more repetition of words, phrases, and sentences. It is important to keep in mind that your audience cannot go back and reread what is not clear. Therefore, you must learn to repeat key points and verbally underscore your main ideas. (Specific techniques of repeating and rephrasing will be discussed later.)

Oral communication should contain words and phrases that are easy to understand. The listener cannot stop and consult a dictionary in the middle of your talk—oral communication is continuous. Therefore, indigenous language should be used whenever possible. A computer expert talking about "chips" to a group of artists might have to stop and explain this word, or else go on with the talk and run the risk of the audience not understanding his language. This would, of course, present a serious problem since understanding is the heart of communication. In fact, the need to be understood is the rationale for the remainder of this chapter.

Language to Represent Reality

Language, in the broad sense, is best defined as a set of symbols used in a common and uniform way by a number of persons able to manipulate these symbols for the purpose of communication. We have already mentioned many of the elements of nonverbal symbols, such as facial expression, gesture, and posture. Now, however, we are concerned with that form of language in which words are the basic symbols. We will discuss aspects of language that can, depending on their use, either help or hinder an accurate symbolic representation of reality. As we have noted, when we use verbal language we are asking words to help describe that which is inside us, something we know or feel. If we wish to share that information (our personal reality), we must describe that reality in ways that will accurately mirror what we "have in mind." If, for example, we see a traffic accident caused by speeding and wish to tell others about the dangers of driving too fast, we must ask our vocabulary to serve as an approximation of what we are experiencing and what we saw. The following discussion focuses on that approximation. Specifically, we will look at those aspects of our language concerned with the accuracy with which our words match reality.

Words Are Symbols

Because words are symbols of verbal language, it is important to remember that they are *arbitrary symbols*. We call them symbols because they *represent* objects, ideas, concepts, and feelings. The word *dog* stands for a four-legged, domesticated animal, but the *word* "dog" is actually *not* the dog, but a sound that our society has decided shall *stand for* that particular thing. You will notice that we used the word *arbitrary*—there is no necessary relationship between the word and the thing it stands for. Persons often forget this fact and confuse a word with the thing for which it stands. They lose sight of the principle that a word exists only as a representation of a fact—a word is not the fact, thing, or occurrence to which it refers. Consequently, there is no assurance that the word selected represents or depicts reality. If Senator X calls his opponent "dishonest" and accuses him of "stealing," these symbols may not accurately represent actuality.

The conscientious communicator must always remember that the word is not the thing itself; it is a symbol. He or she should develop the habit of asking, "Do the words fit the facts?" Irving Lee, in his book *Language Habits in Human Affairs,* summarizes this view when he notes that the communicator should not only be concerned with what *it* was called (symbols), but also what *was* being so called (object).

Words Have Many Uses

It would indeed be convenient if we had one word for each thing or occurrence. But we are faced with the fact that a limited number of words must cover an unlimited number of things. Wendell Johnson, a writer in the field of general semantics, underscores the problem when he writes, "A rather large share of our misunderstanding and disagreement arises not so much because we are constitutionally stupid or stubborn, but simply because we have to use the same words to refer to so many different things."

We could cite an endless number of words that have many uses and meanings. Take the simple word *foot*. It can represent a part of the body, a measurement, or it can be used in a slang expression (to foot the bill). Or take the word *pot*. It can represent a cooking utensil, a rather large stomach, or even something that is rolled in paper and smoked. A glance at any standard dictionary will reveal many words with twenty-five or more meanings.

Due to this multiple-meaning characteristic of language we must be very careful when we use symbols that have a variety of meanings. *Awareness* that any word may have a whole list of uses is the first step in handling the problem. Another step is realizing that what is being said may not represent what the user intended or assumed. In conversation we can also develop the habit of asking directly how a person is using a particular word or phrase. In addition, as speakers, we should try to select words that lend themselves to direct translation and define those words and phrases that have a variety of meanings.

Whenever in a speech or conversation the words or phrases being used are ambiguous or are used in an incorrect sense, they may, if unexplained, produce confusion. Frequently ambiguity stems from inadequate definition, hasty word choice, or loaded language. In each of these instances the words and phrases involved may be interpreted and defined in two or more ways.

In speaking and listening, be watchful of intangible and abstract words and phrases. "Is peace at any price a viable alternative?" "Do sex education classes in schools tear at the moral fiber of our country?" "Economic democracy is desirable for all people." "The new life-style makes one more in tune with the real world." "Sports are necessary for a healthy mind and body." If you look carefully, you will discover that each of these statements lacks precise meaning because key words are undefined. Disputes can also occur over a single word. Notice the lack of specific meaning for words such as *God, happiness, justice, conservative, liberal, Communist, super, socialism,* or *welfare.*

Words Often Omit Essential Details

Whenever we think or talk about a situation, we make decisions about what to include and what to exclude. We abstract some of the details from the total situation and ignore others. This means that when we use language we are only giving a partial picture of what happened. When we say to someone, "Let me tell you about the riot I saw last night," we are about to make certain selections as to what *to* talk about and what *not* to talk about. We cannot, by the very nature of language and our processes of perception, tell our listener each detail we perceived and experienced.

Three problems present themselves as each of us decides what to include in and exclude from our verbal descriptions. First, what is left out—that which is not talked about—is often more important and vital than what is retained. If a speaker says, "Unemployment is not a serious problem; I drove past the shoe factory and noticed a 'help wanted' sign clearly posted," he or she has decided to tell you about the sign. However, because language forces selection and makes it impossible to tell all there is to tell, the speaker did not tell you about the long lines of people waiting to be interviewed. This omitted fact may indeed be more important than what was actually talked about.

Second, our selection of what to share is governed, in part, by our attitudes and experiences —we personally decide what to say and what not to say. Because each of us has certain prejudices and biases, we are inclined to pick those words that have individual appeal. Our speaker's view of unemployment was a factor in the mention of the sign and the omission of any discussion about the large number of persons looking for jobs.

Finally, our vocabularies put limits on the details we can include in our verbal accounts of reality. We cannot talk about what we cannot label. How do we describe something in reality if we are unable to name it? For example, as speakers we would have a difficult time explaining the working of a polar system if our vocabulary did not contain the words necessary to talk about its essential processes and components.

Awareness of the problems, and realization that details are omitted, must be kept uppermost in the minds of both sender and receiver as they engage in communication. Writers in the field of general semantics suggest that as communicators we should learn to wait, stop, and see if more is to be said, and then reach our conclusions; further, that we should develop the use of the *etc.*, silently or orally, to remind us that factors are left out. In short, we should remind ourselves that there is always more than can be said.

Meanings Are in Persons

Words, as language symbols, have no meanings in themselves; their real meanings are in the things and events for which they stand. Each person, acting as an individual, must decide what a symbol means to him or her. Take the word *school*. To the person who likes education it is a place of learning; to the person who hates school it means a place he or she is made to go, and to still another individual, who desires an education, it means a place where he or she would like to go. What the word means depends on an individual's experience with the thing or event the word is representing. No two persons ever have exactly the same experiences; consequently no single word has an identical meaning for two persons. But the speaker must at least try to select words, phrases, and ideas that approach this ideal of common meaning. If understanding, and hence communication, is to take place, sender and receiver must share a reasonably common code.

Sharing a common code is not a simple matter. Because we come to the encounter from a variety of backgrounds, we are apt to find that agreement on the meaning of a word is elusive. For example, to the baseball player a *bird* is a fast runner. A carnival worker uses the word *slum* to talk about cheap prizes. A *monster* in the rock music industry is a successful record. To the person in prison a *hit* means rejection for parole. And *Levi's* are a bad set of sails to the sailor. These, and countless other instances should add credence to our observation that meanings are in persons and not in words.

Words Have Denotative and Connotative Meanings

There is seldom a one-to-one relationship between word and referent. This fact is discussed by students of language in terms of denotative and connotative meanings.

Denotative meanings normally involve those words we learn first (*ball, dada, cat,* and so forth). They refer to words that have a visible connection between the symbol and the object in reality. We can see and touch items that have denotative meanings (*tree, car,* and so forth). Because the word directly denotes, or refers to the object, there is often agreement on denotative meanings.

Connotative meanings, because of their subjective nature, present a more serious problem to the speaker who seeks to have messages accurately represent reality. Connotative meanings are more personal, emotional, and ambiguous. Referents for connotative words are more abstract and, therefore, subject to personal nuance. In fact, a connotative meaning is often so personal and emotional that it may be difficult to agree on a single meaning. How, for example, do we begin to define *democracy, freedom, hope, love, sexuality,* or *censorship*? The task confronting the conscientious communicator is not a simple one. We must be vigilant in our scrutiny of language. Knowing that connotative meanings are abstract and intangible may be the first step toward developing linguistic awareness—an awareness that does not take communication for granted, but instead realizes the nebulous nature of words and uses them with caution and care.

Language Tends to Be Static

Much of our trouble with word usage comes from our forgetting that the world changes faster than words. We often use words that are somewhat out of date and may no longer represent or describe reality. Laura Lee, writing in the *General Semantics Bulletin*, notes:

> The same word stands for a person, thing or activity day after day, although the thing it stands for may change, grow, transform. We do not name the process, the originality, the development, the flux. We speak in static terms and learn to perceive and think that way.

The successful communicator is aware that reality changes and often words do not. The most effective word-symbols we can use are those that take the dynamic nature of life into account. As communicators we may have noble purposes and lofty goals, but if our language does not convey our thoughts, communication is doomed to failure. Good communication uses language that accurately represents reality—and poor communication uses language that distorts, deforms, or fails to correspond to the thing or feeling experienced by the sender.

Language to Induce Desired Responses

The language of speechmaking, in addition to the six features just discussed, has the purpose of making the idea seem real and meaningful. It is not enough to have the idea expressed in everyday language; to have a lasting impression the message must be clear and vivid. The way the speaker selects and uses words— the proper word in the proper place— is often the first method of distinguishing the most able speakers from all the rest. As communication scholar Colin Cherry notes:

> Words can arouse every emotion; awe, hate, nostalgia, grief. . . . Words can demoralize a man into torpor, or they can spring him into delight. They can raise him to heights of spiritual and aesthetic experience. Words have frightening power.

A person's style in using words is a highly personal matter and something developed over a long period of time. This does not mean that a person's language habits cannot be improved with practice. On the contrary, the basic elements of effective style and word choice can be amended and enriched by sincere and careful practice. What follows is a listing and discussion of those language elements that can help the speaker accomplish the overall objective, which, in most instances, is to secure a desired response.

Your Language Should Be Clear

As a speaker you must first know exactly what idea you wish to convey to your listeners. Then you must find those symbols that will enable you to be understood—to be clear. Clear language is *immediately meaningful* to those who hear it. The speaker who can arouse definite and specific meanings has an excellent chance of being understood. Conversely, the speaker whose language suffers from ambiguity and confusion is not easily comprehended. Clarity can be fostered if the speaker's choice of language is *accurate* and *simple*.

Accurate Language

Being accurate involves selecting words that say exactly what you mean. How often we hear someone say, "I read this book one day," never indicating what book and what day; or someone refers to "that thing over there," without ever letting the listener know what "thing" is being talked about. In both cases the language lacks accuracy. Words have been selected that fail to correspond directly with the concept or object discussed.

Inaccurate word choice is normally brought about by carelessness. The speaker often uses technical language or uncommon words without stopping to realize that the symbols he or she has selected have very little meaning for the audience. Laziness may also show itself in our failure to seek definite and exact words. We may use ambiguous words and we may be guilty of omitting essential details. For example, it is not helpful, or accurate, if while explaining the functioning of a new electric automobile motor you say, "This thing produces about the same number of volts as the old one." Words and phrases such as "thing," "about the same," and "old one," are definitely not specific.

Accuracy is specific and concrete. The listener receives a much clearer picture if the speaker uses names, dates, places, facts, and other details. For example, "On Tuesday John and I went to the Main Street exhibit" is certainly more accurate and meaningful than "I went to town with a friend." Or we hear general statements such as, "New York spends a lot on welfare for each family under its plan." The communicator concerned with clarity and comprehension would say, "In 1979 the maximum monthly welfare payment for a family on welfare in the state of New York is three-hundred and fifty dollars." Here we can see the value of being accurate—the listener knows exactly what we mean.

Accuracy in grammar also increases understanding. Mistakes in subject-verb agreement, pronoun case, verb tense, and prepositions may produce audience confusion. Notice how accuracy of meaning is hampered by the following examples: "For what are you waiting?" "His voice fit him perfect." "We should have respect for whomever was in power." "Our college's Graduate School has a difficult job before them."

Our advice to those who wish to achieve greater accuracy of expression is really quite simple—think about what you want to say, think about the persons who will hear your words, and say what you mean. The acid test of human communication is found in your answer to the following question: Do my words accurately represent and reflect my reality?

Simple Language
Equally as important as accuracy of expression is simplicity of expression. Notice the difference in clarity between "moderate" and "abstemious," "money" and "legal tender," "top" and "*ne plus ultra.*" Ask yourself if you think a speaker is concerned with understanding or exhibitionism when he or she uses "edifice" instead of "building," "elucidate" for "explain," "surreptitious" for "secret," and "imbibe" for "drink." In all of these instances the simple word increases understanding and reduces confusion and ambiguity.

The purpose of communication is to share ideas, information, and feelings. If your language distorts the concept you wish to convey, communication will fail. By being an exhibitionist with your vocabulary you run the risk of not being understood and, hence, of not accomplishing your purpose.

Remember that being simple does not mean being infantile and dull. It indicates that the speaker realizes that vague and complicated words can cause serious communication breakdowns.

Your Language Should Be Vivid
Clear language will be understood, but if you wish also to hold attention, maintain interest, and create a favorable impression you must make your language vivid. Vividness and clarity are not separate—to achieve vividness you must first be clear.

When we are being vivid, we are selecting sensory words and phrases. Vivid language appeals to the listener's senses by having the audience see, hear, feel, taste, and smell the images the speaker creates.

Imagery
When employing imagery, we may be asking our listeners to reencounter a past situation, or to experience a new situation that we paint for them. In either case the objective is to have the audience experience, vicariously, the particular sensation being described.

1. *Detail* is essential in painting word pictures for the audience. Notice the difference in effectiveness between "A water-skier hit the dock," and "The water-skier, gliding gracefully over the glass-top lake, failed to see the half-sunken dock protruding into the still water and went crashing into the exposed wood beams."

   Consider these images:
   a. As we drove through the sandy and dusty area, we felt the earth beneath us tremble as the wild boars stampeded in front of us.
   b. I felt as cold as a piece of ice as I approached the half-open door of the broken down cabin.
   c. The dazzling brilliance of the setting sun made it difficult for me to see the large figure moving across the stream.
   d. His face, touched by time, was rough, scarred, and firm.
   e. As we entered the room an odor of sweet peppermint led us to the copper pan sitting on top of the coal-fed stove.
   f. As I left the hospital I could still hear the piercing, penetrating cry of the wounded American.

g. The great peacefulness of the night covered us like a warm quilt.

h. Here and there we could see an angry spot of lightning.

As you would suspect there are occasions when the impression to be communicated takes more detail and development than one can put into a single sentence. In these instances, the singleness of impression might be expressed by an extended illustration. Recently a speaker was trying to convince his listeners that it might be dangerous to ride motorcycles into the Mexican desert without understanding some of the problems of that country. One way he tried to demonstrate this point was by telling his audience about the intense heat in Mexico.

> Our motorcycles broke down the second day we were in Mexico. It was high noon and the rays of the sun that hung directly overhead fell straight as plummets upon the roofs and streets of the small, dry village we found ourselves stranded in. The heat was like fire, and there appeared to be only small, thin lines of shade. The sun was everywhere. The heat rising from brick and plaster and metal met the heat that steadily descended, smothering, from the bright, scorched sky. Only the lizards dared to move. Most of us feared moving because of the stupefying and blazing heat.

There are many occasions when detail is employed in less dramatic ways. In the following example the detail is not as emotional, yet the intent is just as serious as in the previous example. In both cases the speaker wants his listeners to see, experience, and understand the point he is trying to make.

> A course in public speaking is a most desirable training for the professional or commercial person. It will give you training to address a public meeting without being nervous, but it will also greatly improve your conversational powers. It will make you careful in your selection of words, their punctuation, and exact meaning; it will extend your vocabulary and give more power and intonation to your voice. It will also train your mind to quick thinking and to select without hesitation just such words as are best adapted to express your thoughts. Few persons can speak their ideas in a clear, concise manner, and fewer still can ask a good, direct question that goes to the very heart of an issue. And yet, this ability to frame a concise question at the right moment is one of the most desirable attainments for a person who has social intercourse in his job.

2. Using *descriptive adjectives and adverbs* gives the listener a much more complete picture of what is being talked about. "A bitterly cold day," "a studious man," "a damaging admission," and "a sarcastic professor," all offer the listener a more vivid concept of what is being referred to.

Being specific makes your ideas more vivid and interesting, and hence easier to understand. In the following general/specific comparisons notice how a more specific word helps the speaker elicit a more distinct image.

General	Specific
animal	dog, horse, elephant, camel
vehicle	car, bike, motorcycle, coach
workman	plumber, painter, carpenter, mason
color	blue, orange, green, violet, crimson
move	crawl, creep, glide, waddle, run

Description, like detail, takes a variety of forms. In the next example, with just a few sentences, a speaker uses description to explain a complex idea.

> The words steam engine, when used to label an energy source, bring to most of us the idea of a machine of complex nature to be understood only by those who will devote much time to the study of it. However, if you can understand the workings of a common pump you can understand the steam engine. It is, in fact, only a pump in which the fluid passing through it is made to impel the piston instead of being impelled by it—that is to say, in which the fluid acts as the power, instead of being the resistance.

3. In using detailed, vivid images, or specific descriptions, it is important to select your words in light of the listener's *background* and *experiences*. It is hard for someone to appreciate the "blue and rolling waves that break on the Solomon islands" if they have never seen the Solomons. Compare the idea to something from the listener's past and the image will be made more effective.

Figures of Speech

Vividness is also achieved by using figures of speech. As variations from literal or ordinary forms of expression, figures of speech are highly effective, for they not only add vividness, they increase the speech's vigor and beauty. Their use often separates the ordinary speaker from the more advanced communicator.

Simile and *metaphor* are among the most common figures of speech. *Simile* is an expression of the figurative resemblance of one person or thing to another put in the form of an explicit comparison. A simile normally uses *like* or *as* to compare and link similar ideas. One would be using a simile when saying "Our house swarmed with guests like a beehive." Or "At times finding gasoline for our car is like hunting for a place to camp on the Hollywood freeway."

Closely related to simile is *metaphor*, in which one class of things is referred to as though it belonged to another. The simile says one thing is *like* another; the metaphor says one thing *is* another. Thus the simile, "He is *like* the Rock of Gibralter," becomes a metaphor when expressed, "He *is* the Rock of Gibralter." Abraham Lincoln discussing the danger of two Americas used a metaphor: "A house divided against itself cannot stand."

The speaker may also find that his or her style can be made more vivid by using *antithesis*. In this figure of speech, contrast is emphasized by the position of words. For example, "The state exists for man, not man for the state." Former President Kennedy used this technique in his now famous phrase, "Ask not what your country can do for you— ask what you can do for your country."

There are many figures of speech besides the three we have just mentioned. However, because they use language even more figuratively, they are much harder to master. Nevertheless, being aware of a few of them will enable you to practice and eventually work them into your speeches.

Personification is a figure of speech in which life or personality is attributed to inanimate things or abstract ideas. One would be employing personification when saying "Freedom blushed with shame over Watergate," or "The tugboat laughed and said, 'you do the trick first.' "

Hyperbole is a figure of speech that magnifies objects beyond their natural bounds, in order to make them more impressive and more vivid. It is based on exaggeration. "She ran faster than a greyhound." "We live the time that a match flickers."

Using *climax* as a figure of speech, a speaker presents a series of thoughts or statements arranged in order of increasing importance. "She sacrificed her home, her friends, and her family to serve this community."

The last figure of speech we shall look at, *onomatopoeia*, is often thought of as a vocal device instead of a language tool. It is a figure in which the sound of the word or group of words imitates the sound that it names or describes. The following words fall into this category: "rumble," "crash," "splash," "boom," "buzz," "cackle," "hiss," "smack," and "chatter."

Because figures of speech are often the ornaments of the speech, there is a tendency to use them for their own sake. As you would suspect, this may create the impression of merely showing off. Therefore, they should not be used unless they are natural and appropriate and increase the effectiveness of what you have to say.

Language Should Be Appropriate

When we explored audience analysis we stressed the importance of finding out as much as possible about the listener. That information will enable you to adapt your speech to specific audiences. Your language, as one aspect of that adaptation, may well be the most crucial. You know from experience that you often change words and phrases as you move from person to person and place to place. If a professor calls on you in class, you respond with one type of language, yet if a friend asks you a question, your remarks will be far less formal. What you are doing when you move from phrases like "uptight" to "very nervous" is making your language appropriate to the receiver. You run the very real risk of not accomplishing your purpose when you use language that is not suited to your listeners. Imagine how you would feel if you had gone to hear a lecture entitled "An Introduction to Perception" and heard a speaker say, "Once we know that we can see electromagnetic radiation with wavelengths of 380 to 760 millimicrons, we should find out what the subjective experience is at each point between the upper and lower thresholds." If the entire audience was composed of persons with very little background in perception, this would be a blatant example of inappropriate language.

Many of the problems presented by improper word choice could be avoided by a thorough and complete audience analysis. Sex education films, for example, are aimed at different age levels. The notion of reproduction is explained in all the films, whether intended for fifth-grade pupils or college students. Yet the language in each of the films conforms to the educational level of the audience. The principles and the anatomy remain the same, only the words are changed.

When selecting appropriate language, we must also take the occasion into account. As we reflect on our own behavior we know that our vocabulary makes both obvious and subtle changes as we shift from context to context. A small, informal meeting of friends would call for casual language, while a college commencement address would demand a more serious tone. For example, the commencement speaker could say, "The world has turned over many times since you entered these hallowed halls," but in a small group that same phrase might appear pompous, sarcastic, or stupid.

There may be situations where patent attempts at adaptation will hurt rather than aid your cause. Two vivid examples are in the area of culture and age. Many blacks use language to produce group solidarity. A white person using black argot would not be demonstrating ability to "speak the language," but rather a lack of tact. The same is true of the middle-aged person who expresses enthusiasm to a teenage audience by saying "far out." Trying to have our language be something other than what is natural to ourselves produces artificiality. This sham is usually transparent and often results in embarrassment.

There are, of course, other ways of offending an audience besides the misuse of argot and slang. Use of sexist references and obscene language are the two most common ways. Not all persons are troubled by sexist references, yet current trends and propriety suggest that phrases such as "girls," "chairman," "sexy," "dumb broad," and the like should be avoided.

Good taste and a keen audience analysis should be your guide to the use of vulgar references. Obscene language and taboo words, although used by many persons, are usually offensive and inappropriate in the public speaking situation.

One note of caution. We observed at the outset of this section that your speaking style was a highly personal matter. Therefore, use language that is *appropriate to you*. Language that you are comfortable with, that feels as if it is part of your personality, is the language you should use. Admittedly, you should aim for excellence, but excellence within the confines of your background and experience. To do otherwise is artificial and inappropriate.

Language Should Be Free From Distractions

We normally focus our attention on those things in our environment that either interest or distract us. For example, if someone is talking to you on the topic of saving money, you are likely to attend to every word. However, if during the explanation the speaker's fingers start to drum on the table, you are apt to move your focal point from the speaker's ideas to the noise being produced by the nervous mannerism. In many communication situations, words as well as actions serve as the distracting stimulus. All of us have poor language habits that can interfere with our overall communication effectiveness. We inadvertently choose words or phrases that divert attention from our main ideas. Because each of us personally selects the words we utter, it will be useful to examine some of the types of words that often cause communication problems.

Slang

Slang words and phrases, when used for a special effect, might be acceptable, but more often they tend to lower the status of the user and distract from the purpose of the speech. The person who must constantly resort to slang is usually doing so because of laziness. Words and phrases such as "guys," "cool," "ticked off," "far out," "rip off," and "off the wall" do little to clarify an idea, make an image more vivid, or raise the speaker's credibility.

Triteness

Closely related to slang is the problem of trite and hackneyed phrases. Notice how the following list of overused expressions would make one believe that the user of such language lacked imagination and creativity: *pretty as a picture, last but not least, our hour of trial, it gives me great pleasure, busy as a bee, hit the nail on the head, the straight and narrow path, better late than never, green with envy, behind the eight ball.*

Jargon

When addressing a general audience, a speaker must avoid shoptalk, jargon, and highly technical language. Each profession has its own language, and the speaker must remember that what is clear to an engineer may be very confusing to a doctor. If the symbols selected are not easily defined, ambiguity results. "Cognitive dissonance-consonance" may be meaningful to the social psychologist, but only noise to the layman. Knowing the listener's background and defining unfamiliar words will help the speaker overcome many of the problems of jargon.

Loaded Words

There are those who suggest that loaded and emotional words should be used whenever possible. They argue that such words assist the speaker in the goal of "manipulating others." Although loaded words are often colorful, they are in most instances ambiguous and vague. By playing upon emotionalism these words, both implicitly and explicitly, ask the listener to respond on a purely emotional basis. Notice the images called forth by phrases such as "the savage and brutal senator," "the chiseling miser," "the bureaucratic welfare state," and "a fanatical rightwinger." Emotion is important in communication, but the speaker should supply adequate evidence and sound reasoning to justify any loaded word. The speaker should remember that words he or she uses must be consistent with facts. If a colorful word can be selected that does not distort reality, it should be used; but if the appeal is solely irrational, the speaker is violating ethical responsibility.

Empty Words

In this day of the mass appeal we are barraged by superlatives and exaggerations. This overexposure may condition the unsuspecting communicator to lean heavily on overworked and meaningless terms. Notice the empty quality of the following words and phrases: *super, colossal, deluxe, really great, magnificent, terrific, very good, fantastic, extra special, a whole lot*. Many persons have been so bombarded with empty words that they are tempted to discount them and pay little attention to the person using them.

Contractions   Recently it has become popular to use shortened forms of certain words. Although such contractions are derived from words in good use, they often lower the prestige of the speaker and indicate a lack of concern for language. Some common contractions are "exam" for "examination," "condo" for "condominium," "prop" for "proposition," "prof" for "professor," "caf" for "cafeteria," "auto" for "automobile," and "lab" for "laboratory." "Frisco," "Vegas," and "D. C." are poor substitutes for San Francisco, Las Vegas, and Washington, D. C., and their use by visitors to those cities is particularly irritating to local residents.

Improving
Language Habits   Each of us has the freedom to select the words we wish to employ at any particular moment. It is a matter of individual choice as we decide to say "yes" instead of "yeah" or "sailboat" instead of "yacht." Because word selection and style depend, to a large degree, on subjective factors, improvement is not an impossible task. Many persons are guilty of believing the myth that orators are born, that the ability to use language effectively is a genetically endowed characteristic. This notion is simply not true. Even though language habits and vocabulary develop early in life, they are constantly open to change. And this change can be in the direction of improvement. However, this involves more than memorizing a few rules or formulas. It demands practice and hard work. If you are willing to put forth the energy, much of your effort should be channeled into the activities discussed below.

1. *Learn to use a dictionary and a book of synonyms.* These two sources are helpful in providing you with clues to new words that are often more accurate and vivid than the ones you have been using. For example, turning to a book of synonyms and antonyms, such as *Roget's Thesaurus*, will increase your vocabulary while increasing your choices when searching for the right words to share an experience. Instead of having to say, "It was good," you could be more specific by using one of the choices afforded by a *Thesaurus*, such as "beneficial, valuable, edifying, salutary, capital," or even the exotic "*rara avis*."

2. *Be alert to new words as you listen and read.* Listening is an excellent method of improvement, for it allows you to perceive the overall impact of a word. Hearing someone say "glistening" instead of "bright" may persuade you that one strikes the ear more pleasingly than the other.

   Novels, plays, speeches, poetry, and essays illustrate how knowledgeable persons use language. In the correct context a writer might avoid "the road was dangerous," preferring, instead, something like "the precarious nature of the highway made each new curve more menacing than the last."

   Finally, improving your language habits implies that you *remember* the new words or phrases to which you are exposed. Remembering is often aided by the simple act of writing down those expressions that interest you.

Many famous speakers carry a pencil and a pad of paper to jot down fresh and novel words.

3. *Develop a habit of careful writing.* Careful writing and revision develop better expression. A diligent writer will not settle for the first word that comes to mind, but will search for the word or phrase that will promote clarity and convey the desired impression.

4. *Speaking often is one of the obvious ways of learning to use language well.* By actually "doing the thing," the speaker learns which words and phrases help accomplish a purpose and which words retard progress.

5. *Be aware of words and make a study of language itself.* The field of general semantics for example, examines the relationship between language and objects. The sincere student will find this sort of study both rewarding and interesting. There is a whole new world to explore when one investigates how persons use symbols to influence one another and the world they live in.

6. *Have at your command more than one word or expression for the same idea or object.* Truly successful speakers have developed the versatility that enables them to put ideas in many different ways. Saying "thus far it is but a tendency, a symptom, a foreshadowing," enables a speaker to express one concept in a variety of ways. Such a habit is of untold value as a means of both describing reality and having that reality be interesting and exciting to the listener. Learning to use language variations in a skillful manner enriches your thoughts by clarifying your ideas and making them more appealing.

It is obvious by now that a large segment of the study of communication is necessarily a study of language. Therefore, it is well to remember that advice about language is not confined to this chapter alone. For example, our observation in this chapter that "language should be interesting to listen to and easy to comprehend" is treated under "informing" in chapter 8 and under "common language fallacies" in chapter 7. Communication is a highly interrelated, overlapping process and not subject to clear-cut, isolated skills and techniques.

Summary

Keep these general language principles in mind as you engage in both public and private communication: (1) Words are symbols used to represent objects, ideas, concepts, experiences, and feelings. (2) One word can have many meanings and many uses. (3) In using word-symbols as our communication code, we often omit essential details. (4) Word meanings reside within persons; they have meaning only in terms of the associations established between the symbols and the object or concept to which they refer. (5) Words have denotative and connotative meanings. (6) Language tends to be static while reality is dynamic.

Clarity, vividness, and appropriateness characterize effective language usage. Clarity derives from the use of words that are accurate, simple, and precise. Vividness derives from imagery, which is accomplished by use of details and descriptive words, and from figures of speech. Appropriateness is language suited to the audience, occasion, and speaker, and the avoidance of slang, triteness, jargon, loaded words, empty words, and contractions. Language habits can be improved by sincere and conscientious study and practice.

Suggested Readings

Alexander, Hubert G. *Meaning in Language.* Glenview, IL: Scott, Foresman, 1969.

Allen, Ronald R., and McKerrow, Ray E. *The Pragmatics of Public Communication.* Columbus, OH: Charles E. Merrill Publishing, 1977. Chapter 3.

Aly, Bower, and Aly, Lucile F. *A Rhetoric of Public Speaking.* New York: McGraw-Hill, 1973. Chapter 4.

Johnson, Wendell. *People in Quandaries.* New York: Harper and Row, 1946.

Hayakawa, S. I. *Language in Action.* New York: Harcourt, Brace, 1941.

Lee, Irving J. *How to Talk with People.* New York: Harper and Row, 1962.

McCabe, Bernard P., and Bender, Coleman C. *Speaking Is a Practical Matter.* 2d ed. Boston: Holbrook Press, 1973. Part II, Step 3.

Wilson, John F., and Arnold, Carrol C. *Public Speaking As a Liberal Art.* 4th ed. Boston: Allyn and Bacon, 1978. Chapter 9.

Zannes, Estelle, and Goldhaber, Gerald. *Stand Up and Speak Out.* Reading, MA: Addison-Wesley Publishing. 1978, Chapter 8.

Having an Influence

Part 3

Informative Speaking
Being Understood

I attribute the little I know to my not having been ashamed to ask for information, and to my rule of conversing with all descriptions of men on those topics that form their own peculiar professions and pursuits.

John Locke

One of the primary functions of speech is to provide each of us with the means of transferring knowledge from one person to another. What we know individually, and what our culture knows collectively, is passed via language. Our success in making knowledge available to others is a highly valued skill in our complex and ever-changing society. Think how often we are impressed with the person who can say "Let me explain" and then is able to render an idea clear and comprehensible.

Our world is flooded with new data, ideas, and concepts. A high premium is placed on the person able to understand and *share* information. The purpose of this chapter is to offer you theories and principles that will aid you in conveying information to other persons.

Situations requiring this type of discourse are numerous. Almost all teaching can be labeled informative speaking. Likewise, the instructions and training given to work forces and office and sales staffs can be placed in this particular category. Even directions given by one person telling another how to get to Main Street must be labeled informative speaking. At all levels of communication, both formal and informal, informative speaking occurs.

Informative speaking imparts materials that will increase the listener's knowledge of a given subject. If you know a great deal about astronomy and give a speech on the topic, you expect your listeners to know more about the subject when you complete your talk. Therefore, *the primary objective of informative speaking is to present information so that it will be easily understood and remembered by your audience.*

Informing must not be viewed in isolation—it is part of the entire complex process of communication. Principles discussed throughout the text apply to delivering the speech to inform: Any rigid distinction between speeches to inform and other types of speeches is impossible. It is more realistic to view discourse on a continuum with *many* gradations running from informing to persuading. This orientation comes closer to reality than one that sees persuading and informing in tight boxes. The successful communicator realizes the subtleties of communication and the folly of believing that there are not countless occasions when informing and persuading overlap. In the final analysis it is the response of the receiver that determines whether the message is informative or persuasive, and in most instances it will be a bit of both.

Types of Informative Speeches	While all informative speeches are alike in giving information and increasing understanding, they may be separated into the following basic types: (1) *Descriptions*. You may wish to describe an individual, a location, an event, a reaction, or a mood. In each of these instances you are primarily concerned with having the audience see and experience what you are describing. For example, if you wanted your listeners to have greater insight into the personality of Ralph Nader, you might describe his youth, his initial interest in the consumer rights movement, and his later accomplishments. (2) *Reports*. Book reports, reports on articles, committee reports, and so forth, are commonly employed by the college student. You might report, for instance, on what your research group decided to do about creating bicycle lanes on campus. You have the responsibility to transmit what you have read, discovered, or deliberated upon. (3) *Explanations*. This is a general term for information about the functioning of a process or the workings of some agent: You are explaining how something works. A speech explaining the principles involved in the operation of the electric car falls into this category. (4) *Instructions*. You may wish to tell others how to perform a specific act, such as how to administer first aid. Employers use instructions to show new employees how tasks are performed.
Basic Assumptions	Because increased understanding is the primary goal of informative speaking, the successful communicator is aware of the basic principles that contribute to both short- and long-range learning. Educators and psychologists have suggested some basic assumptions about how persons learn and retain information. These assumptions should guide all speakers in selection of topic, and preparation and presentation of material. Let us look at a few of these learning precepts as a preface to a more complete analysis of informative speaking.
Motivation	Common sense, and years of psychological testing, tell us that we learn more, and retain it longer, when we are motivated. When information is relevant to our needs and wants we pay closer attention to the person offering that information. If, for example, you are having some difficulty meeting your college expenses, and a speaker tells you that there is a way for you to earn some extra money without having to leave the campus, you are apt to pay close attention to what is talked about. Part of this chapter will focus on devices that motivate persons and encourage them to pay attention.
Coupling	Learning is facilitated when a presenter of information couples what we already know and understand with unknown information. If we have never ridden horseback, yet can visualize the relationship between steering a car and reining a horse, we might couple these experiences and be able to understand something of elementary horsemanship. Later in this chapter we will present a number of techniques that assist in establishing these important links.
Organization	Persons learn more rapidly when the material presented is arranged in logical sequence, and when that sequence is clearly identified. You know from your own experiences that when a speaker lacks a clear direction, and leaps from point to

Having an Influence

point, your only memory of the talk is frustration over trying to make sense out of the speaker's ramblings. Part of this chapter capitalizes on what researchers now know about the constituents of successful organization.

Frequency

Listeners remember a fact or an idea much longer if it is repeated and reinforced. The person who *says* "I am fond of you" while *placing a hand* on your shoulder, is both repeating and reinforcing a message. A speaker, by using a variety of oral techniques, can do much the same thing. We shall soon look at some of these techniques.

Additional Senses

Educators have known for a long time that learning is fostered when the stimulus is presented in a way that involves more than one of our senses. If you see a visual aid depicting the human heart at the same time a speaker discusses blood circulation, you are apt to have a clearer understanding of the circulatory system because of this dual explanation. Believing in the importance of this multi-sensory approach, we shall offer some specific advice and models that can contribute to increased listener understanding.

Steps in Preparation

In chapters 1 and 2 we discussed preparation necessary for successful speech making. We pointed out that before any behavior can be changed, or any response secured, there must be both analysis and preparation. Much of what we now say about the speech to increase understanding has been examined under other headings. There are, however, several specific principles of preparing the informative speech that bear closer examination.

Determining the Purpose and Selecting a Topic

If you are to make ideas clear to an audience, you must first determine what you want the audience to know about these ideas at the conclusion of your talk. The specific purpose of any given informative speech is a statement of *exactly* what the speaker wants the audience to understand. For example:

1. To have the audience understand how the United Nations is financed.
2. To have the audience understand how to analyze dreams.
3. To have the audience understand the workings of a political party convention.
4. To have the audience understand marijuana laws in California.
5. To have the audience understand how to take better snapshots with a fixed-focus camera.

All of these specific purposes tell precisely what the speaker wishes the audience to understand.

In choosing and narrowing a topic for the informative speech, you should look to many of the criteria presented earlier in the book. Let us briefly review some of them. You should know more about the topic than do the members of the audience. During the course of the speech, and in a manner that does not border on boasting, you should tell them how you came to know as much as you do about the particular subject. For example, you might say, "Having worked as a page in the United States Senate, I was able to learn a great deal about the evolution of a new law, and today I would like to share some of those experiences with you."

The topic selected must be relevant. Intelligent people would not like to hear you talk about the night you raided the cookie jar. A comprehensive audience analysis (coupled with common sense) is perhaps your best guide to determining relevance. As always, we suggest you try to view the topic from the position of your receivers. This listener-centered approach will help you avoid trite and uninteresting subjects.

The topic should be stimulating as well as timely. Remember, you are seeking to increase the listener's fund of knowledge. They have not selected this topic, you have! Therefore, it must be a topic that arouses curiosity at the same time it holds attention. It is an exciting challenge to take what appears to be a dull subject and give it life and vitality.

Locating sufficient material is yet another consideration in selecting and narrowing a topic. Think how frustrating it would be if you wanted to discuss the types of rattlesnakes found in your region but could not find any information. Be assured that your frustrations would be shared by your audience, for they would feel baffled as they listened but failed to hear anything new.

Select a subject appropriate to the occasion. A topic dealing with automation in the restaurant business would be out of place at a Teamsters convention.

Most important, select a subject that interests you. Could there be a more thankless task than having to explain the methods used in mounting butterflies if you are not interested in butterflies? Our pleasure is increased, and our burden lessened, when we deal with issues we enjoy.

Gather and Select Materials

If you are to secure understanding, your speech must contain materials that are clear and comprehensible. In gathering the data for a talk you should be adaptable, selective, accurate, objective, and thorough.

In order to accomplish these objectives you should begin by making an inventory of what you already know and the material you have available to you. You will then be in a position to determine what additional materials you need. After the inventory, you are ready to locate and gather the necessary information. By realizing your aims, personal resources, and limitations, you can select the illustrations, examples, comparisons, definitions, statistical data, interest factors, forms of restatement, and visual aids that will accomplish your specific purpose.

An effective speaker gathers more material than he or she will be able to use. A thorough preparation and analysis will make you more knowledgeable about the topic and enable you to be more selective about what you include and what you exclude.

Objectivity is important in all phases of preparing the speech to inform. The speaker is not trying to convince others of the worth or value of one system over another, but, rather, is trying to expand the knowledge of the listeners. Subjectivity, as we all know, is a characteristic of the human personality; so objectivity must be given special consideration when we try to inform. Unsupported inferences and value judgments must be avoided or at least controlled. In short, the speaker should prepare and present a talk with an attitude of open-mindedness.

Materials of Informative Speaking	Although increased understanding is the primary end of informative discourse, information alone will not capture or hold attention. We need a reason for listening—we have to be motivated. Therefore, the materials of informative speaking must serve two purposes—they must increase comprehension at the same time they hold attention.

There is a great deal of overlapping between the features of a speech that hold attention and those that contribute to learning. What we might label an attention factor might also help to explain a key point in the speech. Nevertheless, we shall divide informative materials into those techniques and principles that foster effective exposition and those that arouse interest and hold attention.

Increased Understanding	Because much of this book is concerned with increased understanding, you have already been exposed to many of the principles that render an idea clearer and easier to comprehend. (For example, in chapters 5 and 7 we examined the content of your ideas.) Hence, many of these same concepts and techniques are now re-visited and amplified, this time from the perspective of informative speaking.

Definition	Many mistakes are made when listeners are confused about meanings. Because the speaker is usually very familiar with the subject matter, he or she may forget to define some of the basic and important terms, phrases, or concepts. In addition, because words are symbols, and usually interpreted differently by different persons, listeners can become confused by the meanings of numerous words.

When trying to decide which words need defining, begin by examining those that are *abstract* or *unfamiliar*. If you were talking about democracy, it would behoove you to define what you mean when you use that particular term. Words such as *democracy, freedom, socialism,* and *liberty* are so abstract that they may evoke any number of meanings. Simply put, by defining such words we tell the listener exactly what we mean when we use the word.

Confusion also results when we employ unfamiliar words or phrases. For example, if we say that "the congruity theory of persuasion is an effective tool for the advertiser," we might be hampering learning. However, if we were to define "congruity," we could make the unfamiliar become clear.

In defining words or phrases, the speaker should observe the following rules: (1) *Define the unknown in terms of the known.* Using language that is simpler than the original expression is an application of this principle. Going from the known to the unknown establishes a common frame of reference and allows the audience to see what you mean. For example, a veteran Navy radarman defined radar by comparing it to the action of a tennis ball being bounced off a garage door. (2) *Define the word by placing it in the context in which it will be used.* For example, you might say, "In discussing the problem of school dropouts we shall concern ourselves with the student who leaves school, for whatever reason, before graduation or before the age of eighteen." In this way the audience knows who you are talking about when you use the term "dropout." (3) *Anticipate the knowledge level of your audience on the particular topic so that you will be in a position to decide which words need defining.* If you were talking to a group of electronics experts and used the simple radar analogy cited above, you might insult them, yet the same radar analogy might be very effective for a group of liberal arts majors.

When we talk about defining we are referring to defining entire concepts as well as single words. There are even occasions when these definitions take the form of lengthy explanations. For example, a speaker discussing "holistic gardening" might want to explain the holistic philosophy of reality as a means of defining this unique approach to gardening.

Example

The value of examples as means of clarification cannot be overemphasized. Examples are not only the simplest and most common of all the devices, they are the easiest to employ. Examples allow you to say, "This is what I mean."

A speaker using examples to clarify an assertion might proceed as follows:

	I. This university is doing a great deal to help the handicapped individual secure a college education.
(example)	A. It has an "out-reach" program that goes into various special education classes and explains admission requirements.
(example)	B. It offers numerous scholarships to handicapped individuals.

The technique of using examples was explained in detail in chapter 5. And although we are now investigating informative speaking, what we said in earlier chapters applies directly to our current discussion. Examples can be helpful if we follow a few guidelines: (1) The example should be brief and pointed. (2) It should be relevant to what the speaker is explaining. (3) It should be adapted to the education and interest levels of the audience. (4) It should be consistent with the tone of the speech and not appear to be something the speaker has added for no apparent reason.

An example may be either a specific instance or a detailed illustration and may appear as real or fictitious, in verbal form or in graphic form. In a speech on water pollution you might employ a graphic example by showing a large picture of some of the foreign matter found in many rivers and streams.

The most important criterion for using examples is that they prove or clarify the generalization being made. For instance, if you were speaking on the topic of the role played by contemporary First Ladies, you could give explicit examples of the activities of Pat Nixon, Betty Ford, and Rosalyn Carter. These examples would explain your point in a vivid and concrete form while holding the attention of your listeners.

Comparison and Contrast

Clarity may be enhanced through the use of comparison and contrast. Comparison shows how two things are alike; contrast shows how they differ. These devices are useful in leading the listener from the known to the unknown. In explaining the functions of the United States' Senate, you might use comparison by explaining the relationship between the Senate and your college's Student Council. By pointing out the duties and functions of the Council (known) you would show the likeness in the Senate (unknown). Analogy is a good form of comparison because it also compares the known with the unknown.

Contrast may be more helpful in some cases than comparison. If the point from which the contrast originates is known by the audience, the contrast will be particularly meaningful. For example, a student in a speech class recently used contrast to show the high increase in the cost of living in the United States. He contrasted the cost in 1979 to the cost in 1978 and 1977.

Statistics

It is frequently useful to explain an idea in terms of size or quantity. For example, if you were talking about income tax in the United States, it would be helpful to offer statistics on the various programs and the numerous methods of calculating percentages.

In informative speaking, statistics are usually used for purposes of *counting* or *measuring*. If you were trying to explain that professional boxing could be considered big business in the United States, you could use statistics to point out that the Leon Spinks–Muhammad Ali fight grossed over 25 million dollars. Counting the number of motorcycles registered in California would be an example of how statistics could be used to clarify the extent of vehicle registration in that state. Measuring is often used as a way of conveying size. You could highlight the vastness of Central Park by noting that it occupies 840 acres.

A few guides should be kept in mind. By themselves statistics are abstract and meaningless. To be useful they must be compared or contrasted with something else to show how many, how few, how large, or how small the idea or thing really is. If you were offering statistics dealing with the number of light-years to the nearest star, you might make such figures meaningful by explaining a light-year in terms of how many trips that would involve between campus and the downtown area. Second, a large list of numbers is hard to comprehend. Whenever possible use round numbers. Third, it is important that you be very selective in citing statistics, for a listener will tire of a lengthy discussion of facts and figures. Fourth, see that your statistics meet the tests advanced in chapter 5. Whether your aim be informative or persuasive, your material should be authentic, complete, and clear.

Description

On certain occasions description will be the best method of explaining and clarifying the thought you are trying to develop. In description the speaker pictures or portrays an object, event, or person by stimulating the listener's sense of sight, sound, smell, taste, or feel. The listener's mind is focused on the object by means of vivid word pictures. A speech on Canadian national forests might well employ descriptions of the wildlife, water resources, and vegetation that constitute the forests. For instance, clarity regarding water resources could be enhanced if a speaker said, "The waterfalls are everywhere; from any mountain or valley you can see and hear the crystal-clear water cascading and tumbling over the rocks."

There are often times when the description is much longer than a sentence or two. When describing what a meteor looks like a speaker noted:

> The luminous streak appeared in the sky all at once. It seemed to be about half the diameter of the full moon and much like a street arc light. Its tail, of brilliant orange, with a sharp blue flame fading out at the extreme end, looked to be ten or twelve times as long and fully as broad as the body. The downward course was leisurely, as if in slow motion.

The successful communicator is not abstract, vague, or general, but offers information and material that is clear, specific, accurate, and appropriate. In informative speaking, when the response sought is understanding, it behooves the speaker to use concrete data. An audience would have a difficult time remembering very much about a speech that tried to explain the entire subject of mental health in ten minutes. There simply would not be time to supply the needed data to make the subject meaningful. Learn to narrow your focus and use detailed descriptions to make the focus clear.

Reinforcement and Emphasis

We can never retain all that we hear. Therefore, by means of reinforcement and emphasis, the successful speaker underscores those materials deemed most important and compelling. Four of the most common reinforcement techniques are discussed below.

Restatement uses new words to convey and echo an idea already discussed in a speech. After giving a speech on the dangers of cigarette smoking you might want to restate your main thesis as "cigarette smoking can cause you great physical harm." In this way the listeners hear the idea again, but expressed this time in a new manner. *Repetition* is the use of identical wording to repeat the idea. Through repetition the main point is better remembered. Both restatement and repetition have their roots in learning theory and should be used frequently in communication.

Calling attention directly to the idea you wish to stress is yet another device available to the speaker. Simply saying "this is important" or "now get this" can focus attention on the point you wish to emphasize. These two obvious phrases tell the audience that they are about to receive some significant information. Imagine how your attention would be arrested if, while you were daydreaming, someone looked directly at you and said, "It is important that you understand this issue."

The way you use your *voice* and *body* can also help reinforce and emphasize those aspects of your speech that you would like listeners to retain. For example, you can reinforce an important idea by changing the loudness of your voice or by pausing. You can often add emphasis by moving toward your listeners. This activity accents the verbal elements of your talk. Even gestures, such as pointing, can stress an important aspect of the message.

Partition, Enumeration, and Summary

Memory is short and, as the speaker moves through the speech, the listener may frequently lose track of the main thesis. It is therefore of prime importance that the speaker aid the listener in remembering the main ideas as they are developed throughout the talk. *Partition, enumeration,* and *summary* are three techniques that increase understanding and retention.

A *partition* (often referred to as an initial summary or "preview") is a list offered early in the speech of the points that will be covered. You simply tell your audience what main ideas you plan to treat in the body of your speech. For example, "In talking about how to insulate a room I shall first take up the procedures for insulating the floor, then those for insulating the walls, and finally the procedures for insulating the ceiling." Having highlighted what you plan to cover, you are now ready to move to the body of your talk.

Enumeration, which occurs during the body of your speech, is the numbering of each point as it is introduced. "First . . . , Second . . . , and Third. . . ." This technique is helpful in increasing clarity by alerting the audience to movements from one idea to another.

Summary is the reiteration of main items at the close of the entire speech. For example, "In insulating a room we looked at the techniques used for insulating the floor, the wall, and the ceiling."

Maintaining Interest

The importance of listening attentively to any form of communication needs no demonstration at this point. We can all accept the premise that where attention is focused, concentration is most acute. The late James Winans of Cornell University built a theory of persuasion around "inducing others to give fair, favorable, or undivided attention to propositions." And you will recall we started this chapter by mentioning that persons learn more when the material is relevant. Interest and attention are simply corollaries of that relevance.

For our analysis, think of attention and interest as interchangeable. Admittedly, the dictionary may offer separate definitions of the two terms, but when we talk about human behavior, attention and interest have interlocking and overlapping meanings. Your own behavior proves that what interests you commands your attention and likewise, what you attend to interests you. In this approach to attention and interest, our awareness of a given stimulus is greatly heightened. All competing stimuli are secondary as the main message goes directly to what psychologist William James called the "focus of consciousness."

We do not pretend to know any magic formula that will transform a dull message into a scintillating experience for the listener. Each speaking situation makes its unique demands; hence, there could hardly be a universal formula for success. But we can profit from the findings of psychologists who have probed the nature of attention and interest. These findings have enabled us to devise guidelines for minimizing the effort our listeners will have to exert in order to stay attentive to our ideas.

Noting That Which Is Impending

Not only are we interested in that which has just happened, but also in that which is soon to happen: the impending. A person who wants to discuss recent improvements in the safety features of automobiles might say, "I heard on the radio this morning that the first of the new model cars are due to hit the dealers' showrooms within the next ten days. It will be interesting to see how they measure up to the safety standards I'd like to discuss with you today." A speaker, giving a talk on one of the current ballot propositions, used "the impending" to arouse and maintain attention in the following manner:

> In just two weeks we shall be asked to decide the fate of this city's hiking trails. For on Tuesday, November 7th, the voters of this community are going to have an opportunity, by means of a ballot proposition, to decide if the State of California should use tax money to purchase several

wilderness areas from the Federal government. This issue has been debated for years, and now it appears that the time for action has arrived. Because you shall be affected by the outcome, and because you shall help determine that outcome, it might be helpful if today I take a few minutes and explain the proposition in some detail.

You have probably noticed how much more interested in college registration students become on the eve of the term opening, or how prognostications about conference football standings take on greater interest closer to the start of the football season. So look for ways of linking your subject to an event in the immediate future.

Alluding to That Which Is Physically Near Your Audience

Just as ideas involving temporal nearness catch interest more readily than those in the distant past or distant future, so ideas involving physical proximity are more compelling than those that are remote. A news item involving your immediate neighborhood probably will capture your attention faster than one concerned with the other side of town.

The immediate physical surroundings in which the communication act takes place also offer possibilities for applying this interest factor. For example, if you were trying to give the audience some conception of the size of the passenger compartment of a new supersonic jet airliner, you might compare its dimensions with the dimensions of the room (or building) in which the audience is situated. If you were discussing the principle of the microwave relay of telephone messages, you might say, "Look out the window at the bank building over there. See that large dish-shaped antenna on the roof? That is part of the coastal network of relay stations enabling you to talk with others in cities 800 miles to the north." Or a speaker who wishes to use a hypothetical illustration to explain some principle of boating safety might say, "Tim and Joan are going out to Mission Bay this weekend and rent one of those small sailboats for a cruise around the bay." Give the audience someone close to identify with and they will likely be more interested in following the illustration. Every teacher soon learns the attention value of a student's name to perk up that person's interest.

Referring to the Familiar

A parachutist once remarked, "Jumping out of a plane gives you somewhat the same sensation you experience when you unexpectedly reach the top step of a dark stairway. You raise your foot for another step, then discover it isn't there." By relating the unfamiliar (jumping out of a plane) to the familiar (reaching for a step that is not there) the speaker enabled listeners to experience vicariously a small part of his favorite pastime.

This technique of relating the unfamiliar to the familiar is basic to effective speaking whether it be persuasive or informative. The listener's frame of reference must always be considered when attempting to explain a new idea or concept. Reference to the familiar, however, does not mean simply telling the audience what it already knows. Rather, tell the audience what it does not know in terms of what it does know.

Invoking the Listener's Personal Needs

Who is the most important person in the world to the listener? It is probably the listener. And what directly affects him or her will be of interest. Does your message have any bearing upon the listener's self-interests? Does it concern, directly or indirectly, the listener's health, safety, family pocketbook, status, personal comforts, or any of a long list of needs and wants? Every listener may subconsciously be asking the speaker, "What's in it for me?" A speaker recently capitalized on the audience's personal needs when he was trying to have a group of college students pay attention to a speech on "making effective use of our study time." He noted:

> Each one of us in this room has given up something to be here. We have given up activities ranging from making money on a job, to playing tennis during this lovely sunny day. So why are we here in college instead of doing something else with these four years? If we reflect on it the answer is very simple—we came here because we believe that a college education has both immediate and long-range rewards that we deem important. However, to be the recipient of these rewards we not only give certain things up, but we have to attend classes and spend a great many hours studying. This study time comes from time when we could be socializing or engaging in some other leisure activity. Knowing that we all want more time for various occasions, I would like to talk to you today about how you can improve your grades and at the same time have more freedom to have fun. Specifically: How to make more effective use of your existing study time.

A speech concerning a nuclear power plant might be prefaced by remarks concerning possible cuts in the listener's light bill or new conveniences to enjoy as a result of cheaper electricity. Allusions to new food additives that will cut cooking time drastically might enhance listener interest in an explanation of chemical compounds. A discussion of the proposed state budget takes on added impact when the speaker suggests that the children of the listeners may not enjoy "free" public education if certain amendments are adopted. Never overlook the possibility of relating your message to the personal concerns of the audience. In his book, *Persuasive Speaking*, Thomas Scheidel observes this of the listener:

> He will hear best those statements which are relevant to his needs, his expectations, and his experiences. They will be emphasized by him. The skillful speaker, aware of this fact, will take these sources of emphasis into account in adapting his message to his audience.

Imparting Activity

In our chapter on delivery, we pointed out how the speaker who uses meaningful bodily action and vocal variety holds attention more readily than the speaker who fails to employ them. The content of the speech can also be infused with activity. If the speaker arranges ideas in a logical, easy-to-follow sequence, those ideas seem to *move* for the listener. A jumbled, helter-skelter lack of arrangement is one of the surest techniques for losing audience interest.

Words that suggest action should be fully employed by the speaker. "He staggered home" is more compelling than "He went home drunk." "The old pickup truck was doing seventy-five when it drifted over the divider strip into the oncoming lane" is more meaningful and interesting than "She was going too fast in that old truck."

The authors recall a classroom speech on memory improvement in which the speaker demonstrated a technique for memorizing a list of items. Among other things, the speaker asked the audience to visualize each item in motion—the more absurd and exaggerated the motion the better. He explained that we tend to remember moving objects more readily than stationary ones.

Varying your developmental materials also imparts a feeling of activity to your message. Rather than dwelling at length on sets of statistics, add variety by inserting appropriate examples, analogies, and quotations from authorities. If you happen to be discussing a serious topic, avoid falling into a pattern of unrelieved sobriety. Insert a light note here and there (consistent with your purpose, of course) to lend refreshing variety. This is a good place to remind you that these attention and interest factors we have been discussing should be used *throughout* the speech. They not only *secure attention* at the start of your presentation, but when used at the right times they *maintain interest* during your entire speech.

Using Reality

A student speaker was relating anecdotes about famous film comedians of the thirties. As he turned to W.C. Fields he unrolled a yellowing playbill he had found in the basement of a local movie theater where he was working. It advertised as "an outstanding coming attraction" one of Fields' early films. In another more somber speech, the sister of an American student being held prisoner in Turkey for alleged possession of illegal drugs recounted the anguish of her brother's confinement. "This envelope I'm holding brought the first letter he was allowed to write from prison." Still another speaker, an apprentice bank teller, was explaining to an evening speech class how to recognize counterfeit currency. She asked each listener to take a dollar bill out of his or her wallet and examine it closely as she explained the telltale clues.

The film buff did not need to display the W.C. Fields playbill in order to recount some of that comedian's hilarious escapades. The sister of the jailed student did not need to hold up the envelope from her brother to make clear his ordeal. And the bank teller could have drawn a representation of the dollar bill on the board and made her instructions for counterfeit detection just as clear. But in all three cases a striking heightening of interest resulted from the use of an *actual* object. The real item is almost always more compelling than the best verbal description, pictorial representation, or mock-up that can be devised. By the same token, reference to an actual example tends to be more compelling than reference to a hypothetical example.

It is not always possible or practical to produce "the real thing," whether it be an object or an example. In such cases we have to substitute that which is *realistic* for that which is *real*. For example, if we are trying to get our audience to visualize some circumstance in the future, we obviously cannot produce the actual circumstance. But we can provide *lifelike* details that will cause the listener to respond, "Yes, that could very well happen." Putting real persons in hypothetical circumstances or hypothetical people into an actual setting lends credibility *and interest* to such examples. You will recall our example of a few pages back where the speaker said, "Tim and Joan are going out to Mission Bay this weekend and rent one of those small sailboats for a cruise around the bay." While the event depicted was hypothetical, the persons and places were real. Thus the event bore a resemblance to reality.

Pointing Out Conflict

The speaker should be aware of the value of conflict as a means of holding audience interest on a subject. Perhaps conflict is implicit in the subject itself. A speech opposing a proposed course of action has built-in conflict. A problem-solving speech has built-in conflict. Subjects in which conflict is not implicit, on the other hand, require that the speaker superimpose it. A speech explaining what happens to a letter from the time it is mailed to the time it reaches its destination does not seem to have a built-in element of conflict. But by skillful use of a hypothetical illustration a postal worker did introduce conflict into that subject. He asked the audience to imagine that one of the men in the front row was carrying in his suit pocket an insurance premium he had forgotten to mail. To keep his insurance in effect the premium would have to reach the home office twelve hundred miles away within thirty-six hours. Would mailing the premium at this moment enable it to reach the company in time? For the remainder of the speech he followed the progress of that particular piece of mail until, happily, it reached its destination in the nick of time. The twin ingredients of conflict and suspense kept the audience interested throughout the entire speech.

Using Humor

Judicious use of humor can be a most effective means of holding audience interest. However, its effective employment requires skill. Because of its unpredictable nature, we caution you to use it sparingly and with propriety. Sometimes it succeeds too well, so that the audience's attention becomes focused upon the humor as an end in itself rather than as a means of making the message interesting.

In chapter 10, when we discuss special speech types, we shall treat humor in some detail. However, because humor can aid you in making your informative presentation more interesting, we will offer a few positive suggestions and possible dangers inherent in using humor. (Remember that the audience's reactions to your attempts at humor are apt to take a variety of forms. Humor can be successful without your listeners falling off their chairs in wild abandon. They may simply smile or take inward pleasure from your statements.)

When using humor as an attention device, think of something novel and original. Look to the possibilities offered by exaggeration, incongruity, and sarcasm. A student, informing her listeners about the history and functions of the Salvation Army, used exaggeration as a form of humor when she told the following joke:

A man came into the Salvation Army mission and asked, 'Is this the Salvation Army's mission?' 'Yes, of course,' the officer replied. 'Do you save bad women?' the visitor then asked. Again the officer replied with a 'Yes.' 'Good,' came the response, 'Will you save me three for Saturday night?'

Likewise, incongruity, presenting the familiar in an unfamiliar manner has humorous overtones. Speaking on the P.T.A. a student said, "My mother used to visit my teacher so often that the other kids elected her class president."

Sarcasm, if used carefully, can also be an effective humorous technique. While informing a class about the Women's Rights Movement a speaker told the following story as a means of recapturing attention:

The feminist who was giving a speech in support of the Equal Rights Amendment was interrupted by the deep voice of a heckler from the crowd: 'Don't you wish you were a man?' 'No,' she replied without missing a beat. 'How about you?'

When using humor in the informative speech it is important to remember that your main purpose is still increased understanding. Stringing a series of unrelated jokes together would be highly inappropriate. In addition, an analysis of both your audience and your occasion are crucial in using humor. Because humor has the potential of being offensive, you must carefully consider how your efforts will be received.

Organizing the Speech to Inform

Systematic arrangement of material is crucial in informative speaking if the listener is to retain the information presented. Listen carefully the next time you hear an informative talk and you will discover that there are occasions when the educated as well as the uneducated forget the importance of organization and clarity. Speeches that seem to leap from point to point without offering internal or external clues seldom leave the listener with anything meaningful.

The Introduction

The introduction to the speech to inform has three interrelated purposes: (1) to arouse attention, (2) to create a desire for the detailed information contained in the body of the speech, and (3) to preview the main points of the speech.

Specific methods of starting a speech were discussed in detail in chapter 6. The selection of a method will be determined by factors relating to topic, audience interest, audience knowledge level, speaking time available, and speaking occasion. When listeners are not vitally concerned with the topic, it is quite often profitable to begin with a rhetorical question, startling statement, or unusual illustration. These devices arouse the apathetic and disinterested listener. For example, to stimulate audience interest in a speech dealing with hang gliding a speaker used the following introduction:

The other day, while I was driving home from school, I noticed an extremely large bird gliding gracefully through the sky. As I looked again I realized that this was truly the largest bird I had ever seen. I pulled my car over to the side of the road so that I could get a closer look. As I gazed into the sky this third time I thought that I must be dreaming—

for what was flying over my head was not a bird, but a person. A person with wings.

Another speaker, talking on the topic of solid waste disposal, began by trying to secure attention with a series of startling statistics. He noted:

In the next year we have to decide what to do with two million tons of major appliances, twenty-two million tons of food, ten million tons of newspapers, three million tons of paper plates, towels, and napkins, and fifty-two million tons of bottles and containers. Do you have any ideas where we can put all this? Suggestions now range from putting it all in satellites and sending it into outer space, to making a large island out of it and calling it Son of Big Mac.

In selecting any introductory device it is important to remember that if you fail to arouse interest at the outset, you are apt to deliver the entire speech to an audience that has its attention focused elsewhere.

In all communication situations it is to your advantage if you can stimulate a desire on the part of the audience to want to listen to your presentation. In the introduction to the informative speech make it clear to your audience that your topic holds significance for them and that they will benefit by listening. For instance, recently a speaker used an introduction to demonstrate that paying attention to the speech could save the listener a great deal of money. The topic was gasoline conservation, and the speaker said, "By following the few simple suggestions I will discuss today, you should be able to save enough money each week to treat yourself to a T-bone steak."

Other methods of stimulating interest in your topic can, of course, be much more elaborate. A student, trying to explain how to take better photographs, showed the audience some prints that were obviously examples of poor photography. While thumbing through the enlarged photos, she asked her listeners, "How many of you take photographs that turn out like these?" The audience laughed. She then said, "How many of you would like to take photos that look like this?" Now she started to hold up and display some beautiful specimens of outstanding photography. She added, "You can all take photographs similar to these if you can learn to follow a few simple steps. I have been an amateur photographer for six years and would like to share some of these steps with you now."

There are also occasions when the curiosity of the listeners is appealed to as a way of arousing interest in what is to follow. When speaking on the philosophy of Francis Bacon, a student read the following paragraph as a way of pointing the audience to the body of the speech.

Reading maketh a full man, conference a ready man, and writing an exact man; and, therefore, if a man write little, he had need have a great memory; if he confer little he had need have a present wit; and if he read little he had need have much cunning, to seem to know that he doth not. Histories make men wise; poems witty; the mathematics subtle; natural philosophy deep; moral grave; logic and rhetoric, able to contend.

Informative Speaking: Being Understood

He then added, in his own words, "What does this mean for us three hundred and fifty years later?"

You can better hold attention during the body of your speech if you have already created an atmosphere of curiosity and interest. By motivating the audience early in the speech you also increase the probability that they will learn something by the conclusion of your talk.

We started this chapter by noting that persons learn more when they know what they are going to be asked to learn. Your introduction should provide a brief initial summary (preview) of the main points to be taken up in the body of your speech. By telling your audience that your speech on the subject of how to swing a golf club will deal with the grip, the stance, and the swing, you are allowing them to glimpse your organizational pattern as a means of making their job of listening easier. You are preparing them for what is coming, and they will find it much simpler to locate your main ideas. As another good example, the speaker we mentioned who was seeking to have the audience understand how to take better photographs, had a preview that stated, "In looking at these simple steps for improved photo taking I should like to talk about composition, lighting, and equipment."

The Body

Since the introduction has (1) captured the listener's attention, (2) aroused interest in the information to come, and (3) previewed main points, you are ready to present the information itself. To promote the listener's comprehension of your ideas, and to maintain attention at a high level, you should organize the body of your speech into meaningful groupings. The division of the whole into its parts is an essential step in explaining any complex concept. No one, for example, can understand all aspects of public welfare, but most persons could assimilate certain features if the features were presented and explained separately. In most instances the classification and division of the speech is inevitable in light of the subject matter. These groupings will be more easily remembered if they can be worded in a logical pattern. Let us reexamine some of the patterns of arrangement discussed in chapter 6 in light of their application to informative speaking.

Chronological Pattern

The chronological, or time pattern, has its greatest value in explaining processes, presenting historic events, and relating personal experiences. Discussing the history of air travel you might develop your material under three headings:

I. Early attempts at flying
II. Air travel today
III. The future of air travel

Giving a speech on the legislative process the order might well be:

I. Drafting a bill
II. Committee hearings
III. Debate on the floor of Congress

Spatial Pattern

Spatial order is especially effective in speeches describing a scene, a location, or a geographical distribution. For instance, the body of your speech could be arranged from North to South, from top to bottom, or from center to outside. In talking on the topic of weather in the United States, your order might be:

I. Weather on the East Coast
II. Weather in the Middle West
III. Weather on the West Coast

For a speech on life under the sea you might select the following order:

I. Surface sea life
II. Sea life twenty feet below the ocean surface
III. Sea life on the ocean floor

Causal Order

Causal order tells of the causes of certain effects, or tells of the effects resulting from various causes. In giving a talk entitled "The Sun and the Individual," your pattern might appear:

I. The effects of the sun on the skin
II. The effects of the sun on the eyes
III. The effects of the sun on the hair

When treating the topic "Why World War II?" you might select the following arrangement:

I. United States and German relations before 1941
II. United States and Italian relations before 1941
III. United States and Japanese relations before 1941

By examining the relationship of the United States to each of these countries, one is able to point out possible causes of World War II.

Topical Pattern

Topical pattern is probably the most frequently used of all patterns. This arrangement sets out several facets of a topic that are obviously related and consistent. If you are talking about the financial structure of your university, your pattern might include:

I. The university's assets
II. The university's liabilities
III. The university's endowments

The key to the topical pattern is that the arrangement is rather apparent and the one an audience most likely expects.

You may wish to order the material so that it moves from the simplest to the most complex, the most familiar to the least familiar, the least important to the most important, or the most acceptable to the least acceptable.

The Conclusion   Methods of concluding a speech were explained in some detail in chapter 6 and can profitably be reviewed as part of your training for informative speaking. There are, however, certain techniques of concluding that are especially valuable for the speech to inform. For example, it may be helpful to restate your message and summarize its main points. You may desire to heighten audience interest once again and suggest areas that will add to or clarify concepts you mentioned.

The most popular concluding technique is the final summary (or reiteration). Persons tend to pay close attention when they feel the end of the speech is near. The final summary takes advantage of this captured attention by reviewing the main ideas in the *same* order they were presented in the initial summary and in the body of the speech. In speaking on the topic of college registration, you might conclude by saying, "So we have seen that you can register for classes in three ways. First, you can register by mail; second, you can make special arrangements with the specific instructors; and finally, you can sign in the Registration office on the first day of classes."

A Sample Outline   One form that organizational scheme often takes is the outline.

(Title)	Who Pays?
(General Purpose)	To Inform
(Specific Purpose)	To have the audience understand the major arguments for and against state aid to parochial schools.

Introduction

(Rhetorical question)

  I. How many of you realize that one of the crucial battles raging during the founding of this country remains an unresolved issue even today?
    A. The early colonists were determined to separate church and state.
    B. Yet compulsory school attendance laws meant that some parents, who desired private schools, were forced into financing two separate institutions.

(Motivation toward topic)

  II. This highly emotional issue affects us today as much as it did over two hundred years ago.
    A. If the state began to pay tuition fees for private schools, it would mean that millions of additional dollars would have to be found.
      1. Some of the money would come from our taxes.
      2. Money now being used to pay for public education would be rechanneled into parochial schools.
    B. If the state supported parochial schools, some say it would bring church and state closer together.
    C. Yet what about the person who believes that under the Fourteenth Amendment we can educate a child in any way we deem appropriate?
      1. Is it not a denial of our freedom to be forced to pay dual taxation?
      2. What if you believe that our public schools are "Godless?"

(Preview)

    III. To better understand this important issue of state aid to parochial schools, I should like to look at the arguments frequently made in favor of tax support for these schools and then examine the arguments advanced by those who oppose such aid.

Core Statement: Opinion is strongly divided on the issue of state aid to parochial schools.

Body

    IV. Arguments that support tax aid for parochial schools are twofold.
        A. Denominational schools offer an important religious, spiritual, and ethical element not found in public schools.
          1. Only religious schools can teach Christian values.
          2. Public schools are Godless.
        B. The right of parents to determine the education and religious instruction of their children is a fundamental one.
          1. Failure to provide public funds for denominational schools is a partial denial of that right.
          2. This denial may well make some families second-class citizens who are not benefiting from their taxes.

    V. Arguments advanced by those who oppose tax support for parochial schools are threefold.
        A. It is urged that the appropriation of public funds for denominational schools would be a long step toward breaking down the unique American policy of separation of church and state.
          1. It was part of an early colonial policy.
          2. It was an idea contained in the First Amendment to the Constitution.
        B. It is contended that the organization of American public schools along denominational lines would make education a divisive rather than a unifying factor in our life.
          1. Schools now teach a variety of opinions and views.
          2. Denominational schools would tend to teach dogma and one-dimensional attitudes.
        C. It is argued that the present arrangements promote healthy growth among various religions.

(Use visual aids)

          1. A recent religious census reveals that fifty-three percent of the population hold church membership—the highest mark in U.S. history.
          2. Approximately seventy-eight million persons now belong to various religious groups.

(Summary)

VI. Today, by looking at both sides of an important issue, we have gained some insight into the pros and cons of tax support for parochial schools.
   A. Those in favor of tax support suggest the following:
      1. Denominational schools can do a better job of teaching values and ethics.
      2. It is unfair to deny a basic right to persons who select parochial schools.
   B. Those opposed counter by saying:
      1. Granting funds for these schools would bring church and state closer together.
      2. Denominational education is divisive.
      3. The status quo is beneficial to both church and state.
VII. In the final analysis you must seek additional information before deciding how you personally feel about this important historical and religious problem.

Visual Aids

The value of visual aids as a means of support was suggested in chapter 5 when we discussed the various forms of support. Visual aids are useful in informative discourse to make ideas more vivid, more lasting, and more understandable. Visual aids help clarify new terms or ideas that are not readily understood or meaningful to many in the audience. The word "larynx" might be unfamiliar to the listeners, but a model or diagram would quickly offer the audience a definition of the term, and "steam generating plan" would be more meaningful when accompanied by a diagram. A common principle of learning maintains that it is worthwhile to employ as many physical senses as possible, that the more associations one has with an idea the better are one's chances of remembering the idea. Being able to see the idea, as well as hear it, contributes to both of these objectives. We have stressed throughout this chapter the importance of interest and attention as part of the informative process. A pretty picture, a shiny object, or a drawing provides the listener with an object upon which attention can be focused, and the listener is usually anxious to hear what the speaker has to say about it.

Types of
Visual Aids

Objects,
Specimens, and
Models

If at all possible, use the *actual object*. Reality is usually more compelling than a mere representation of that reality. If the actual object can be seen, it can help explain an idea or a principle while it captures and maintains attention. An audience can better understand how to develop film if all of the essential objects (trays, solutions, and so forth) are in front of them. Or a speech on football protection gear can be aided by displaying a football player's shoulder pads, hip pads, and helmet. Effective communicators are not content to merely talk about an idea, they want the listeners to see the actual object in question.

There will be times when you cannot bring the actual object to the speech. On these occasions you will have to settle for a *specimen*, a sample of the real object. The speaker who cannot bring the audience an entire rock collection has to be satisfied with showing a few specimens. Even so, these specimens are useful for shortening the time needed to explain how certain rocks look.

Because they are replicas of the real thing, *models* can serve three useful purposes. First, they help *explain* a complex idea. For example, a model of the human heart can greatly simplify this intricate organ without distorting any of the heart's main functions. Second, models can be made into any size or shape; therefore, they can be *moved* from place to place. We could not bring the *U.S.S. Nautilus* to class, yet seeing a disassembled model of that nuclear submarine would be helpful to any audience. Third, because models have to be constructed, the model-makers can *emphasize* whatever aspect of the process they wish. Notice in the communication model below how messages and feedback are

Figure 8.1
Feedback Model

emphasized while such concepts as encoding, decoding, and channels are not even shown.

In this particular visual aid the speaker was concerned with defining feedback. As you can see, the model helped demonstrate that feedback is the response the receiver makes to the sender's messages.

Posters, Diagrams, Paintings, and Photographs

Speakers who want to make their own visual aids find that *posters* are very useful. Posters can clarify and reinforce any idea selected by the speaker. For example, if you are using statistics in your speech you might well say, "In 1971 the price for a gallon of regular gasoline in our city was 33.9¢, in 1973 it was 44.7¢, in 1975 it was up to 55.9¢, in 1977 it reached 63.9¢, and (at this moment) in 1979 it is 94.9¢" This same point could be given added emphasis by using a poster.

Speakers use posters to help their listeners remember key elements in the speech. Figure 8.3 demonstrates how a speaker, talking on the subject of fire prevention, used a poster to stress important ideas he wanted the audience to retain

Diagrams are like models—both attempt to explain and clarify that which is complex. However, models are three-dimensional while diagrams are two-dimensional line forms. The blueprints for an underground watering system would be an example of a diagram. A student recently used a diagram when she was talking on the subject of planting a vegetable garden. She was using her visual aid to help demonstrate the importance of what to plant in each row and

Figure 8.2
Poster

Prices of Regular Gasoline in Our City

Year	Price
1971	33.9¢
1973	44.7¢
1975	55.9¢
1977	63.9¢
1979	94.9¢

Figure 8.3
Poster

Home Fire Prevention Plan

1. Eliminate rubbish in halls and closets.
2. Use container when storing inflammable materials.
3. Check all electrical wiring.

the distance needed between these rows. Her points were that some vegetables needed more room than others and some plants would grow so large they would rob the sunlight from the smaller plants. Her diagram helped clarify these points.

Paintings (also sketches and cartoons) and *photographs* are extremely helpful and are readily available to all speakers. Imagine how clarity would be enhanced by these visual aids if you were speaking on either the history of the American automobile or modern architecture for the 1980s.

Charts and Graphs

Abstract or complicated ideas can often be made more understandable through the use of *charts* and *graphs*. The increase in personal income taxes over the last twenty years, for instance, can be well illustrated on a graph that shows, on the vertical axis, the years involved and, on the horizontal axis, the average amount of taxes paid by each individual. The four most common charts and graphs are: (a) the *organizational chart*, which shows, by means of blocks and interconnecting lines, the hierarchy of control and responsibility; (b) the *comparison chart*, which compares or contrasts two or more quantities, usually of a statistical nature, in terms of each other or in terms of other predetermined quantities; (c) the *pie graph*, which is a circle divided into several pie-shaped segments, each segment representing a classified item and its relationship to the other items; (d) the *bar graph* and the *line graph*, which are usually employed to represent trends, as in a sales graph.

Figure 8.4
Organizational Chart

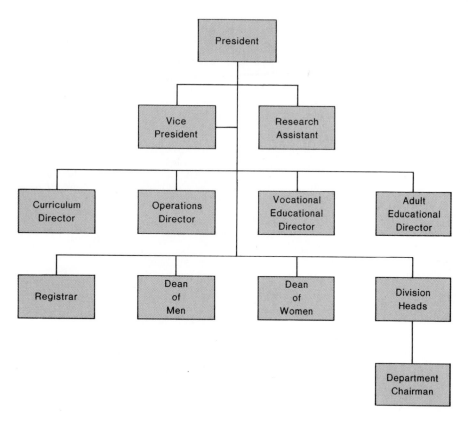

Figure 8.5
Comparison Chart

Major U.S. Weapons Systems

Item	Estimated Cost (in millions)	Number to Be Produced
F-14 Tomcat	$10,564.0	580
F-15 Eagle	$12,603.4	729
F-16 Condor	$13,833.3	1,730
F-18 Hornet	$12,815.8	811

Figure 8.6
Pie Graph

Average Day for Working College Student

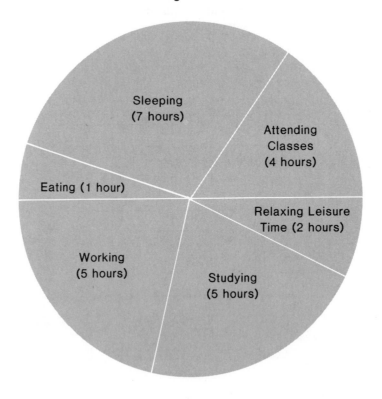

Sleeping (7 hours)

Attending Classes (4 hours)

Eating (1 hour)

Relaxing Leisure Time (2 hours)

Working (5 hours)

Studying (5 hours)

Figure 8.7
Bar Graph

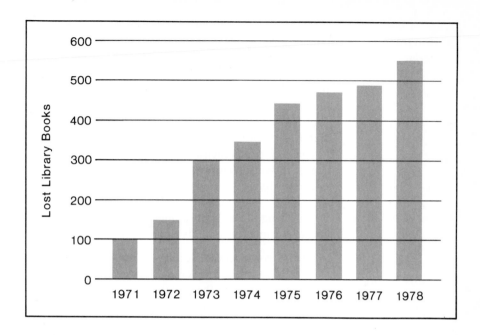

Blackboards

The main advantage of blackboards as visual aids should be obvious to anyone who has attended school: they are *convenient*; items can easily be added or removed at any time. They are usually found in conference rooms and auditoriums as well as in classrooms. We caution the conscientious speaker to check the speaking environment before the speech to be sure that a chalkboard will be available. The authors remember one speaker who very casually said, "Now let me diagram how this system will work," only to turn around and find there was not a blackboard in the room. Both the speaker and the audience were greatly embarrassed.

There are occasions when the blackboard offers an opportunity to present a step-by-step development of the process you are explaining. By adding material as you go along, you can visually demonstrate how a ship is built from the inside to the outside. Moreover, because chalk is erasable, you can eliminate certain items as a means of clarifying your point.

Blackboards are handy and helpful, but some words of advice are in order concerning their use and abuse. Remember that it takes time to write, and you may lose the audience's attention while you are lettering and diagramming. Therefore, you should continue talking and maintaining eye-contact while you are at the board. If you put your material on the board before you speak, your audience may spend more time looking at it than at you.

The content and mechanics of a particular chalk drawing should be planned well in advance of your presentation. You may want your drawing to appear spontaneous, but in actuality you should be as rehearsed with your drawings as you are with your speaking.

Duplicated or Mimeographed Material

On occasion you may want everyone in the audience to have a copy of a long quotation, diagram, chart, or other illustration. Many business meetings call for materials to be in everyone's hands. When this is the case, you may find these suggestions helpful. First, if possible do not distribute the material until you are ready to use it. Circulated material offers listeners an easy excuse to stop listening. Second, make sure to give each person a copy of the material. Trying to read over someone's shoulder can cause confusion in the audience. Third, your material should be neat and readable. It is of little value if your words contribute to audience comprehension at the same time the printed material is distracting and perplexing. One will counter the other, and the result may be a lack of understanding.

Using Visual Aids

By following these simple guidelines in the use of visual aids, your material will be clearer, more meaningful, and more interesting.

1. In preparing and selecting your visual aid make certain that the aid is pertinent to the subject and serves a real purpose.
2. The material on the visual aid should be completely accurate in both representation and authenticity. This does not mean that some forms of exaggeration cannot be used for emphasis.
3. The visual aid should not contain any distracting elements. For example, nonessential details or details that are so poorly depicted that they cannot be accurately interpreted may obscure rather than clarify your ideas.
4. In most instances it is best to display only one visual aid at a time. To have more than one aid in front of the audience at one time encourages the listeners to divide their attention between the aids and perhaps miss certain important points about the one you happen to be discussing.
5. Be sure that the lettering, artwork, or other main features are large enough, clear enough, and of sufficient contrast for all viewers to see.
6. Make the aid attractive so that it adds to clarity and understanding while helping you secure and hold attention. Try to use color and other creative techniques that can keep your aid from being dull and ordinary.
7. Remember the necessity of maintaining contact with your audience. Too many speakers enjoy their visual aid so much that they forget their audience and end up talking to the aid.
8. Be sure to coordinate your visual aid with your words. Do not point to a wheel of a car when you are talking about the fenders, or show one aid while talking about something shown by another.
9. Check the physical surroundings and furnishings so that you will not discover, when it is too late, that there is no place to put your chart, or no electrical outlet available for your tape recorder. Many speakers have had to hold their aids throughout their talks because they failed to investigate the accommodations available.

10. Conduct an audience analysis for your visual aids in much the same way you would for the verbal content of your speech. Ask yourself this important question: "Is *this visual aid* suited, in both content and form, for *this audience*?" A visual aid that insults your audience's intelligence, or one that is much too complex for their backgrounds, will hinder instead of help your speech.

Summary

The principles of communication discussed throughout this book are directly applicable to informative speaking. However, certain steps must be applied when sending a message intended to increase knowledge of a particular subject. In outline form, these steps are:

I. Introduction
    A. Arouse attention.
    B. Stimulate interest.
    C. Summarize the main points to be covered in the speech.
II. Body
    A. Adapt material to the audience—audience analysis.
    B. Employ clear organization.
    C. Strive for audience comprehension.
        1. Use definitions.
        2. Employ concrete examples.
        3. Use comparisons and contrasts.
        4. Dramatize essential points with statistics.
        5. Use vivid and complete descriptions.
        6. Emphasize and reinforce main points.
        7. Use partitions, enumerations, and summaries.
    D. Arouse and maintain interest and attention.
        1. Note that which is impending.
        2. Allude to that which is physically near the audience.
        3. Refer to the familiar.
        4. Invoke the personal needs of the audience.
        5. Impart activity in body, voice, and content.
        6. Use reality.
        7. Point out conflict.
        8. Use humor.
    E. Employ effective visual aids.
III. Conclusion
    A. Present summary of the main points.
    B. Arouse interest in further investigation.

Suggested Readings

Dale, Edgar. *Audio-Visual Methods in Teaching.* Revised Edition. New York: Holt, Rinehart and Winston, 1946.

McCabe, Bernard P., and Bender, Coleman C. *Speaking Is a Practical Matter.* 3d ed. Boston: Holbrook Press, 1976. Part IV.

Monroe, Alan H.; Ehninger, Douglas; Gronbeck, Bruce E. *Principles and Types of Speech Communication.* 8th ed. Glenview, IL: Scott, Foresman, 1978. Chapter 19.

Olbricht, Thomas. *Informative Speaking.* Glenview, IL: Scott, Foresman, 1968.

Reid, Loren. *Speaking Well.* 3d ed. New York: McGraw-Hill, 1977. Chapters 14–17.

Wittich, Walter A., and Schuller, Charles F. *Audio-Visual Materials.* 4th ed. New York: Harper and Row, 1967.

Zelko, Harold P., and Dance, Frank E. *Business and Professional Speech Communication.* 2d ed. New York: Holt, Rinehart and Winston, 1978. Chapter 5.

Persuasive Speaking
Changing Beliefs, Attitudes, and Behavior

One fact stands out in bold relief in the history of man's attempt for betterment. That is that when compulsion is used, only resentment is aroused, and the end is not gained. Only through moral suasion and appeal to man's reason can a movement succeed.

Samuel Gompers

If you were to move the channel selector on your TV set through its full spectrum, there is a good chance that you would encounter messages such as these: a politician arguing that thousands of American workers are being displaced by illegal aliens willing to work for less pay; a distinguished actor philosophizing about the integrity of a tire manufacturing firm; a clothing salesman urging you to take advantage of a "limited time only" sale. These all-too-typical examples represent attempts to influence you in persuasive ways. The politician is trying to make you believe in the existence of a condition, the actor is trying to generate in your mind a favorable image of the tire company, and the clothing salesman obviously is trying to get you to buy his merchandise. They are all trying to *change* you in some way.

All speeches seek to change the listener. As we noted in the previous chapter, the speech to inform seeks to increase the listener's understanding. The speech to entertain seeks to divert the listener's interest. But the change sought by the persuader is a change in the listener's beliefs, attitudes, and behavior. Moreover, it is a *willing* change that the persuader seeks. Unwilling changes are products of coercion, not persuasion. "He that complies against his will/Is of his own opinion still" is a true couplet today—as it was when Samuel Butler composed it over three hundred years ago. Changes brought about by coercive tactics—threats, "arm twisting," and the like—are apt to be short-lived, while changes that are willingly undertaken may very well endure.

In this chapter we shall focus upon communication consciously aimed at inducing willing changes of belief, attitude, and behavior in the listener. We shall be discussing the elements the speaker wishes to change, various ways of inducing the desired changes, and the prospects of achieving change.

Targets and Topics of Persuasion

When we say that the targets of our persuasive efforts are beliefs, attitudes, and behavior of others, what do we mean by these terms? *Belief* is defined in *Webster's New Collegiate Dictionary* as "a conviction of the truth of some statement or reality of a fact, especially when well grounded." Martin Fishbein (see Suggested Readings) maintains that we display *beliefs in* and *beliefs about* objects. Thus, if you were to say, "Poverty exists in the United States," you would be expressing a *belief in* the probability of its existence. If you were to say, "Poverty in the United States is intolerable," you would be expressing a *belief about* its existence.

Attitudes, according to Fishbein, "are learned predispositions to respond to an object or class of objects in a favorable or unfavorable way." How do you react when you find out that the friendly stranger seated next to you at the lunch counter is an off-duty police officer? An undertaker? A minister? An ex-convict? A debt collector? Your instinctive reaction probably reflects a learned predisposition toward the person's particular occupation or status.

Behavior, as we shall use the term, refers to the listener's observable state of activity. The observable state ranges between inactivity and hyperactivity. Changes in behavior may be from action to inaction or vice versa, or they may involve an increase or decrease in the intensity, duration, or magnitude of an action. For example, if you were to urge a friend to stop smoking, you might observe one of these changes in behavior: your friend might give up smoking entirely, might cut down on consumption, might ignore your advice, or might increase consumption out of defiance. Furthermore, your friend's behavioral change might take place immediately, or it might be delayed. The change might be short-lived or permanent.

If beliefs, attitudes, and behavior are the targets of change, with what fundamental issues do we wish to effect change? Generally speaking, persons hold differing views on (1) the reality of facts, (2) the validity of value judgments, and (3) the advisability of adopting proposed courses of action. If a speaker and a listener differ over the reality of an alleged fact, the speaker's core statement will probably be worded as a *proposition of fact*; he will attempt to prove or disprove the existence of something. For example:

> The de-programming of religious cultists is a violation of their constitutional rights.
>
> UFOs are earthly phenomena.
>
> Atlantic City gambling casinos will outdraw Las Vegas casinos within five years.
>
> The death penalty has never deterred the commission of crimes of passion.
>
> Multinational corporations control the world's economy.
>
> Anti-American sentiment in the Middle East is subsiding.
>
> President Kennedy was struck by bullets fired from two separate locations.

It is important to bear in mind that propositions of fact deal with *alleged* facts—matters whose reality is disputed. Moreover, propositions of fact may deal with past, present, and future circumstances. "The movie *Jaws* caused a decline in the number of swimmers at the nation's beaches in the summer of 1975" alleges the existence of a circumstance in the past. "TV violence is causing an increase in juvenile crime" asserts a present condition. "The Communists will control all of the Middle East in two years" alleges a future condition.

If speaker and listener differ over the validity of a value judgment, the speaker espouses a *proposition of value*; that is, the speaker maintains that something is good or bad, is better or worse than something else, is right or wrong, is justified or unjustified, and so forth. The following core statements are examples of propositions of value:

The U. S. decision to recognize Red China was wise.

Hang gliding is no more dangerous than surfing.

Penalties for possession of "Angel Dust" are too lenient.

Solar energy is better than geothermal energy.

The passage of Proposition 13 was the best way to curb government spending.

The national defense budget is too big.

The president was justified in asking for salary increases for members of the armed forces.

Like the proposition of fact, the proposition of value may concern itself with judgments about something in the past, the present, and the future, as can be seen in the examples cited above.

If speaker and listener differ over the advisability of adopting a proposed course of action, the speaker espouses a *proposition of policy*; that is, the speaker argues that something should or should not be done. Thus, one might recommend or oppose the following proposals:

Mercury vapor lamps should be installed in all campus parking lots.

Dogs should be allowed on Mission Beach each weekday morning during the winter months.

The sale of garments made from the skins of animals on the endangered species list should be prohibited by international agreement.

Federal funding of the Amtrak system should be doubled.

Admission standards to state medical schools should be made more lenient.

The construction of buildings in excess of thirty feet in height should be prohibited in any area within five hundred yards of the seashore.

"Junk food" vending machines should be removed from campus.

Issues of fact, value, and policy constitute the common topics of persuasion. Within the compass of a single speech, the speaker may be called upon to defend all three kinds of propositions. For example, a speaker trying to win support for a proposed policy will have to prove several propositions of fact and value in the process:

A need exists for the policy. (proposition of fact)

The proposed policy will fulfill the need. (proposition of fact)

The proposed policy is better than any other proposals advanced. (proposition of value)

The foregoing example by no means exhausts the list of propositions of fact and value that have to be established before a proposition of policy can be proved.

Types of Persuasive Speeches

Persuasive speeches may be classified according to the types of audience response sought. If your aim is to secure audience agreement with your position on a proposition of fact, value, or policy, we say that you are making a *speech to convince*. Thus, you might want your audience to agree that industrial spying is taking place, or that industrial spying is bad, or that industrial spying should be declared illegal. In each case you would be trying to convince your audience. If your aim is to get audience action on some matter, we say that you are making a *speech to actuate*. If you want your listener to sign a petition, donate to a charity, write to a legislator, buy an insurance policy, take a course, or see a play, you are attempting to actuate that listener. If your aim is to reinforce or rejuvenate existing attitudes or beliefs held by the listener, we say you are making a *speech to stimulate*. Inspirational messages, ranging from sermons to pep talks to commencement addresses, are usually concerned with stimulating audience attitudes, beliefs, and emotions.

There will be occasions when it is necessary to convince, stimulate, and actuate all within the same speech, but only one of these will constitute your *ultimate* aim. A sales presentation is an example of a speech whose ultimate aim is to actuate—to get the customer to buy the product or service. In the course of the presentation the salesperson will probably have to convince the customer of a number of points—that the product is needed, that its purchase is feasible, that it is better than competing products—and will probably have to stimulate existing attitudes and beliefs in order to intensify the customer's desire for the product. But the acts of convincing and stimulating are merely instrumental to the ultimate aim, which is to actuate.

Preparing the Persuasive Speech

The process of preparing a persuasive speech is in many respects similar to that used in preparing an informative speech. The topic is chosen, the audience is analyzed, the specific purpose is determined, the materials for achieving the specific purpose are discovered, the speech is organized and rehearsed, but the application of each of the steps of the process to persuasion involves certain unique procedures.

Choosing the Topic and Position

Ideally, the choice of a topic for a persuasive speech should arise from the speaker's recognition of some condition that requires change and the further recognition that change cannot be effected without the help of others. Perhaps you feel that student activity fees at your school are too high, but you despair of ever seeing a reduction until students get together to bring pressure on those responsible for setting the fees. Such a situation calls for a persuasive speech. Or perhaps you live near a pulp mill and suffer from the odor of its operation. You want the odor reduced but know that such a reduction will not take place until people unite to bring pressure on the management. Again, the need for a persuasive speech arises. In each case you become aware of a disturbing element. Then you take a *position* or *stance* with regard to the correction of that disturbing element.

Doubtless you have already taken a position on a number of analogous disturbances. Why not draw upon one of them as the topic for a persuasive speech? As we observed in chapter 1, one of the basic principles of subject selection is to choose a subject that interests you—that *involves* you.

There may be times when the topic and position is chosen for you. Perhaps a friend will ask you to solicit for a worthy cause. Perhaps you will become a salesperson and will be told what to sell. But regardless of whether you originate the subject or someone else does, you should not undertake a persuasive task unless you are interested in the subject and motivated to persuade.

Analyzing the Audience

If the aim of persuasion is to induce a change in the listener, it behooves us to place particular emphasis upon knowing the listener. The majority of failures in persuasive attempts can probably be traced to insufficient or inaccurate analysis of those whom the speaker wishes to influence. Perhaps the speaker has taken pains to find out about his listeners as individuals but has failed to take into account what they are like when they become members of a group. The group imposes codes of behavior upon the individual not necessarily operative when he or she is removed from the group. The salesperson accustomed to dealing with one person at a time sometimes finds it a difficult experience to deal with a group, so different are persons in their public and private behavior. On the other hand, some speakers find it easier to deal with the group than with the individual because of the tendency of most persons to become less critical in their thinking when they become members of a group. Whatever the case, the speaker should become familiar with what *motivates* the listener as an individual and as a member of a group.

In analyzing your audience for a persuasive speech, seek answers to these questions: (1) What is the audience's general attitude toward my topic and position? (2) What is the audience's attitude toward me as a spokesperson? (3) What beliefs does the audience hold about my topic? (4) What has influenced the audience to take its current position on the topic?

1. *Audience attitude toward topic and position.* Following are some of the possible individual and group attitudes confronting the speaker at the outset of a persuasive speech. (1) Individual listeners or the audience as a whole may have a "don't care" attitude about your proposition. If that is the case, you may have to place particular stress upon the link between your proposition and the listener's self-interests in order to overcome the apathy. (2) Individual listeners or the audience as a whole may be hostile toward the point of view you are upholding. This may involve your starting with those items which you and the audience agree upon and then moving on to the areas of disagreement. (3) Individual listeners or the audience as a whole may be interested but undecided, in which case you may decide to place particular emphasis upon the use of factual evidence supporting your position. (4) Individual listeners or the audience as a whole may be favorably inclined toward your position. Your job, in that case, is to reaffirm for the listeners their basis for agreeing with you.

2. *Audience attitude toward the speaker.* Individual listeners or the audience as a whole may be primarily concerned with your personal credibility. If you have a good reputation preceding you to the platform, your task is to confirm that reputation. If you have a negative reputation before the speech, your job is to supplant it with a positive reputation. If you have no reputation preceding you to the platform, your job is to create a good one through the speech itself.

3. *Audience beliefs.* The precise issues with which you should deal in a given communication depend upon the audience. Through careful analysis of the audience you should determine *what their thinking is about the subject.* What beliefs do they presently hold? If you are planning to urge the adoption of a policy, you should ask:

Does the audience know that a problem exists? Do they doubt that a problem exists? Do they deny the existence of a problem?

Are they aware of the seriousness of the problem? Do they doubt the seriousness of the problem? Do they deny its seriousness?

Are they aware of the causes of the problem? Are they likely to doubt my interpretation of the causes?

Are they aware of the possibility of solving the problem? Do they doubt that a solution can be found? Do they deny that a solution can be found?

Are they aware of the various solutions that have been advanced? Are they aware of the advantages and disadvantages of some or all of the proposed solutions?

Do they doubt the workability of my proposed solution?

Do they doubt the superiority of my proposed solution over other proposed solutions?

It should be evident that persuasion should not be attempted until you have tried to secure an answer to the foregoing questions. It would be folly to try to convince an audience that you have the best solution when they do not believe that a problem even exists. Your answers to these questions may tell you that more than one speech will be required before the audience is ready to accept your proposal. Finding what the audience is thinking will tell you the point at which you should launch your argument and will enable you to make a more reliable prediction of just how far you can move the audience from its present position.

If you are planning to limit your purpose to winning audience agreement on a proposition of fact or value, you should try to find answers to these questions:

By what criteria does the audience measure the truth of the fact in question (or the value judgment in question)?

Is each criterion valid?

Are there criteria that the audience has overlooked?

Are there better criteria available?

For example, if you wanted to convince an audience that the Mercedes is superior to the Cadillac, you would be well advised to discover how your audience measures a car's superiority. By its economy? Stability? Comfort? Safety? Beauty? Speed? Its aura of prestige? Unless you discover the criteria (and the *priority* of criteria) that the audience uses, you may be wasting your time. This does not mean that you will necessarily *use* the audience's criteria. You may try to convince them that other criteria are even more important. For example, you might convince the audience that the efficiency of a car's smog control equipment is a more significant criterion of superiority than the car's beauty, speed, comfort, or economy.

A criminal court case furnishes a good example of criteria used to measure the truth of an alleged fact. The prosecution contends that the defendant is guilty, offering as criteria of guilt such elements as motive, means, and opportunity: "He is guilty of kidnapping the banker because he needed the $50,000 ransom to pay off a gambling debt. He owns a panel truck, equipped with a police radio—ideal as a getaway vehicle. Inside the truck police found bandages, adhesive tape, a half-full bottle of chloroform, a map with the banker's street marked with a 'highlighter' pen. Then to clinch it all, he had a set of keys to the banker's house and cars." The defense counsel concedes that motive, means, and opportunity are indeed criteria for measuring guilt but adds that they are not the only criteria or necessarily the *important* criteria: "Even though my client may have had a means, an opportunity, and a motive to commit kidnapping, he did not possess the physical ability to carry it through." Thus proceeds the tug-of-war of justice.

So discover whether your audience has criteria for measuring the truth of the fact you are alleging or the value judgment you are urging. Then you will be in a much better position to offer your audience convincing reasons for agreeing with you.

4. *Forces influencing audience position.* While it is of great importance to discover what your audience feels and believes, it is of equal importance to ascertain the principal sources of influence operating upon the listener. *Why* does the listener believe and feel a certain way? While there are any number of forces that may be influencing the listener's position, we will point out two categories for discussion. The first deals with pressures brought upon the listener from without, and the second deals with pressures brought upon the listener from within.

Group membership and audience position. Much interest has been shown in the social pressures influencing the adoption, retention, modification, and abandonment of attitudes. The *reference groups* with which we identify, the *small groups* with which we interact directly, and *leaders* to whom we look for guidance exert pressures upon us to believe, feel, and act in certain ways.

Each of us probably identifies with numerous reference groups. Maybe we identify with Mexican Americans or blacks or Anglos, with Republicans or Democrats, with Catholics or Protestants or Jews, with the elderly or young adults, with the wealthy or the poor or the middle income group, with blue collar workers or white collar workers, with Southerners or Westerners or Easterners, with idealists or pragmatists—to cite examples of common reference groups. Some groups have no determinate structure or goal, such as age group, economic class, or regional group. Others display varying degrees of organization and orientation. Our "membership" in a particular group may be by reason of our parentage—religious and political affiliations are often inherited; our membership in others may be the result of voluntary actions that place us within the group. Whatever the circumstances of our "joining," a feeling of kinship with the *group* (but not necessarily with the *individuals* within the group) develops, in some instances resulting in a kind of blind loyalty. Donald K. Smith (see Suggested Readings) points out that the "individual's perception of his membership in certain groups is likely to be accompanied by a contrasting recognition of groups with which he feels little or no identification." In fact, he points out, it "may sometimes be accompanied by hostility toward other groups."

We also belong to small groups that involve us in direct interaction with other members of that group. Our families, our circle of friends, our associates at work, our fellow club members, our church congregation are representative groups exerting direct pressure upon our behavior.

Our leaders in all those areas where we join others in a group exert varying degrees of influence upon our attitudes, beliefs, and behavior. The greater the confidence we place in the leader, the greater our propensity to emulate that person's behavior and accept his or her attitudes and beliefs on certain matters as our own. The mass suicides of religious cultists in Guyana in 1978 offer a tragic example of the powerful influence that can be exerted by a leader.

What are the implications for persuasion in the social pressures exerted by reference groups, small groups, and leaders? Depending upon the particular circumstances involved, the speaker may find that the listener's consciousness of group pressure is an asset that can be used or is a detriment that must be offset. In some situations an individual may consent to believe, feel, or act in a particular way if informed that others of the group are doing likewise or have given approval to such behavior. The "bandwagon technique" of the propagandist is built upon this very principle. It attempts to intensify the listener's awareness of membership in the group. In those situations where the speaker's proposal runs afoul of the social pressures operating upon the listener, the speaker must minimize those pressures. The speaker will attempt to get the listener to disassociate from the force bringing pressure.

It is important, then, for the speaker to discover the identity of the reference groups, small groups, and leaders that may be exerting an influence upon the listener's position.

Ego-involvement and audience position. Muzafer Sherif and his associates have conducted extensive investigations into the relationship between our ego-involvement with an issue and our willingness to modify our position on that issue. Sherif maintains that the greater the degree of ego-involvement we experience, the narrower are our "latitudes of acceptance," and hence the less likely we are to change our existing opinions on the issue.

It appears that the listener who has a vested interest in the matter at issue poses a considerable problem for the persuader who wants to change that listener's position on the issue. Imagine the difficulty of an employer trying to convince an employee that he should accept less pay for more work. The employee would probably maintain that it should be the other way around.

Our degree of familiarity with an issue and our willingness to change position was also studied by Sherif. His findings suggest that the less familiar we are with an issue, the more amenable we are to changes in our position on that issue (if, indeed, we hold a position at all).

Extreme devotion to a position, he maintains, virtually blinds us to any suggestion of change. Even a moderate point of view is perceived with some hostility by the fierce believer, because "it falls squarely within his latitude of rejection."

Discover, then, what "vested interest" your listeners may have in the issue under consideration. This information will enable you to set a more realistic persuasive goal.

Determining the Specific Purpose

Having analyzed the audience carefully, you are now in a position to devise a strategy of persuasion. You know what beliefs and attitudes have to be modified or overturned, you know what influences have to be enlisted or counteracted, you know how the audience perceives your personal credibility—you know the magnitude of the task that lies ahead. You may decide that more than one speech will be necessary to attain your ultimate persuasive goal. Your audience analysis has equipped you to determine how much you can accomplish in a given communication encounter. Therefore, your next move is to formulate a statement of the specific purpose of the upcoming speech.

In a persuasive speech, the statement of the specific purpose indicates exactly what you want the audience to believe, feel, or do. For example:

To have my audience believe that the proposed LNG terminal should be located at least seventy miles north of Los Angeles.

To have my audience feel that the school administration is acting in the best interests of the students.

To have my audience purchase tickets to the Renaissance Faire.

To have my audience believe that steel animal traps are inhumane.

To have my audience sign a petition urging the instructor to re-schedule the mid-term examination.

Once you have formulated your specific purpose you can begin the selection of materials that will best enable you to accomplish that purpose.

Persuasive Speaking: Changing Beliefs, Attitudes, and Behavior 185

Choosing the Means of Persuasion

Twenty-four centuries ago Aristotle in his *Rhetoric* observed that there are three instruments of persuasion: (1) "Persuasion is effected by the *arguments*, when we demonstrate the truth, real or apparent, by such means as inhere in particular cases." (2) "Persuasion is effected through the audience, when they are brought by the speech into a state of *emotion*; for we give very different decisions under the sway of pain or joy, and liking or hatred." (3) "The *character* of the speaker is a cause of persuasion when the speech is so uttered as to make him worthy of belief; for as a rule we trust men of probity more, and more quickly, about things in general, while on points outside the realm of exact knowledge, where opinion is divided, we trust them absolutely" (italics added). The durability of Aristotle's classification may be seen by a cursory examination of rhetorical treatises from his day to the present. Perhaps different labels are affixed to the modes of persuasion, and perhaps some of the modes have been subdivided, but all are essentially Aristotelian in their origin. In this section we shall be concerned with finding convincing arguments, impelling psychological appeals, and ways of manifesting personal credibility.

It should be emphasized that the separation of persuasion into three modes is arbitrary. In most communication situations the speaker's persuasive attempts will be a composite of all the modes. So we suggest that you view these three as being fused in practice, even though we are analyzing them separately.

I. Convincing Arguments

To be convincing an argument must meet the audience's test of reasonableness. We all like to think that any action we take or any belief or attitude we hold rests upon a rational foundation. In fact, we search for reasons to justify our behavior, whether past, present, or future behavior. The speaker, then, is obliged to meet the listener's rational requirements.

Let us examine now the materials of argument—evidence and reasoning—and some of the possible requirements for a rational argument.

Evidence

A thorough analysis of evidence (forms of support) was undertaken in chapter 5. It would be well for you to review that material as part of your introduction to this view of persuasive communication. What follows is a description of how various forms of evidence apply specifically to persuasive speaking. We shall group the forms of evidence into the following two general categories: (1) evidence of *fact*, and (2) evidence of *opinion*.

Factual evidence may be drawn from the speaker's own personal observations or from external sources. Each of us has witnessed an event and reported to others what we witnessed. Perhaps we saw a man with a gun run out of a corner grocery, and we tell a police officer what we saw. Or we argue with a friend over which moped gets the best mileage, and we cite figures compiled from our own experience.

The validity of factual evidence drawn from our own personal observation is dependent upon two factors. First, how well equipped are we to be good witnesses of the "facts" we report? Do we have the necessary physical capacities, such as keen eyesight, or acute hearing? Is our perception colored by the emotional state we happen to be in? Do we see only what we want to see? In short, are we objective observers? Second, how well equipped are we to report what we have seen? Do we alter the story from telling to telling to make it more interesting? Do we relish the lurid details out of proportion to their importance? Do we possess the vocabulary needed for relatively objective reporting?

Factual evidence drawn from external sources must meet these and other tests of validity. Is the fact being reported by the original observer directly? If so, that observer should be judged in light of the same questions we ask ourselves when we are the primary observers. Is the fact being reported by a secondary source? If so, what is the secondary source's reputation for reliability? When was the fact observed and when was it reported? What is fact today may not be fact tomorrow (witness population figures). Is the fact represented out of context? Do other sources report the same fact?

Opinion evidence has two sources also—the speaker's own personal opinions based upon direct experience and the opinions of others, presumably experts. The acceptability of the "educated guess" is, of course, dependent upon whether the audience views the speaker as a person qualified to voice an informed opinion. If by reason of your occupation or your major field of study, you do possess the necessary qualifications for expertise—and if your audience recognizes these qualifications as adequate—you may with impunity use yourself as a source of opinion. By and large, however, the student speaker should use the testimony of a recognized authority. Whether the opinion cited is his own or an expert's it should meet the criteria for valid testimony discussed in chapter 5.

Reasoning

The mere possession of valid evidence of fact and opinion is, of course, valueless unless we do something with it. The process of doing something with evidence— that is, drawing conclusions from it—is called *reasoning*. As you have doubtless seen, the same set of facts and opinions can lead to more than one conclusion. The persuasive speaker attempts to show that his or her conclusions are nearer to truth than the opponent's.

We generally recognize four forms of reasoning: (1) deduction, (2) induction, (3) reasoning from analogy, and (4) reasoning from causation.

1. *Deduction*. This is also called reasoning from axiom and reasoning from the general to the particular. The syllogism,

   All men are mortals.
   Socrates is a man.
   Therefore, Socrates is a mortal.

   is often cited as an example of deductive reasoning. The first line, "All men are mortals," is the axiom, or general statement. The second line is the particular case in point, "Socrates is a man." The third line states the conclusion, which shows the relationship of the particular to the general. Much of our reasoning follows this pattern. We have countless axioms that we employ in making everyday decisions. We have axioms to guide us in selecting a movie to see—"Movies starring Woody Allen are funny. I see one is playing at the Orpheum. Let's go!" Others guide us in dining—"The seafood at Malone's is fabulous. I'm in the mood for a swordfish steak. Let's go to Malone's." Others guide us in choosing professors—"The Fraternity Faculty Guide is a reliable source. I'm going to follow its advice and crash Dr. Elliot's class." If only such reasoning were always valid!

Several tests should be applied to detect weaknesses in our deductions. First, is the guiding rule usually accurate? Are Woody Allen's movies usually funny? Why do you say so? How many of his movies have you seen? Is your guiding rule based on personal experience or on the judgment of a friend or perhaps a professional movie critic? (You will notice that we use the word *usually*, because the persuasive speaker deals mainly with what is probable rather than what is certain.)

Second, does the particular case in point fall within the scope of the guiding rule? Does the movie playing at the Orpheum really *star* Woody Allen? Maybe he is playing a cameo role. Is it a feature he made sometime before achieving stardom? Unless the case in point falls within the scope of the guiding rule, we cannot reasonably conclude that the movie at the Orpheum will probably be funny.

Persuasion abounds in the use of deductive reasoning. When we urge others to defeat a tax reform measure "because it is reactionary," we are implying the following:

Things that are reactionary are bad.
This measure is reactionary.
Therefore, it is bad. (And we do not support bad measures.)

As speakers and listeners we should examine critically any use of deductive reasoning. Unless the deduction can meet the tests we have mentioned, it lacks validity.

2. *Induction.* Also called reasoning from examples, reasoning from the particular to the general, or simply generalization, induction is the reverse of deduction. The pollster interviews five hundred voters and concludes that "The American voter is more conservative today than ten years ago." We read that four locals of a trade union are rife with corruption and conclude that all the other locals are probably corrupt, or possibly that all labor unions are corrupt. We meet an exchange student from Sweden and tell our friends that Sweden has the most beautiful people in the world. All these examples are imperfect inductions because the generalization is based upon a limited number of examples. However, it is usually impossible for us to investigate every single part of the whole; so we must rely upon what we feel is a representative sample. The current vogue of professional pollsters as a source of social information (particularly during political campaigns) is due in great part to their professed accuracy in obtaining representative samples.

All of us engage in inductive reasoning. In fact, many of the axioms we employ in deductive reasoning have been arrived at through a prior process of induction. The axiom, "Movies starring Woody Allen are funny," was probably arrived at after the viewer had witnessed three or four of his movies.

Since we all use induction we should be familiar with the tests of its validity. The following questions are pertinent. (1) How many examples are used in arriving at the generalization? To sample two watermelons from an entire truckload and generalize about the whole truckload is to trust to luck rather than to logical reasoning. There must be *enough* examples to warrant the conclusion drawn. (2) How representative of the whole class are the examples used in generalizing about the class? While the *quantity* of examples is important, even more important is the *quality* of the examples. If you could sample three apples from a bushel basket, could you choose a representative sample of the entire basket? Perhaps not, because of the limited quantity. But at least you could make an intelligent attempt. Would you choose your three apples from the top? From the middle layer? From the bottom layer? Very likely you would choose one from each layer. Or if the storekeeper has a reputation for packing fruit of uniform quality, then conceivably one apple from the basket might warrant a generalization about the whole. (3) Is the generalization confined to the class from which the examples were drawn? Alluding to our apple-sampling example, any generalization we draw should be concerned only with the basket from which the sampling was made, not with all the baskets in the store. Yet this is a common error in induction. One renegade labor union gives a black eye to all organized labor. The misbehavior of a few local teenagers is used as the basis for a generalization about all teenagers, when at best it should be used only as a basis for generalizing about certain local problems. As a listener you should apply these tests of inductive logic to the remarks of the speaker. As a speaker you should make certain that your inductive reasoning meets these tests before employing it.

3. *Reasoning from analogy.* "It will never work here. It didn't work in England." "Try my headache remedy. It'll make you feel better in a hurry." "I don't see why I can't have a new car. George's dad bought him one." In each of the examples cited, the speaker is drawing upon comparisons to reach a conclusion. In the first example there is an implied comparison between England and here. In the second, there is a comparison between you and me or my headache and yours. And in the final example, George and I or George's dad and my dad are the persons compared. Reasoning from analogy, then, suggests that because two things are alike in certain known respects, they will also be alike with respect to the issue in question. Of all the forms of reasoning, this is perhaps the one most subject to error—and for a very simple reason. The validity of any argument based upon comparison is dependent upon a high degree of similarity between the circumstances compared. A perfect analogy would demand identical circumstances with no variables involved. Such circumstances are seldom ever found. Thus, the person using analogical reasoning must be extremely careful to avoid overlooking pertinent points of *dissimilarity* between two otherwise comparable things.

What are the *relevant* points of similarity that should exist in the items compared? The physician is trained to recognize relevant points of similarity between the patient at hand and a patient already treated. Thus, Dr. Evans can reason that "Joe has the same symptoms as Harry; penicillin treatment worked for Harry; so I'll prescribe it for Joe." But speakers all too often do not take the time to analyze the constituents of relevance. Noting that a great *number* of similarities exist between two situations, they do not take the time to ask if the similarities are pertinent. Do not be fooled by quantity; look for quality.

If you expect to employ reasoning from analogy in a speech, it is advisable to use one or more of the other forms of reasoning as well because of their higher probative value. If you rely solely upon analogy, your audience may note points of dissimilarity that you have overlooked.

4. *Reasoning from causation.* Causation may appear in at least three forms. We may reason from a known set of circumstances to a probable set of consequences, cause-to-effect. We may reason from a known set of consequences back to their probable cause, effect-to-cause. Or we may reason from one set of consequences to another set of consequences, effect-to-effect.

Cause-to-effect reasoning can be readily illustrated. We read in the newspaper that auto workers have been granted a wage hike; so we predict that new-model car prices will be higher. Or in election years we hear Democrats saying, "Don't elect the Republicans unless you want another depression." The Republicans, in turn, say, "Don't elect the Democrats unless you want to get us in another war."

Effect-to-cause reasoning is just as common. The accident scene smells of alcohol; so we reason the accident was the result of drunken driving. The next-door neighbor sports a beet-red complexion; so we reason he stayed too long at the beach. The stock market moves sharply upward; so we conclude it is the result of the president's latest observation on the nation's economy.

Effect-to-effect reasoning is a special form of reasoning from analogy. It says that because two sets of circumstances are similar (similar causes), their consequences will be similar. The doctor who prescribed penicillin for Joe because it worked for Harry (who exhibited the same symptoms) was using both analogical and causal reasoning.

Reasoning from causation should be subjected to the following tests. (1) Does the alleged cause always produce the same effect? (2) Can the effect result from more than one cause? (3) Are there any conditions that can interfere with a causal connection?

Thus, we have examined some of the ways persons reason and the kinds of evidence from which they reason. As you frame arguments to support your persuasive proposition, bear in mind the tests of reasonableness that your audience may require you to meet.

There is only one answer to the question, "How much proof will an audience require before it believes something?" That answer is, "Enough." If you have studied your audience well, if you have tried to put yourself in the role of the listener, then you have a pretty fair idea of what constitutes "enough."

II. Impelling Psychological Appeals

A speaker may, with faultless reasoning and unimpeachable evidence, convince you that a problem exists and that there is an ideal solution to the problem. Yet you may fail to take the steps necessary to implement that solution. You have been convinced, but you have not been actuated. Why? The answer may be that the speaker talked in terms of "a problem," rather than *your* problem, and offered a solution to "a problem" rather than a solution to *your* problem. In short, the speaker has overlooked the psychologically impelling reasons that spur persons to action. Unless the listener can feel some identification with the problem, action is not likely to be taken to solve the problem however logical a given solution might be.

How does the speaker get the listener to *identify* with the problem and the solution? There are two general means. First, if the problem and its solution have a direct bearing upon the life and welfare of the listener, the speaker simply has to point this out. Second, if the problem and its solution affects the listener only indirectly, the speaker may point out how someone close to the listener is affected (or possibly how someone *who can be made to seem close* to the listener is affected).

Perhaps an illustration will clarify these avenues of identification. If you are making a plea for contributions to the cancer fund, and your listeners are themselves cancer victims, your approach will probably be to point out that augmenting the cancer fund may mean direct assistance to the listeners. If the audience is made of those who have relatives or friends who are sufferers, you will probably stress the warmth of helping a loved one. If the audience is made of those who have no connection with anyone afflicted, you may, through a vivid narrative, introduce them to a "typical" cancer victim through whom they can identify with the problem and its solution. *The listener should be made to feel the problem directly or vicariously if action is to be forthcoming.*

An examination of some of the basic needs and wants lying behind human actions may suggest ways in which you can get the audience to identify with your persuasive messages.

1. *Self-preservation.* Safety devices, physical fitness courses, and life-prolonging medications are examples of goods and services that provide a partial answer to our need to stay alive and enjoy physical well-being. Persons using automobile seat belts are typical of those acting out of a desire for self-preservation. Pleas to control population growth may be rooted in our desire to preserve the sources of survival. The familiar tactic of those soliciting support for an increase in military expenditures is to use self-preservation as the appeal: "With the enemy stockpiling nuclear warheads twice as fast as we are, we stand to move into a hot war unless we build up an equivalent deterrent."

   A note of caution: Appeals designed to frighten the listener into compliance tend to be short-lived in their effectiveness unless coupled with more positive motivations. The "one shot" salesman may be effective in using fear appeals the first time around, but he will get few repeat sales.

2. *Sex attraction.* A cursory glance at any magazine, newspaper, billboard, or television advertisement confirms the power of sex attraction as a motive impelling us to buy an astonishingly wide range of goods and services. Purchase of that new car suggests a bevy of glamorous companions. The new electric typewriter conjures fantasies of a happy, and hence glamorous, secretary. The public speaker, however, is well advised to employ this motive more discreetly than the advertiser. Persons in a group would probably be made to feel uncomfortable by an overt appeal to the sex motive while the same appeal appearing in print would not raise an eyebrow. The difference probably lies in our reluctance to acknowledge publicly our susceptibility to this appeal. Therefore, it is preferable to plant a suggestion rather than to openly link your argument with sex attraction.

3. *Acquisition of property.* The appeal to the pocketbook is as popular as the appeal to sex attraction in advertising. Bargain sales, "giant, economy sizes," higher interest rates on savings accounts, and real estate speculation are manifestations of the universal desire of persons to acquire property. The spokesperson for the school bond drive points out that a better educated citizenry will be a more prosperous citizenry, suggesting that money spent now will be returned many times over as a result of a healthier economy. Even Rolls Royce ads have occasionally appealed to our desire to save money—in the long run.

4. *Self-esteem.* Sometimes we will sacrifice personal safety, sublimate sex attraction, and disdain the acquisition of property if it means that our self-esteem can be increased. The desire to be "looked-up-to," to be well regarded by our peers, or our superiors, is a powerful motivating force. It may be manifest in such diverse actions as enrolling in night school, swimming the English Channel, donating a large sum to charity, or indulging in conspicuous consumption. Self-esteem, extended to groups, takes the form of civic pride, the desire to be "first in the nation," to be the alfalfa-baling center of the country, to have the world's finest zoo.

5. *Personal enjoyment.* Our love of good food and drink, of comfortable accommodations, of labor-saving devices, of all the so-called "good things in life" becomes a dominant motive once our basic needs for food, clothing, and shelter have been satisfied. We do not buy sugar for its life-sustaining qualities but for its power to bring pleasure to our taste buds. We do not buy a hundred thousand dollar home just to keep out the elements but to satisfy our love of the "nicer things." Trailers, campers, power boats, works of art, and video-tape recorders are acquired primarily to satisfy our need for personal enjoyment.

6. *Constructiveness.* The speaker enlists support for a community cleanup campaign by appealing to the civic club's collective desire for constructive projects. The weekend mason building a concrete-block retaining wall, the mother making dresses for her daughters, the retired captain fashioning a brigantine from toothpicks, cloth, and pasteboard exemplify the human desire to be constructive, creative, inventive.

7. *Destructiveness*. We are also motivated by an urge to destroy that which is felt to be detrimental to self, to family, to society. So we are urged to "stamp out crime," conquer disease, rid the nation of poverty, fight pollution and break down the barriers of race, creed, and color. In short, we are asked to put our destructive instincts to constructive use.

8. *Curiosity*. We undertake many things not simply for tangible benefit, but to satisfy our sense of curiosity. We flock to the balloon-launching, patronize the wax museum, buy the paperback book with the enticing cover, or try a "new taste sensation" because we find the unusual and the novel so alluring.

9. *Imitation*. The desire to "be just like" a person we admire may prompt us to buy the breakfast food recommended by the Olympic gold medalist, to acquire the same kind of color television as our neighbor, to vote for the political candidate recommended by our favorite movie actor. The speaker must be cautious, however, in appealing to imitative instincts. Pains should be taken to discover whether or not the model is really admired by the listener. If the model is envied instead, the listener may go to great lengths to avoid imitation.

10. *Altruism*. We like to think that some of our actions are not selfishly motivated. We make anonymous donations to charity, we send CARE packages abroad, we volunteer to read to the blind.

The speaker should consider using as many appropriate appeals as possible, for not all members of an audience are motivated by the same appeal. Needs and wants differ from one individual to another. Furthermore, most of us are occasionally impelled by motives we would rather not admit; so we appreciate the speaker who gives us a "legitimate" motive for doing what we already want to do. Our propensity to rationalize has long been recognized by persuaders on and off the platform.

Though we have discussed the preceding ten motive appeals as if they were separate entities, they are, in reality, seldom as simple or fixed as we have, for explanatory purposes, suggested. Human beings are complicated creatures and not subject to simple stimulus-response relationships.

Most human behavior is motivated not by a single act, but by a large complex of behavior patterns. For example, most of our actions are related to our past experiences, our emotional tendencies of fighting, fleeing, and pairing, our biological needs, our psychological needs (such as security, recognition, affection, and new experiences), our personal goals and beliefs, and, most of all, our self-concept. It should be obvious, therefore, to the trained speaker that the listener must not be viewed as a simple responding organism but as a highly intricate individual.

Before leaving the area of psychological influences that may be made operative in persuasion, we will examine two other phenomena: (1) our need for consistency, and (2) our susceptibility to suggestion.

1. *Our need for consistency*. Theories of attitude change advanced by such men as Fritz Heider with his "balance" theory, Leon Festinger with his theory of "cognitive dissonance," and Charles Osgood and Percy Tannenbaum with

their "congruity" theory are all concerned essentially with our apparent need to maintain consistency within our beliefs, attitudes, and knowledge—"cognitions." If something acts to introduce an element of inconsistency (imbalance, incongruity, or dissonance), according to these theories, we make adjustments necessary to restore a state of consistency.

For example, if we believe that lawyers are not to be trusted and then we are told that one of our trusted childhood friends has become a lawyer, an element of inconsistency has been introduced into our cognitions. Perhaps we will resolve this inconsistency by changing our belief about lawyers or our attitude toward them. Thus, our unfavorable predisposition toward lawyers may be transformed into a neutral or (conceivably) favorable disposition. Our belief that all lawyers are untrustworthy may be transformed into the belief that most, or some, or a few of them are untrustworthy. We might resolve the inconsistency by rationalizing that our old friend does not really fit into our concept of "lawyer," and thus our old beliefs and attitudes are allowed to remain intact. Or we might resolve it by refusing to believe the news that he has become a lawyer. We might say to our informant, "You're mistaken," or "My friend was kidding you when he told you he'd become a lawyer," or "You're lying!" Or, conceivably, we might start disliking our old friend if our beliefs and attitudes about lawyers as a class are deeply entrenched.

The application of the consistency principle to persuasion can readily be seen in selling. Much selling is rooted in the introduction of a dissonant note to the prospective buyer. Let us say that Charlie is happy with the set of tires on his car because he believes them to be safe. Into this picture of contentment intrudes the salesperson who raises serious questions about the durability of the tires. Charlie's cognitions are thus thrown out of balance. The salesperson has the answer that will restore the balance (or, at least hopes to).

Sometimes the job of the persuader is to help the listener live with an existing inconsistency by offering a means of reducing its intensity or rationalizing its existence. Wartime propaganda furnishes an example. The people of a peace-loving nation are besieged with a sense of guilt at becoming involved in a war. They are offered the palliatives, "This is the war to end all wars," or "We must not desert the cause for which so many of our people have died," or "We must fight so that our children can live in peace," or "If we don't stop them here, we'll have to stop them somewhere else." In these instances the persuaders have attempted to offset the severity of the listener's cognitive dissonance—"I don't believe in war, but here I am supporting a war"—by reminding the listeners of other beliefs or attitudes they hold that are consistent with supporting the war—"I believe in safeguarding our children," or "I believe in honoring our dead," or "I believe that the achievement of peace is worth any price," or "A stitch in time saves nine."

Our apparent need to maintain consistency offers a wellspring of opportunities for the person who would alter our beliefs, attitudes, and behavior.

2. *Our susceptibility to suggestion.* We are all familiar with the chain reaction set off by the first person in a group to yawn. We recall the delight of "conning" our elders into looking upward at an imaginary object. We have experienced the magnetic pull toward the carnival barker as we see a small crowd gathering. And the sight of a child carrying a box of popcorn stirs our desire for the same treat. The power of *suggestion* is operative in all of these cases.

Suggestion is the arousal of a response by indirect means. It may operate through channels external to the message, such as the decor of the surroundings, flags, paintings, posters, giant photographs, acts of ritual, music, and prominently displayed collection plates or cannisters. These factors may operate to condition the listener to respond positively to the speaker's message.

Suggestion operates as well through your appearance, your voice and your manner on the platform. If you appear to be confident (but not arrogant), you tend to inspire confidence in what you have to say. If you *seem* to lack assurance (whether you actually do or not), the listener tends to be wary of your message. If your posture is slouchy, your ideas, by association, may seem superficial or your thinking sloppy.

Suggestion operates through your message. If you stress positive ideas, if you avoid mentioning ideas contrary to your position, if you keep "personalities" out of controversy, you condition the audience to respond favorably to your point of view (or at least you condition them against a negative response).

Further ramifications of suggestion will be apparent in our discussion of the next means of persuasion.

III. Manifesting Personal Credibility

"What you are stands over you the while, and thunders so that I cannot hear what you say to the contrary." Emerson's statement epitomizes the impact of the speaker's *ethos* upon the listener's reception of the message. The way the audience perceives the speaker, as well as the way it perceives the message, determines the nature of its response.

Why do you take your television set to a certain shop for repairs? If you know something of the intricacies of electronics, your selection may rest on logical grounds. But if you are like many of us, who are naive about electronics, you may have chosen that repair shop because *something about* the technician inspired confidence.

Speakers on two separate occasions attempt to convince you that a right-to-work law in your state should be repealed. Both use essentially the same arguments and the same evidence. But you want to agree with one of the speakers, while the other speaker cannot manage to budge your convictions. What is the difference? *Something about* the former speaker inspired believability.

What are the constituents of personal credibility? What are the clues we as listeners subconsciously look for in speakers? The following list, by no means exhaustive, suggests several facets of speaker behavior to which audiences respond favorably.

1. *Intelligence.* The extent to which a speaker seems to have mastery of the subject matter is a determinant of our response. If the speaker marshalls an impressive amount of evidence, shows insight into all aspects of the question, uses reasoning that meets the tests of logical validity, and displays "common sense," the speaker's believability is enhanced.

2. *Poise.* The speaker who seems to be in command of himself inspires confidence. President Kennedy inspired confidence in his answers to hostile questions because he never appeared to become unsettled by the hostility.

3. *Modesty.* This trait should not be confused with self-effacement or "false" modesty. In the sense in which we use it here, it suggests the absence of self-congratulation in any form. Genuinely great people do not have to tell others of their greatness. Speakers who take themselves too seriously may only inspire contempt.

4. *Moderation.* We tend to be wary of those who indulge in overstatement, in personal abuse, in unseemly emotional displays. Moderation is usually equated with reasonableness.

5. *Tact.* Closely associated with moderation is tact. It is the ability to deal with others without giving offense. In application to persuasion, it means such things as disagreeing without being disagreeable, admonishing without scolding, enlightening without insulting the audience's intelligence.

6. *Friendliness.* Goodwill is contagious. The speaker who shows a good disposition toward the listeners, even though there may be matters on which they disagree, clears one of the obstacles to persuasion. It is well to remember, however, that a mere *pose* of friendliness can have extremely adverse effects, if the audience detects it as a pose.

7. *Sincerity.* The used-car salesperson tells the customer, "I'd like to sell you this car because, quite frankly, I stand to earn a good commission. Furthermore, you stand to get a good car in the process." The salesperson's candid disclosure of the real motives may well have a disarming effect upon the customer because most of us place credence in the remarks of those we regard as sincere and open in their dealings with others. Of all the traits of character, sincerity may be the most important to persuasion.

8. *Genuine concern for the listener's welfare.* The speaker who seems motivated by something more than personal gain, who shows a genuine concern for us as listeners, will more readily receive our confidence than the speaker we suspect of selfish motives. Here again, the concern should be *sincere.*

These, then, are several of the marks of personal credibility. A word of caution is in order. Speakers who wish to show themselves worthy of respect and emulation must not, in the process, place themselves beyond the possibility of emulation.

Organizing the
Persuasive
Speech

Every persuasive situation has unique demands. The organization of one persuasive speech may radically differ from that of another. One may be organized as if it were an informational speech while another may be as obviously manipulative as a television commercial. We simply cannot say to you, here is *the* way to organize a persuasive speech. What we shall attempt to do instead is suggest some of the more popular organizational strategies. Your good judgment will tell you if a given strategy is applicable to the persuasive situation you are facing.

As we indicated in chapter 6, most speeches do have one structural characteristic in common—they are divided into three parts. Let us explore briefly the principal functions of the introduction, the body, and the conclusion of the persuasive speech.

The basic functions of the introduction to any speech are getting attention and preparing the audience for what is to follow. In the persuasive speech these two functions have to be accomplished in a way that creates a climate of acceptance. It is usually a good policy for the speaker to refrain from assertiveness in the early stages of a persuasive speech because such behavior may generate suspicion and hostility. A spirit of inquiry is much less likely to erect barriers. If the speaker decides to announce the core statement in the introduction, he or she should consider putting it into the form of a question. Compare these two ways of orienting your audience to the nature of your talk:

1. Today I would like to discuss with you the question, "Are prisons justified in a modern society?"

2. Today I will attempt to demonstrate that prisons are not justified in a modern society.

The body of the persuasive speech contains the defense of the persuasive proposition or core statement. For example, if you are defending a proposition of policy, you will probably offer arguments that show the need for a policy and demonstrate the capacity of your policy to satisfy that need. If you are defending a proposition of fact or value, you will probably offer criteria for measuring the truth of the fact or value judgment in question and then apply those criteria. In the next segment of this chapter we shall discuss in much greater detail some of the possibilities for designing the body of the speech.

The conclusion to the persuasive speech should place the audience in the state of mind most conducive to the accomplishment of the speaker's purpose. For example, if your purpose is to actuate, the audience should be ready to act. If your purpose is to convince, the audience should be ready to assent.

With these general considerations before us, let us turn now to some specific strategies of design.

1. *Organizational strategies for propositions of policy.* In chapter 6 we discussed two organizational patterns that can be used when urging adoption of a policy, the Problem-Solution Order and the Motivated Sequence.
    a. *The Problem-Solution Order.* This pattern is based upon a tripartite division of the body of the speech. After an introduction designed to gain attention and orient the listener, the speaker moves into the body of the speech where (1) the problem area is presented, (2) the solution to the

problem is explained, and (3) the solution is defended. The speech concludes with a call for appropriate belief or action. An example of proposition of policy organized around the Problem-Solution Order follows:

Introduction

I. The six-car pile-up at Grand and Main last Tuesday underscores the existence of a long-standing problem in that area.

Body

I. The intersection of Grand and Main is a traffic nightmare.
  A. It is the scene of numerous collisions. (support)
  B. It is a bottleneck during morning and afternoon rush hours. (support)
II. The cause of this problem is the lack of a left-turn traffic light at the intersection.
  A. Cars attempting left turns from Grand onto westbound Main are targets of cars southbound on Grand.
  B. Cars waiting to turn left produce a back-up of homebound traffic on Grand.

Core Statement: A left-turn traffic light should be installed at the intersection of Grand and Main.

III. A left-turn traffic light would correct the existing problem.
  A. It would minimize collisions. (support)
  B. It would speed northbound traffic on Grand. (support)
IV. A left-turn traffic light would be practical to install.
  A. It would be practical from an engineering standpoint. (support)
  B. It would be practical from a financial standpoint. (support)
V. A left-turn traffic light would not introduce disadvantages.
  A. It would not introduce hazards. (support)
  B. It would not be aesthetically unpleasing. (support)
VI. A left-turn traffic light is the best solution to the problem.
  A. It would be less costly than an overpass. (support)
  B. It would be more convenient than re-routing northbound traffic onto Cisco Avenue.

Conclusion

I. You can help this proposal become a reality by signing the petition I am about to circulate.

b. *The Motivated Sequence.* This organizational strategy is a variant of the Problem-Solution order. As its name suggests, the Motivated Sequence has a psychological orientation. It consists of five steps taken in this order: Attention, Need, Satisfaction, Visualization, and Action. Attention must be the speaker's first concern. Unless the listeners are made to focus their attention on the speaker, all else is to no avail. Need involves the introduction of an element of dissonance. The listeners must be made aware of the existence of a problem that affects them in some way. Satisfaction is that segment of the speech in which the solution to the problem is explained and defended. Visualization projects the listeners into the future where they are made to picture the solution in operation, especially as the solution concerns the listeners personally. Action calls upon the listeners to implement the solution. Here is an example of the Motivated Sequence in skeletal form:

Attention

Fifteen hundred of your fellow citizens are suffering from a form of pollution that cannot be seen, smelled, tasted, or touched.

Need

Statement of Problem: The noise level at the assembly plant is dangerous to the workers.

I. The one hundred fifteen decibel noise level is thirty decibels higher than the maximum level set by the Industrial Safety Commission.
II. It can cause hearing loss, cardiovascular problems, partial loss of vision, and mental disturbance.
III. Many of your neighbors are in the affected work force.

Satisfaction

Statement of Solution: Acoustic shielding of the metal presses would reduce the noise to a safe level.

Core Statement: Acoustic shielding of metal presses should be implemented in our plant.

I. Acoustic shielding is feasible.
II. Acoustic shielding is advantageous.
III. Acoustic shielding is the best solution to the problem.

Visualization

Many of your neighbors will suffer needlessly if this problem is not corrected. If acoustic shielding is provided, those same neighbors will be healthier, more productive, and happier workers.

Action

Join me in writing to Don George, General Manager, Ajax Motors.

2. *Organizational strategies for propositions of fact and value.* In chapter 6 we discussed two patterns commonly employed in the development of propositions of fact and value, the Deductive Order and the Inductive Order.

a. *Deductive Order.* This mode of organization involves disclosure of the proposition prior to the presentation of materials supporting the proposition. For example, if a speaker wished the audience to agree with the proposition, "Magum X is better heating fuel for our clubhouse than Sagum Y," the speech might be organized in this order:

Introduction

I. By the end of this month we have to make a decision about heating fuel for our clubhouse.
II. There are two alternatives available to us, Magum X and Sagum Y.

Core Statement: Magum X is superior to Sagum Y.

I. Magum X is cleaner.
II. Magum X is cheaper.
III. Magum X is safer.

Conclusion

I hope you will give careful consideration to Magum X.

      b. *Inductive Order.* When using this mode of organization, the speaker withholds disclosure of the proposition until *after* the presentation of materials supporting the proposition. Using the same proposition, "Magum X is superior to Sagum Y," the Inductive Order of presentation might appear this way.

Introduction

I. By the end of this month we have to make a decision about heating fuel for our clubhouse.

Body

I. The heating fuel we choose should have these qualities:
    A. It should be clean.
    B. It should be cheap.
    C. It should be safe.
II. We have two fuels from which to choose, Magum X and Sagum Y.
III. Magum X is cleaner, cheaper, and safer.

Core Statement: Magum X is superior to Sagum Y.

Conclusion

I hope you will give careful consideration to Magum X.

    When choosing between Deductive Order and Inductive Order the speaker should be guided by knowledge of the audience's predispositions. If the speaker feels the direct approach exemplified by Deductive Order would make the audience defensive, then Inductive Order should be chosen. There are occasions when the direct approach is to be preferred. For example, if two speakers are debating a proposition of fact or value, the audience might view a late disclosure of position as ridiculous.

    3. *Further consideration of idea placement.* Behavioral scientists have attempted to answer the persistent questions of organizational strategy. Of particular interest to students of persuasion are their *tentative* answers to the following questions:

        Does an argument exert a more lasting influence if it is heard first or heard last in a series of arguments? If the audience is familiar with the issue or if it is involved in the controversy, it is influenced more by the argument heard first. If the audience is disinterested or if it is relatively uninformed about the issue prior to hearing the arguments, it will be influenced more by the argument heard last.

When both sides of a controversy are presented in succession, will the side presented first or the side presented last be in the more advantageous position? Some studies have concluded that the side presented first has the "natural" advantage. Other studies, however, were inconclusive.

Are attempts to persuade helped or hindered when "the other side" is presented as well as the speaker's own side? If listeners are initially opposed to the speaker's position, the strategem exerts a persuasive effect. The same is true if listeners are well educated. Less educated listeners, however, are moved more rapidly by a one-sided presentation.

Is it more effective to imply the conclusion one wishes the audience to accept or to state it explicitly? Results indicate that an explicit statement exerts a more persuasive effect upon the majority of listeners.

Remember that the foregoing answers are tentative. Many variables operate in any communication situation; it is virtually impossible to design an experiment that will take them all into account.

One final opinion concerning the overall structure of the persuasive message: Jesse Delia, writing in the *Quarterly Journal of Speech*, visualizes a persuasive structure "beginning with arguments highly congruent with the existing predispositions [of the audience] and gradually moving through a series of accepted linkages to the persuader's recommended opinion or course of action."

Expectations

If a speaker commands all pertinent information about the listeners, subject, and occasion, what are the chances of persuading? They will probably be good—if the speaker remembers that beliefs and attitudes are not apt to change suddenly and dramatically and that many attempts may have to be made before signs of change become evident; if realistic goals are set for each encounter with the listeners; if intelligence, patience, and persistence are exercised; and if the speaker has a little luck as well.

Summary

Persuasion is the process of inducing willing changes in the listener's beliefs, attitudes, and behavior. Successful persuasion rests upon a thorough knowledge of the audience and its attitudes toward the speech topic, the speech purpose, and the speaker. The objects of change are the listener's learned predispositions, convictions, and manifest behavior—particularly with respect to issues of policy, fact, and value. The speaker's position should rest upon a knowledge of the audience's thinking about the subject. The means of persuasion, according to rhetorical tradition, lies in logical appeals, psychological appeals, and the listener's perception of the speaker's personal credibility. The constituents of logical persuasion are evidence and reasoning. Evidence should be derived from an authoritative source, fairly presented, recent, and capable of corroboration. Reasoning takes four forms, according to the traditional view. Deductive reasoning moves from the general rule or axiom to the specific case at hand. Inductive reasoning proceeds from particular cases to a generalization about all cases.

Reasoning from analogy is based on the supposition that because two things are alike in certain known respects, they will also be alike in the point at issue. Causal reasoning may appear in at least three forms—cause-to-effect, effect-to-cause, or effect-to-effect.

Persuasion through psychological appeals traditionally is thought to involve the use of motivation and suggestion. The needs and wants to which the speaker may link the message include self-preservation, sex attraction, acquisition of property, self-esteem, personal enjoyment, constructiveness, curiosity, imitation, and altruism. Suggestion is the arousal of a response by indirect means. It may operate through channels external to the speaker, through the speaker's delivery, and through the verbal message.

Persuasion through personal credibility is possible when the speaker manifests poise, modesty, moderation, tact, friendliness, sincerity, and genuine concern for the listener's welfare—provided the listener perceives these factors.

While the persuasive speech may be organized in a variety of ways, certain methods seem to enjoy high popularity. The Problem-Solution Order and the Motivated Sequence are particularly appropriate for developing propositions of policy. Deductive Order and Inductive Order are among patterns well suited to develop propositions of fact and value.

Suggested Readings

Auer, J. Jeffery. "The Persuasive Speaker and His Audience." *The Rhetoric of Our Times*. Edited by J. Jeffery Auer, pp. 255–75. New York: Appleton-Century-Crofts, 1969.

Bryant, Donald C., and Wallace, Karl R. *Fundamentals of Public Speaking*. 4th ed. New York: Appleton-Century-Crofts, 1969. Chapters 16–21.

Cronkhite, Gary. *Persuasion*. Indianapolis: Bobbs-Merrill, 1969.

Fishbein, Martin. "A Consideration of Beliefs, Attitudes, and Their Relationships." *Current Studies in Social Psychology*. Edited by Ivan D. Steiner and Martin Fishbein. New York: Holt, Rinehart and Winston, 1965.

Fisher, Walter R. "A Motive View of Communication." *Quarterly Journal of Speech* 56 (April 1970): 140–48.

Hovland, Carl I.; Janis, Irving L.; and Kelley, Harold H. *Communication and Persuasion*. New Haven: Yale University Press, 1953. Chapter 3.

Monroe, Alan H.; Ehninger, Douglas; Gronbeck, Bruce E. *Principles and Types of Speech Communication*. 8th ed. Glenview, IL: Scott, Foresman, 1978. Chapters 18, 19.

Scheidel, Thomas M. *Persuasive Speaking*. Glenview, IL: Scott, Foresman, 1967.

Sherif, Muzafer; Sherif, Carolyn W.; and Nebergall, Roger E. *Attitude and Attitude Change*. Philadelphia: W.B. Saunders, 1965.

Smith, Donald K. *Man Speaking*. New York: Dodd, Mead, 1969. Chapter 7.

Changing Environments

Part 4

Special Occasions
The Unique Communication Situation

A good speaker is one who rises to the occasion and promptly sits down.

O.A. Battista

Informing and persuading are the chief purposes behind most messages designed for public or private occasions. We have assumed that the principles and techniques of informing and persuading remain basically the same regardless of the occasion dictating the message. After all, most occasions call for messages using supporting details or evidence, factors of interest and attention, organization, language, and delivery. There are occasions, however, when the situation demands an extension or combination of the basic elements found in informing and persuading. Knowing that all forms of communication have a great deal in common, the trained and conscientious communicator can quickly adapt skills to many varied situations.

No list or treatment of special occasions could be complete, for in one sense each communication situation and occasion is novel and original. Yet there are some specific occasions we might be in when moving from one environment to another. On these occasions we must remember all of the past speech training while using the items that relate directly to the special occasion.

Students show the most concern about situations calling for an impromptu speech, a speech from manuscript, an entertaining speech, an after-dinner speech, or a speech of introduction. They are also concerned about how to handle questions from the audience after a speech. (And they are interested in learning how to cope with one of the most important communication situations they will ever face, the job interview. The job interview is discussed in Appendix A.)

The Impromptu Speech

There will be occasions when you are called upon to deliver an offhand response to a demand or a request for a "few remarks" on a specific subject. The *impromptu* (or spur-of-the-moment) speech is delivered in just such situations. It is a speech that simply cannot be thoroughly prepared. We see this type of speaking every day. In meetings, at conferences, in classes, and in conversations, we are asked to give our ideas and opinions on countless subjects. Because of the lack of specific preparation, many view impromptu speaking as the most difficult of all speech forms. If you can learn to remain calm when called upon to give a talk, you will discover that the impromptu situation is not nearly as menacing as first anticipated.

There are three different times when you can prepare for the impromptu speech. First, if you are fortunate enough to possess a large storehouse of information, you can usually find something worthwhile to say. A broad background of reading and experience are invaluable in meeting the challenge of impromptu speaking. Second, if you suspect that you might be called upon, you can pay close attention to what is going on at the meeting and what is being said at the platform. By observing closely you may consider what you would say if called upon. Third, you can learn to use the brief period between the time you are called upon and the time you have to utter your first words. Although this period of time may range from a few seconds to a few minutes, it can still be put to good use.

The following suggestions, if practiced, will help you overcome your fears and get on to accomplishing your purpose.

1. Adopt a positive mental attitude toward the impromptu situation. Remember, those who ask you to speak impromptu do not expect you to produce a polished oration on the spot; listener expectations are not as demanding as they would be under different circumstances. They are more concerned with hearing your off-the-cuff observations about the subject than they are about watching a display of speaking skill.

   Consider, also, that when someone asks you to speak on the spur of the moment it is because that person knows you are knowledgeable about the topic. Otherwise, why should your comments be solicited?

2. Listen carefully to the remarks of others. Often you can build upon their remarks when you are called upon to speak. Avoid daydreaming to spare yourself the agony that comes when you are jolted into the present by someone's announcing, "Let's hear what your opinion is." Listening is a part of the preparation for any speech and especially so for the impromptu speech.

3. When called upon to speak, you should first try to formulate a central statement or position on the subject. Perhaps you can agree with a previous speaker's position and add more examples, statistics, or testimony. Or you might disagree with another and build your speech around the reasons for your disagreement. What if you happen to be the first or only speaker? Then perhaps you can design a speech that answers one of these stock questions about the general topic on which you are asked to speak: What is it? Who is connected with it? Where can it be found? When did it come into being? Why should you be concerned with it? How can you cope with it?

   Of course, there are many other questions that could be applied to a given topic, the answers to which could provide the main theme for an impromptu speech. The important thing is to try to confine yourself to one main theme so that your speech will have unity.

4. Select an organizational plan that will let you develop your main point. Here are a few commonly used patterns:
   a. Refer to what has been said by a previous speaker. State your position on the issue. Develop your position by illustration, analogy, or any appropriate form of support.
   b. Tell the audience what you plan to do. Tell them why it is important. Carry out your plan.

c. Start with an illustration. Explain how it clarifies or proves your point.

d. Develop the theme chronologically—such as, past history, present state, future prospects.

e. Develop the theme according to spatial or geographical considerations—such as, impact on Europe, Asia, or Africa.

f. Divide the topic into component parts—such as, economic, social, and political aspects or mental, moral, and physical aspects.

5. Try not to hurry into the main part of your presentation. This will give you valuable time to think of what to say and will help you relax and gain your composure.

6. Do not prolong the conclusion. Too many impromptu speeches are characterized by the conclusion that is apologetic and embarrassed. Why not simply summarize what you have said, restate your position, and sit down?

7. The ability to cope with an impromptu speaking situation can be greatly improved if you are willing to practice. One good method is to read the editorial page of your local newspaper and frame a reaction to each of the editorials or letters to the editor dealing with subjects about which you feel strongly. Valuable, too, are speeches developed around a word or phrase—such as, sexism, integrity in public office, consumerism, or business ethics.

The Manuscript Speech

Reading a written speech is more popular today than ever before. Professional conventions, business meetings, and appearances before government agencies are all occasions when you can benefit from a "polished" speech, a speech where every word is carefully selected for accuracy. Such a speech is the manuscript occasion.

Preparing the Speech

Remember that you are preparing a *speech*, not an essay. The characteristics of good speechmaking and good writing differ. The principles of successful speaking, discussed throughout this book, apply directly to speech manuscript preparation.

Because the occasion that calls for the manuscript speech is special, most speakers are willing to put a great deal of energy into preparing their manuscript. The following sequence, though time consuming, is helpful in preparing the manuscript.

Developing the Outline

Begin by going through many of the same steps we discussed in the section titled "The Organization of Your Ideas" (chapter 1). After questions of purpose, audience analysis, and analysis of occasion are addressed, begin developing the outline. The outline for the manuscript, like the outline for the extemporized speech, should be concerned with matters such as introduction, body, and conclusion.

Writing the First Draft

Once the outline is researched and completed, you are ready to write your first draft of the manuscript. Given the luxury of time in preparation, your speech should have excellent vocabulary and vivid images.

Revising the First Draft	After reading the first draft aloud you will want to make changes. Many sections that would be acceptable in an essay fail to have the effect you want when read aloud. Having a friend listen to an early draft of the speech is also valuable.
Developing the Final Draft	After making the necessary corrections and additions you should now have a well-written and highly polished speech. The manuscript from which you read can be made even more useful if you follow a few simple guidelines: (1) Use stiff paper, (2) write on only one side of the paper, (3) number the pages, (4) type the manuscript using triple spacing, and (5) use short paragraphs—they are easier to locate when you return to the manuscript after establishing and maintaining eye contact.
	Practice using the final draft a number of times. This will enable you to become familiar with the material and will develop dexterity in handling the paper. You might also find it helpful to mark the manuscript where you want to pause or provide special vocal emphasis and variety.
Delivering the Manuscript Speech	In addition to recalling the principles of good delivery discussed in chapter 3, you should also be aware of practices unique to manuscript delivery.

1. Do not try to conceal the manuscript. Many speakers have tried to feign total spontaneity only to discover that such deception works against them. In addition to having trouble locating their places in the speech, they incurred audience displeasure at being deceived.
2. Establish and maintain eye contact. The fact that you have a manuscript should in no way detract from your initiating and maintaining rapport with the audience. Eye contact can be fostered by becoming very familiar with your speech.
3. Concentrate on ideas rather than words. You must keep in mind that it is a speech you are delivering. If you start to read every word and forget the influence of ideas, you will no longer have the unique effect of speech communication.

The Entertaining Speech	All speeches, to some extent, may entertain the listener. Yet there are specific occasions when the objective is not to increase knowledge or change the destiny of civilization, but rather to have the audience relax in a lighthearted mood and in an enjoyable atmosphere. Perhaps you will belong to an organization or club that has occasional meetings of a purely social nature where speeches provide part of the entertainment. Maybe you will be asked to recount an interesting experience you have had, or tell about an unusual person you have met, or perhaps help "roast" a fellow club member. Then again you may be asked to talk on a subject of your own choosing. Whatever the case, a careful audience analysis is one of the most important steps in the preparation of the speech to entertain.

Characteristics of Entertaining	The speech to entertain may be humorous, but all speeches to entertain need not be funny. The one basic requirement for all speeches of *entertainment* is that *they must hold attention and interest in themselves*. The speaker can best accomplish this objective by incorporating into the speech many of the factors of attention and interest discussed in the chapter on informational speaking.

The dominant characteristics of the speech to entertain are as follows: |

1. *The delivery should be lively, enthusiastic, and animated.* If the speech is delivered extemporaneously, a spontaneous and natural effect will be produced.
2. *Stories, illustrations, and humorous anecdotes are liberally used.* The fully developed example is often so vivid it captures and maintains attention. Remember these illustrations should be fresh and original and free from triteness. Furthermore, avoid "canned" illustrations and anecdotes.
3. The speech to entertain, like all speeches, is *well organized and easy to follow, and is normally constructed around a central theme or idea.* The theme should be appropriate to the audience and occasion. In many instances it may deal with a common topic in a different manner—such as, the problems of eating three meals a day while orbiting the earth in a space capsule.
4. *The response sought is immediate and momentary.* The audience may remember some of the information long after the speech, but the speaker's primary concern is the audience's covert or overt behavior *at the time* of the talk.

The Use of Humor	Humor is the most common ingredient of entertaining speeches. It holds our attention and, if used correctly, creates an enjoyable and friendly atmosphere. The problem of what constitutes humor has been discussed for centuries. What makes us laugh? The more common aspects of pleasure and enjoyment will be examined as a means of supplying the speaker with guidelines for the selection and use of humor.
Exaggeration	Take a possible occurrence, make it larger, overstate it, and you have a potentially humorous situation. As long as the exaggeration has a touch of reality, the audience can enjoy its obvious distortion. To describe the successful assembly of a child's toy as though it were a major scientific achievement would be perceived as obvious exaggeration (and if all goes well, as humorous). One of the tactics used by "roasters" is to seize some very minor fault of the "roastee" and make a major crime of it.
Incongruity	In a literal sense, incongruity is present in any situation in which the parts do not fit together. The unusual, the sudden and unexpected twist, and the inconsistency are all potential sources of humor. You have probably heard sportscasts in which the final score of a game involving two little-known schools was used to conclude a "roundup of the major games of the day." To hear the Hueyville-Lukenburg score immediately after the USC-Ohio State score is probably going to startle the listeners (unless they happen to live in Hueyville or Lukenburg).

A meal of caviar and Fritos topped off by rare-vintage champagne and Twinkies is incongruous because of the casual mixing of exotic and ordinary items.

Attacking Authority

We all enjoy seeing the boss, the sergeant, the police officer, or some other figure of authority as the target of a joke. Even mother-in-law jokes are instances of having fun at the expense of someone or something that is normally regarded reverently. In poking fun at others it is always important to use good taste and not offend the audience's morals or standards.

Many other devices lend themselves to humor. For example, *pun, irony, sarcasm,* and *burlesque* can all be effectively used. Yet the greatest source of humor comes from the creative and imaginative work all of us do when we sit and reflect. *Thinking* about what is humorous usually produces some excellent and rewarding examples and situations.

Developing the Speech

A primary consideration in developing the entertaining speech is your knowing the exact makeup of the audience. In addition, your audience analysis should include some information on the occasion. It is important to know if the audience came only to listen to you, to laugh, or if they expect some concrete information to take home. Once these questions have been answered you are ready to determine the central theme, decide upon an introduction, an organizational pattern for the body, and a conclusion.

Introduction

Your opening remarks in the entertaining speech have the task of arousing attention, setting the mood, and establishing the main point. In the speech to entertain you must make it quite clear that you do not plan to develop any profound concepts, for if the audience expects you to "get somewhere," they will be confused as you continue to provide only entertainment. You will find a discussion of some of the methods used in starting the speech to entertain in chapter 6. (The illustration is a very popular opening device in entertaining.)

Body

When choosing your speech plan, or approach, you must keep in mind the nature of the audience, the occasion, and your speaking talent and limitations. There are endless varieties in the organization of the speech to entertain. The topical order or the chronological order are especially appropriate. A review of chapter 6 might be helpful in adapting these two patterns.

The single, long narrative is a popular device in entertaining. As we noted in chapter 5, the narrative, when presented as an illustration, holds attention, makes a point, and is interesting. A good narrative tells a story; for the entertaining speech, the story should be humorous.

You can also use a series of short narratives developed around a central theme. A series illustrating registration problems in college is an example of this approach. In any case, the speech to entertain should not lead in many different directions, but should be built around a central theme. Remember also that interest may be derived from associating your ideas with things that are recent, impending, physically near, familiar, vital, active, unusual, suspenseful, concrete, real, humorous, or conflicting.

Conclusion

The conclusion is usually very brief and continues to carry the general mood. The devices for concluding were discussed in chapter 6 and should be reviewed as a means of determining which technique best applies to the specific communication situation the speaker faces.

Presenting the
Speech to
Entertain

Although delivery was discussed in some detail in chapter 3, some special features of the entertaining speech influence the way it is presented.

The speaker's mental set is vitally important. The speaker must *want* to give the talk and enjoy the experience as well, or the audience will miss the humor and the spirit of the talk. Moods are contagious, and if the speaker is not relaxed and at ease, it will detract from the mood of enjoyment.

Also, the speaker must try to be animated. A lively feeling must be communicated to the audience, and animation contributes to that atmosphere.

**The After-Dinner
Speech**

The after-dinner speech is perhaps the most widely used occasional speech. Many speeches after a meal may be serious. Yet there seems to be a tradition that seeks to establish a relaxed and friendly atmosphere after a meal. In these cases, *the after-dinner speech is a short, genial, and humorous talk*. Note its similarity to the entertaining speech.

There are a few special considerations to keep in mind as you prepare and deliver an after-dinner talk.

1. Having enjoyed a meal and conversation with friends, an audience is normally in a good mood by the time the after-dinner speaker begins. Because this friendly atmosphere prevails, the speaker should be optimistic and good-humored. Pessimism, bitterness, gloom, and denunciation combine poorly with a full stomach. Therefore, the selection of an appropriate topic is essential in after-dinner speaking. This puts an added emphasis on audience analysis. A story or a joke that is funny to one group of individuals may fail to arouse even a smile from another group.
2. The relationship between speaker and audience should be informal in organization, language, and delivery.
3. The after-dinner talk is normally quite brief. Attention spans grow short after a pleasant meal.
4. Material should be interesting and easy to understand. Humor, interesting stories, examples, and unique experiences are at the heart of after-dinner speaking.
5. Most after-dinner speeches are well prepared. The speaker does not have to hesitate or grope for ideas or words. The speaker, however, must be careful not to let this thoroughness impair spontaneity and thus destroy the friendly and casual mood essential to effective after-dinner speaking.

Making Introductions

The *speech of introduction* is a common occasional speech, yet it is often poorly done. Some speakers forget that the introduction links the guest speaker with the audience. It should not be used to demonstrate the introducer's cleverness or "superior knowledge."

The introduction has two main purposes—to acquaint the audience with the guest speaker and to arouse interest in the talk. To see that the speaker and the speech secure a favorable reception, the introducer can follow a few simple rules.

1. *Be brief.* The introducer subordinates his or her own speech for the sake of the main talk. In most instances, thirty seconds to two minutes is the time allotted to the person making the introduction.
2. Make sure that your information concerning the speaker and his or her background and topic *is accurate.* Errors in pronunciation, particularly of the speaker's name or personal data, can cause a great deal of embarrassment to you, the speaker, and the audience. Secure the essential and personal information from the speaker well in advance of your formal introduction.
3. It is often effective to begin the introduction with a brief reference to the nature of the occasion. This may serve as a bond between the speaker and the listeners. Also, there may be occasions when it will be valuable to emphasize the importance of the subject.
4. Once you have established rapport with the audience by humor, reference to occasion, or some other form of motivation, you are ready to give the biographical data necessary to identify the speaker and to make that person sound interesting and authoritative to the audience. In most cases the biography should include (a) the speaker's place of residence, (b) achievements (publications, honors, and awards), (c) background on the topic (professional and educational), (d) relationship to the audience, and (e) the reason this person was selected to deliver the talk.
5. If the occasion allows, hold the speaker's full name and subject until the end. In this way the speaker's name and topic can be presented as a climax.
6. Avoid hackneyed words and phrases. Introductions such as "Our speaker needs no introduction," and "without further ado" are too common.
7. Pay close attention to the speech so that at its close you can refer the ideas and their value to the audience as you thank the speaker.

Answering Questions

Cathleen Bohnsack is demonstrating a portable television camera with an automatic focusing feature to a group of audiovisual specialists at an educator's convention. She is interrupted by a member of the group: "Is it possible to override the automatic focus in case you want to create a special effect by manual focusing?"

Tim Lofton is urging a group of spectators to boycott a chain of retail liquor stores for selling wine produced by a vintner who allegedly refuses to hire union farm workers. As he concludes, one of the spectators asks: "Since when has a boycott ever benefitted the consumer?"

Kjell Linker has just finished a classroom speech on vegetarianism. A number of students call out questions simultaneously. "Doesn't it cost a lot?" "Can you get good vegetables the year round?" "What does the A.M.A. say about a vegetarian diet?"

Fielding questions from the audience is often a routine part of communication encounters. The speaker seeking to instruct will often invite the audience to pose questions whenever appropriate; the speaker attempting to persuade will very likely be questioned or challenged by some listeners; the speaker rousing the curiosity of the audience with unusual subject matter may be bombarded by questions after the address. In fact, except for speeches delivered under circumstances that preclude immediate feedback, such as televised and broadcast messages, almost all speech situations lend themselves to a question-and-answer session. Because the audience's impression of a speaker is based not only upon what happens during the speech but also upon the speaker's prespeech and postspeech behavior, it is important to examine ways in which the question-and-answer session can promote a favorable impression of the speaker.

Characteristics of the Effective Reply

The ideal reply to a question is polite, straightforward, and brief. *Politeness* cannot be overstressed in replying to the questions of another. Every person who asks a question feels it is important. So regardless of how naive, irrelevant, or poorly worded the question might be, always treat the questioner with dignity. If other members of the audience laugh in derision at a poor question, it is wise for the speaker to refrain from joining in that laughter. Show that you respect the questioner's feelings, and you will deserve the goodwill that follows from such a gesture. Even hostile questions should be answered without rancor. You can disagree politely with your questioner, but issues, not personalities, should be the substance of your replies. Moreover, meeting hostility with politeness may serve to disarm the hostile questioner while minimizing that person's influence upon other listeners. Let your answer be logical enough to satisfy a cynic and congenial enough to satisfy a friend.

Straightforwardness is another desirable feature in answering questions. Audiences are usually quick to sense evasiveness; sometimes the favorable impression left by a speech can be negated by a shifty answer to a question asked afterward. If you do not know the answer to a question, it is better to say so than to try to divert the issue elsewhere. Likewise, if you do not wish to answer a question, then say so, adding an explanation for declining. When a question is asked, come directly to grips with it and avoid diversionary tactics.

Brevity should characterize your answers, too—that is, brevity consistent with completeness. Some speakers are guilty of "overkill" in their answers. Not only do they reply to the question asked, they move off the track and answer questions that have not even been asked. If there appear to be a number of questions forthcoming from the audience, brevity is a necessity.

Organizing the Reply

The nature and scope of the question will probably dictate the organizational format most appropriate for your answer. In all instances, however, you should make a practice of repeating the question before beginning your reply. This gives your audience a chance to hear the question again in case it was inaudible when posed. It also lets the questioner know whether you heard the question correctly.

Moreover, the few moments spent in repeating the question may give you valuable time in which to formulate an answer.

Here are some general suggestions for organizing answers to the three principal kinds of questions:

Request for Clarification

1. Refer to the section of your speech requiring clarification.
2. Use the appropriate clarifying devices—such as, definition, restatement, example, illustration, analogy, diagram, or demonstration.
3. Ask the questioner if the point is sufficiently clarified.

For example: "I've just been asked to define the word 'decibel,' which I used earlier in describing the noise level at the assembly plant. A decibel is a unit for measuring the relative loudness of sounds. The faintest audible sound detectable by the human ear is placed at 1 decibel. Then the range runs upward to about 130 decibels. So when I said that the noise next to the metal press was about 115 decibels, I meant it was really loud. Does that explain it clearly enough?"

Request for More Information

1. Refer to the point on which you have been requested to offer further information.
2. Relate the information using an appropriate sequence—such as, chronological, spatial, topical, or logical order.
3. Ask the questioner if you have answered the request sufficiently.

For example: "Bill asked where the nuclear generating plant is located in relation to Camp Pendleton. Bill, since Camp Pendleton runs for a number of miles along the coast, I'll use the main gate as a reference point. As you know, the main gate is located at the northeast edge of Oceanside. Well, the plant is approximately fifteen miles northwest of that gate, right on the oceanfront. Can you see that now?"

Challenge to Your Position

1. Refer to the point that has been challenged.
2. State the nature of the challenge.
3. Answer the challenge by offering additional evidence in support of your position and by showing the fallacious character of the questioner's objections.

For example: "The gentleman in the back row has challenged the source of my data on the number of missiles deployed along the coastline of our state. If he questions the source I cited, let me refer him to a statement made by Senator Neeland that was quoted in the most recent issue of *U.S. News and World Report*. I think he'll find the identical figure cited by the senator, who is a member of the Senate Armed Services Committee."

Summary

In this chapter we dealt with special communication situations. Although all communication is in a sense special, and therefore uses similarities in form and style, certain situations demand a different degree of proficiency if the speaker is to accomplish a given purpose. The situations dealt with were those calling for impromptu speeches, manuscript speeches, entertaining speeches, after-dinner speeches, speeches of introduction, and question-and-answer sessions.

The impromptu speech is given on the "spur-of-the-moment" or when the speaker has little time to prepare. To keep from being completely overwhelmed, the speaker can call forth a few simple techniques; such as, remembering what was said just before being asked to speak, thinking about past reading and speaking experiences, or working out a suitable organizational pattern.

The manuscript speech is unique in offering the speaker an opportunity to write out the speech in detail before delivering it. In preparing this type of speech it is important to remember that it is a speech and not an essay. Once an outline is completed, the speaker is in a position to start the manuscript. Rewriting is always beneficial. The final draft should be highly refined and polished. In presenting the speech, the essentials of good delivery must be kept in mind. Eye contact, vocal variety, and gestures are as important to good manuscript speaking as they are to good extemporaneous speaking.

The major purpose of the speech to entertain is to have the listeners enjoy themselves. The speaker, by employing the concepts of attention and interest, has the audience relax in an enjoyable atmosphere. Humor is often a trademark of entertaining. This means that the successful speaker must learn to use the humorous illustration, exaggeration, incongruity, attacking of authority, and other such devices.

The after-dinner speech is similar to the speech to entertain. Here again the speaker strives for a lighthearted and congenial atmosphere. This speech is usually brief and "fun to listen to."

The main task of the speech of introduction is to create a rapport between speaker, subject, and audience. By stimulating interest in both the speaker and topic, you will create a friendly climate and one in which the audience is interested in hearing what the guest speaker has to say.

The question-and-answer session is a common part of communication encounters. Politeness, straightforwardness, and brevity are desirable qualities in replying to questions. The nature and specificity of the question as well as the perceived motive of the questioner will affect the speaker's strategy of reply.

Suggested Readings

Barrett, Harold. *Practical Methods in Speech*. 2d ed. New York: Holt, Rinehart and Winston, 1968. Chapter 13.

Brooks, William D. *Speech Communication*. 3d ed. Dubuque, IA: Wm. C. Brown Company Publishers, 1978. Chapter 8.

Huston, Alfred D.; Sandberg, Robert A.; and Mills, Jack. *Effective Speaking in Business*. New York: Prentice-Hall, 1955. Chapter 10.

Reid, Loren. *Speaking Well*. 3d ed. New York: McGraw-Hill, 1977. Chapter 4.

Discussion
Group Communication

Light is the task where
many share the toil.
                 Homer

Willingly or unwillingly, we spend the bulk of our waking hours communicating. And, as you have undoubtedly realized by now, this book's chief concern is the effectiveness of those communications. We now continue this pursuit with the topic of improving communication within the small group.

Many communication situations call for a *sharing* of ideas and a willingness to "talk things over." Whether it be in business, at school, at church, or at social functions, we are constantly having to get together with other individuals to discuss items of business or to solve mutual problems. When you engage in a situation that brings you face-to-face with others, you should be aware of the influence of communication upon the outcome of the meeting. Being able to communicate effectively on these occasions can make the difference between an "aimless bull session" or productive communication.

Interacting as members of a group brings us a variety of personal and collective rewards. We all know the feelings of cohesiveness and solidarity associated with being part of a successful group experience. In fact, the concept of group thinking is fundamental to the democratic process. In a democratic society it is only natural that decisions should be made after considerable deliberation and discussion. We pride ourselves on being fair—that various points of view are presented and considered before a judgment is given or a decision rendered. We maintain, as part of our democratic philosophy, that each person counts and has the right and the responsibility to contribute to the resolution of both individual and public problems. Group discussion affords an opportunity to conduct our own social, political, and vocational affairs in a democratic manner using maximum participation of other trained and interested citizens. *Discussion is the systematic and objective sharing of ideas and information by two or more persons who work together in an effort to solve a problem or to gain a better understanding of a problem.*

The uses of discussion are obvious when we reflect on the occasions and situations when we are in the position of sharing ideas and information with others. In education, for example, many classes function by means of the discussion process. In countless situations, by either chance or design, we meet with others to resolve problems, share feelings, or gather information. Reflect for a moment on the many uses of group communication within a major organization. Members of that organization would not only solve problems via the discussion method, but they might also make important policy decisions, generate and share information, and use discussion as a training tool. All of us face situations involving group communication and this chapter seeks to make those situations more creative and constructive.

Speech Communication and Group Communication

Before embarking on a detailed analysis of group communication it will be valuable to explain briefly the relationship between speech communication and group communication. We would not, for example, want to imply that what has transpired to this point has not prepared us for interaction within the small group. In fact, quite the opposite is true. This entire book applies to the small group setting, for what each of us does as discussants is simply to make various adaptations to those speech communication principles advanced in other chapters. Although the units of speech presented by any given discussant might, by necessity, be shorter and more fragmented than in solitary public speaking, much of what is being done still uses the skills, principles, and techniques of oral communication. On the platform, or sitting with others in a group, one must pay attention to such matters as audience adaptation, feedback, preparation and research, having concrete ideas and supporting them in an organized manner, and language usage. Now we will discuss how speech communication principles can be applied to those communication situations in which speaking time is shared and exchanged, rather than formally limited to one person for a definite, uninterrupted period of time.

Types of Group Discussion

Public discussion may be classified into various types and forms. These classifications are not hard and fast, for in many instances one form may overlap another.

1. *Lecture-forum.* This is the simplest form of public group discussion. The speaker of the evening, the lecturer, addresses the audience. After the speech the lecturer is expected to answer questions directed by members of the audience. The audience may contribute opinions of their own during this period. Hence, we have discussion—ideas are being exchanged. Normally a chairperson introduces the speaker and guides the discussion period.
2. *Symposium.* In the symposium each of several speakers, generally two to five, delivers a talk. These speeches center around one topic, theme, or issue. Each speaker may explain the position and thoughts on the subject as a whole, or perhaps may be limited to a specific phase of the subject. Frequently the audience is allowed the privilege of asking questions at the conclusion of all of the talks.
3. *Panel.* During the last few years the panel has become a very popular method of group discussion. A panel is a discussion within a discussion. In this arrangement a limited number of persons, usually four to seven, sit before the audience and discuss a given topic. There are no planned and set speeches; all the remarks are short and spontaneous. When the panel finishes its discussion, questions from the floor are answered by the panel members.

4. *Informal group discussion (round table)*. This is the most common of all the forms of discussion. It is frequently a nonaudience discussion and tends to be more informal than the other methods. It consists of a small group seated around a table. In this setting they exchange their views and their information in a spontaneous and free manner. The stimulus-response pattern is constantly changing as attention is directed from one person to another. This pattern is well suited for either decision-making or information-sharing and is the discussion situation in which we most often find ourselves.

The four types of discussion mentioned above represent what we call *public discussion*. They are often held before audiences and are usually somewhat formal. We also engage in many discussions that take a more common and less formal procedure. We can call these *private discussions*. These may have overlapping purposes, but as a means of classification we will list two of the most common types.

1. *Therapy groups*. This form of group discussion has many different names—encounter group, sensitivity session, T-group training. These are groups composed of persons who have come together to study themselves and group interaction. No group solution is sought, but rather the aim is to learn about such questions as, "How do I function in groups?" (group interaction), "How do I communicate?" and "What do others think of my communication behavior?" There are times when many of these same questions should be asked in other types of groups.
2. *Problem-solving groups*. Problem-solving groups can take many forms. The form may be a committee, a conference, or simply a group of individuals who share a common problem and join together as a means of solving their problem. This is by far the most common of all group discussions.

   Because of the widespread nature of problem-solving groups, we shall make this group activity the focus of this chapter.

Characteristics of Successful Problem-Solving Groups

Although problem-solving groups share many common features with other groups, they are characterized by several distinguishing features.

1. *Cooperation is stressed in group discussion*. Cooperation and not competition are the attributes of good problem-solving discussions. The rationale for cooperation is built into the very fiber of problem-solving discussion. The members have gathered together because they share a common concern, and it is this concern that is manifest in a spirit of cooperation.
2. *Analysis and investigation are part of the discussion process*. The various members of the group have joined together because they are vexed by the same problem. To find the best answer to that problem the members must be willing to analyze and investigate the issues involved. The person who already has all the answers does not belong in the group, for it is the analytic and systematic search for those answers that gives the problem-solving group its life.

3. *Group discussion is objective.* Members of the group should be willing to examine all sides of issues and questions. They should be open-minded and not fearful of giving all points of view a fair and just hearing.

4. *Discussion is a method of reflective thinking.* Rather than engaging in random and aimless behavior, the problem-solving group follows a thought process that is purposeful, systematic, and organized. The most common pattern of group reflective thinking is one developed from the phases of reflective thought described by the American educator and philosopher John Dewey. These phases, which will be discussed later in the chapter, consist of (1) defining and limiting the problem, (2) analyzing evidence for causes and effects of the problem, (3) proposing solutions for the problems, (4) evaluating and analyzing *all* solutions, and (5) deciding upon ways to put the chosen solution into operation.

5. *Discussion groups attempt to strike a balance between the emotional and the rational.* This balancing of feelings with logical arguments is essential if the group is working toward the resolution of real-life problems. Imagine how difficult it would be to talk about an emotional problem, such as abortion laws, without having personal feelings fusing with rational research. This blending is one of the essential components of successful problem solving.

6. *Sincere skepticism is encouraged.* Although the group strives for a high degree of solidarity, individuals should feel free to question and criticize ideas they believe are weak or insubstantial. A group of individuals that spends all their time simply nodding heads in agreement ends with rather shallow conclusions. Therefore, phrases such as "I'm not sure that is a very good plan," or "Are you certain of that?" should be encouraged by all members.

7. *Discussion groups are in touch with their immediate needs.* Successful groups can detect, and respond to, mood shifts, fatigue, and tension. Being able to take the necessary measures to control these rhythms demands that each member be aware of what is going on within the group.

8. *All members are aware of the wide range of roles that must be performed.* A group does not move toward its goal by centrifugal force; the members supply the energy that enables things to happen. This energy reflects itself through various group roles. These roles range from leadership duties to asking questions. What is important is that these roles be manifest to all members and the acting out of these roles diffused throughout the group. For example, everyone must know and be willing to perform the role of arbitrator if interpersonal conflicts are to be resolved.

9. *Intergroup communication channels are informal and open.* The members must feel free to say what they want. If, for any reason, participants become reluctant to take part, the entire group suffers. This freedom to communicate is stimulated and nurtured when the group climate is informal.

10. *Individual needs are integrated with group goals.* Group productivity and member satisfaction is hampered if the group fails to strike a balance between its members' personal needs and the overall goal of the group. We

all know from personal experience that our enthusiasm is diminished when we are in groups that do not offer us some positive motivation. What we strive for in any group experience is an atmosphere that enables us to accomplish personal aims and desires at the same time we are working with others to solve a mutual problem.

11. *Group cohesion is an important element in successful problem-solving groups.* Although group cohesion may appear to be only an extension of cooperation, it is much more complicated than simply trying to cooperate. Cohesion is the special ingredient that molds a group of individuals together into a unit. It tends to be contagious, and once trust is established, cohesiveness permeates all of the group's activities. This bond, which is so very important to the group, is encouraged when members share a common concern. Reflect on your own motivations in a group, and you will surely realize that you feel enthusiastic when you believe that other persons share your concerns and your involvement. It is on those occasions when cohesiveness is strongest, that openness and high productivity characterize the group.

12. *Group norms are clearly identified.* Each group, as communication patterns evolve, establishes various rules of conduct. These rules (or norms) help members decide how they should behave. Norms are guidelines that all of the group's members should clearly perceive. In the most successful groups these norms are quite evident, and members follow them as a means of reducing uncertainty. These norms also contribute to cohesiveness and increased productivity. However, there are instances when these norms are not as transparent as they should be, and when this happens, frustration, tension, and anxiety become part of the group's experience. Hence, it is important to work for realistic norms and to see that all members recognize the norms.

Limitations of Group Discussion

We would be remiss if we did not mention a few of the limitations and potential weaknesses of the discussion process. First, all of us realize that certain conditions and topics do not lend themselves to group deliberations. There are occasions, for example, when one person, rather than an entire group, is all that is needed to solve a problem or answer a question. It would be a waste of everyone's time to have a group decide "how many parking places exist on our college campus?" A simple phone call to the Security Office would answer such an inquiry.

Second, as you shall see when we describe the steps employed by problem-solving groups, good group discussion takes time. If an immediate decision is needed, group discussion may not be the most efficient method.

Finally, because the human personality is individualistic, it must not be assumed that cohesion and harmony are always the rule. Not everyone in the group will become "great friends" and there are situations when personality clashes can foster hostility and ill feelings. On these occasions withdrawal from the group might be a better solution than trying to act out the myth that "talking makes everything right." There are times when silence and solitude are more effective than words.

Preparing for Discussion	Discussion will be an aimless, purposeless activity if the participants engage in conversation without preparation and forethought. Preparing for discussion involves three closely related activities—selecting the subject, wording the subject, and gathering material.

Selecting the Subject

On most occasions members of a private discussion group will be in a position to select their own subjects. In deciding what to talk about, and what problem to investigate, participants will find it helpful to follow a few guidelines.

1. *Select problems in which the participants are interested.* If the members of the group feel personally involved, they will be far more active in both research and participation. There is ample experimental evidence to point out that we work harder for causes we feel most strongly about. In addition, we enjoy the experience with added enthusiasm if we are sincerely committed.

2. *The topic should be important and worth discussing.* Time is too precious and serious questions too numerous to waste time on trivial and frivolous matters. "What are the best rides at Disneyland?" might be an interesting topic, but certainly not worthy of our time and research efforts.

3. *Choose a topic on which ample resource material is available.* Sitting around and offering information "off the top of our heads" will result in a "pooling of ignorance."

4. *Problems should be selected that can be investigated prior to the discussion and that can be discussed in the time allotted to the group.* A group that is rushed, both before and during the discussion, will usually produce a solution that reflects just such a hasty analysis and lack of deliberation.

5. *The subject selected should present a problem.* If the group is going to be motivated in the problem-solving discussion, they should feel a common need to find a solution. The topic should provide *at least* two sides of investigation. If the solution is obvious at the outset, there is no valid reason to engage in the time-consuming steps of the reflective process.

Wording the Subject

Correct wording and statement of the problem area is as important as the problem itself. For if the group formulates the problem in a way that distorts the real issue, confusion and misunderstanding will result. In addition, the general subject area must be worded into a workable topic if all members of the group are to deal with the same problem. The student of discussion should consider the following suggestions for wording the subject.

1. *The subject-problem should be phrased as a question.* The question highlights a specific problem while it motivates persons to seek answers to the problem. Phrasing such as "price fixing" and "war and peace" are so general and vague that they cannot be discussed in a specific manner. On the other hand, a question such as "What should be the economic role of the United States in Israel?" or "What can our college do to improve the registration

process for entering freshmen?" call for an answer—hence, discussion can take place.

2. *The question should be clearly phrased.* If the wording is ambiguous, the group may have to spend long periods of time trying to decide what to talk about. A question such as "What should be the current status of business?" is an example of ambiguity. The group must stop and decide what "business" and "current status" mean before they can even start working on the problem. Careful wording of the problem, even before the group begins discussion, also serves the dual role of limiting and restricting the scope of the problem. A topic worded "How can we best secure an additional one hundred graduate fellowships at San Diego State University?" indicates precisely what the group will talk about.

3. *Whenever possible avoid wording the problem-question in a "yes-or-no" form.* The "yes-or-no" response limits the available solutions and also leads to debate instead of cooperation. Questions such as "Should our school adopt a year-round session?" places restrictions on the group and limits the responses participants can make.

4. *The topic should be worded in an impartial way.* We all know that one can state a topic in such a manner that it favors one side or the other. We can also word a topic so that the conclusion appears obvious at the start. Both of these evils should be avoided. "Since all students would like a Democrat to be elected president, how can we raise money for the campaign of our Democratic governor?" This example, and others like it, reflect partiality, state the conclusion at the start, and therefore greatly limit the group's latitude.

Gathering Material   *The amount and depth of preparation is as vital in a discussion as in a speech.* If the participants are ill-informed and poorly researched, very little productive deliberation can take place. Each member of a group depends on the other members for different and fresh ideas; if one member fails to gather specific and concrete data, the entire group suffers.

In chapter 5 we discussed the processes of gathering and preparing material. The same principles apply to discussion: (1) Think carefully on the subject before starting your research; (2) decide what you already know on the subject and what you must research further; (3) gather the additional information you need; (4) accurately record your findings; and (5) organize your material in a purposeful and meaningful pattern.

You will notice that the fifth principle in the preceding paragraph suggests that the material should be built "in a purposeful and meaningful pattern." This means that the materials you gather should be organized in the same general order that the group deliberations will follow. Most problem-solving groups use the reflective pattern as their organizational scheme. If you are going to be in a group whose basic aim is problem-solving, it will be helpful to organize your research into the following phases:

I. Define and limit the problem.
   A. Provide definitions of important words and phrases found in the problem.
      1. You can use the dictionary.
      2. You will want to use authoritative sources and experts as a means of defining the topic.
   B. Find materials that help limit the scope and range of the problem area.
II. Analyze the problem.
   A. Material related to the history of the problem should be researched and placed next in your outline.
   B. Information, evidence, and the like must be provided to highlight specific incidents of the problem. (These are usually called effects or symptoms of the problem.)
   C. Evidence must be gathered that reveals and explains the causes of the problem.
III. List all possible solutions.
IV. Evaluate and analyze the solutions.
   A. Exploring the advantages and disadvantages is often helpful.
   B. Evidence that examines the effects of all the solutions is normally treated in this portion of the outline.
V. Treat evidence and research that discusses the best method of putting the solution into practice.

Using Reflective Thinking

In most instances group discussion follows the steps of problem-solving developed by John Dewey. Dewey developed a simple pattern allowing discussants to adapt the steps of problem-solving to group deliberation. These are (1) recognition of the problem, (2) description of the problem, (3) discovery of possible solutions, (4) evaluation of solutions and acceptance of the best solution, and (5) planning action for the preferred solution.

Most problem-solving groups can derive numerous benefits from using the steps of reflective thinking. Two of the more common advantages are worth mentioning. First, it is assumed that by treating each of the five phases in a systematic order we will progress *logically* from a problem to a solution. By analyzing the key issues step by step, reflective thinking seeks to eliminate the random and haphazard decision-making processes characteristic of many deliberations. Think of all those occasions when you were in a group that chose the first solution proposed only to find later that the decision would have been much better, had judgment been suspended until all alternatives had been examined.

A second advantage of Dewey's five steps is manifest within the group itself. Considering that all the members are concerned with the same step of the reflective thinking process at any given moment, we can be assured that all participants will be talking about the same issues at the same time. We hope to be spared the person who begins the discussion by saying, "Now the best way to solve this problem is. . . ." Because each person knows what phase the group is in at every instance, it is a simple matter to tell this person that he or she is well ahead of the appropriate beginning step of the problem-solving process, "We should define our terms at the start of the discussion."

Recognition of the Problem

Before we can solve a problem we must be aware that a problem exists. Therefore, the first step in trying to resolve or understand a problem is defining and limiting the specific problem. By defining the problem early in the discussion, the group can set certain limits if the topic is too broad for the amount of time allotted. By analyzing certain crucial terms and key concepts, the group is also in a better position to comprehend the scope and seriousness of the problem. For example, if a group was to discuss the topic of high school dropouts, it should use the initial period of its discussion to decide such things as a definition of "high school dropouts." Is it anyone under sixteen years old, or is the age to be eighteen and younger? Deciding issues such as these early in the discussion helps a group avoid the all too common problem of nearing the end of the discussion only to discover that there was not a common definition agreed upon.

Description of the Problem

Now that the members of the group have stated, defined, and limited their problem they are ready to analyze the nature of the problem. This analysis and evaluation normally demands that the participants discuss and exchange ideas and information on three topics—history of the problem, effects of the problem, and causes of the problem.

1. *History*. What has led to a situation may offer insight into how that situation can be remedied. If, for instance, a group is discussing student parking fees, it might be helpful to explore the history of these fees as a method of finding when they were first initiated and the rationale behind their introduction. Whenever possible the history of the problem should extend as far forward as the *status quo*.

     On occasion the history phase will have to be omitted. Problems that call for immediate action may not offer a group the luxury of historical review. In addition, problems that are very new may not have a substantial history.

2. *Effects*. Using the various forms of support mentioned in chapter 5, the group should discuss how serious the problem is and who is being affected. By reporting observed effects the members can see the outward manifestations of the problem and how widespread it is. For example, if the group was discussing "What can be done about the increased crime rate among teenagers?" someone might ask if the problem was serious; in response, another participant would attempt to substantiate the seriousness of the problem by stating that "The governor indicated the crime rate among teenagers has doubled in the last ten years." By knowing *what is happening* (effects of the problem), the group can later decide how to remedy the problem.

3. *Causes*. The group, having examined and verified the effects of the problem, now concerns itself with the conditions that caused the effects. In deciding what caused the increased crime rate (effect), someone might offer support that establishes broken homes as a cause of teenage crime.

Discovery of Possible Solutions

After the group has determined the specific problem to be solved and has examined the effects and causes of the problem, it is ready to suggest possible solutions. *All* possible solutions should be identified. Solutions suggested can be singular in nature ("The courts should be stricter with teenage offenders."). Multiple solutions can also be listed ("Stricter courts, better probation procedures, and parent counseling programs are what is needed.").

Evaluation of Solutions

One of the most important characteristics of reflective thinking is the practice of withholding judgment until all possible solutions can be objectively and completely considered (a concept often referred to in the literature of group processes as "suspended conclusions"). The participants should talk about each solution in detail, testing their remarks with concrete evidence, and analyzing their conclusions in light of logical reasoning. In this deliberation the advantages and disadvantages of each solution should be discussed and evaluated. How will the solution offered solve the problem? What will the solution do to the causes and effects mentioned earlier in the discussion? What will the solution do to the *status quo*? Once these, and other questions, have been answered, the group is ready to decide which of the solutions will best eliminate, or at least minimize, the problem. The acceptance of the best solution is tentative and related only to the problem mentioned in the discussion. It does not necessarily represent a fixed decision.

Plan of Action

As a final step the group must decide whether or not its preferred solution can be put into effect. If the solution seems workable, desirable, and practicable, the group should determine the most effective means of implementing their findings and conclusions.

Specific plans are influenced by such factors as the topic, time, and the power of the group. For example, a group discussing a local campus problem might present its solution to the college administration or to the student council. By contrast, a group dealing with an international topic might write a letter to representatives in Washington.

Other Discussion Patterns

The reflective process, although it is the most widely used discussion pattern, is by no means the only organizational scheme available to potential group participants. Two additional patterns may increase your ability to practice successful small group communication in a variety of settings.

| Creative Problem-Solving Sequence | A variation of Dewey's reflective process is one developed by Osborn and Parnes. This sequence seems most suited to situations with many possible solutions. Like Dewey's pattern, this organizational scheme uses five steps. Each step takes the form of a question. |

I. What is the nature of the problem—what are we here to talk about?
   A. Do we need to define any terms?
   B. How much freedom and latitude do we have?
   C. What has been happening that is unsatisfactory?
      1. What are the manifestations and effects of the problem?
      2. What has been tried in the past to correct the problem?
      3. What additional information do we need to assess the problem?
   D. What goal would we like to achieve?
   E. What factors (causes) have brought about this problem?
   F. What is the best summary of the problem we can offer?
      1. Do we all agree on this summary?
      2. Should we divide the problem into sub-areas and sub-problems?
II. What should be done to solve the problem? (A brainstorming session is often employed at this juncture.)
III. What standards and criteria shall we use to judge the merits of our possible solutions?
IV. What are the merits of each of our solutions?
   A. What solutions can be eliminated?
   B. Can we combine any of our solutions?
   C. How do our solutions match our criteria?
V. How do we put our solution into operation?
   A. Who will do what, when, and how?
   B. Shall we follow-up and check our procedures?

| Brainstorming | In its simplest form, brainstorming is a technique that generates the free expression of ideas within a group setting. Those who favor this particular discussion style maintain it fosters creativity because it is not as rigid and structured as the other patterns. Its main goal is directed to the solution of specific problems. |

Members are encouraged to make contributions as rapidly as possible, and no ideas are barred. In fact, there are certain "Brainstorming Rules" that a group adopts as a way of supporting this open and loosely structured orientation.

1. All adverse criticism is forbidden. One is not to criticize ideas or personalities.
2. "Free-wheeling" is welcomed. Members are urged to submit even the most bizarre and remote ideas and suggestions.
3. Quantity of ideas is encouraged. Members are asked to submit long lists of ideas; the theory being "the more the better."
4. Combination and improvement of ideas is one of the chief goals of brainstorming; therefore each member feels free to add to any idea being discussed.

Although this technique is loosely structured, and at times appears chaotic, it often has the effect of "getting the group moving" at the same time it is generating ideas. As noted in the last pattern, some groups insert a brief brainstorming session into their regular discussion.

Communicating in Small Groups

Although we have been talking about group structure and procedure, it should be stressed again that *this book is about human communication.* It is about the ways we send and receive messages. Because of this focus the section on communicating in small groups serves as the main thrust of this chapter. For whatever else group discussion may be, it is primarily concerned with the activity we call human communication.

Group interaction, personal relations, and sensitivity are highly complex concepts and cannot accurately be taught in a single session or by reading a few pages of techniques. However, most writers in the area of small group communication agree that there are certain communication requirements for successful small group communication, and that these behaviors can be learned and practiced by the motivated participant. These behaviors are usually divided into two interrelated categories and roles—(1) Functional and Task Roles, and (2) Maintenance and Supportive Roles. The first set of roles, or behaviors, centers around those communication functions that must be performed if the group is to achieve its desired purpose. These roles primarily concentrate on the "duties and responsibilities" of the members to get the discussion started and keep it moving toward its goal. The second set, the maintenance and supportive roles, has a more personal behavior associated with it as it endeavors to establish and preserve group and individual harmony.

Placing communicative behavior into two categories is a very subjective assignment. Inevitably there is overlapping of categories and in some instances a single sentence might serve in both functional and supportive roles. For example, one might be performing both roles if one said, "John, your ideas are normally very helpful; can you tell us what you think we should do about this solution?" Granting that the two categories are often alike, let us examine some ways in which you can improve your communication within the small group by carrying out both types of roles.

Task and Functional Roles

1. *Adhere to the logical pattern selected by the group.* If Dewey's reflective pattern is selected, see to it that the group "stays on the track." Jumping from effects to solutions and back to definition of terms will only waste time and frustrate the participants.
2. *Each member of the group should be well informed on the topic.* Research is everyone's job. Unsupported generalizations and unwarranted assertions harm the entire group. A successful participant brings not only ideas to the group, but information that he or she has gathered from sources other than personal experiences.
3. *Make your presence known throughout the discussion.* The amount of time the group has and the number of participants will obviously influence the

frequency and length of your contributions, but you should feel free to participate as often as you have something to say. However, when possible you should keep your contributions and exchanges brief and precise. Long and detailed contributions, although sometimes needed, frequently bore the other participants and keep others from getting their turn to talk.

4. *Your contributions should relate to what is being said or to something that has already been said.* Remarks that are simply "tossed out to the group" will often result in confusion or force the group to depart from their established agenda. Think of how frustrating it is for the entire group when progress is interrupted by someone who begins to recount a personal experience completely off the subject. On those occasions all members have the responsibility to see that the transgression is noted and the group is returned to the topic.

5. *Use index numbers and dates as reminders that no word has exactly the same meaning twice.* Make all remarks as specific as possible. For example, "a few weeks ago" is not the same as "January 7, 1979." To say "that man" is not the same as "Dr. John Jones." The other participants in a discussion must know exactly what the contribution means. Narrow and define the symbols used so that they will call up specific images to all who hear it.

6. *Many controversies among participants in a group discussion are accompanied by assertions.* The problem for participants in a group discussion is one of determining how controversies based on assertions can be solved. Two of the many methods of resolving these conflicts are worth noting. First, it is necessary to know what the controversy is, in other words, what the assertions assert. This involves a critical examination of basic premises inherent in the assertions. Second, the participants must be sure that they are not mistaking assertions about the speaker for assertions about things. It is confusing to listeners if we say "Nancy, you are wrong," when in reality we should have said "Nancy, your *information* is wrong."

7. *Discussants should establish an atmosphere that stresses questioning.* The various participants must realize that a lack of understanding about what is said and what is meant hampers the reflective process. By asking questions of one another whenever there is a basic misunderstanding or need for information, the group can overcome many obstacles. Many groups move ahead in the discussion only to discover later that they did not understand the earlier premises that led to the current stage of the discussion. By raising questions, the group can also encourage silent members to take part. For example, someone might say to a reticent member, "Roger, what did you find when you looked at the effects of the problem?" Roger would have a difficult time remaining silent.

8. *Supply leadership for the group whenever needed.* Many participants rely solely on the judgment of the leader for decisions that should be the responsibility of participants. There are, in addition, many functions of a leader that can easily be performed by *any* alert member of the group. For example, any participant can offer summaries whenever that person feels they are

appropriate and would aid the group. Do not make the mistake of assuming that the leader, because of the title held, has all the answers.

9. *Though questioning and skepticism are healthy aspects of group discussion, remember that discussion should be a reflection of the democratic process, and as such everyone should try to cooperate.* Everyone must accept the notion of a "common problem" and the responsibilities inherent in that acceptance. These responsibilities ask all participants to expend energy and often to subjugate personal needs and wants.

10. *The way we communicate is often as important as what we communicate.* Our best ideas can be lost if our delivery is distracting or dull. We all know how hard it is to listen to someone who speaks in a monotone or who shifts aimlessly in the chair. These violations of basic communication skills, the improper use of voice and body, can often obstruct communication.

Maintenance and Supportive Roles

1. *All of us work very hard to protect, enhance, and maintain our self-concept and problems may arise from this.* If someone sends us a message that we interpret as an attack on our ego, we immediately call forth our entire arsenal of defensive strategies to protect ourselves. In a group we face a number of challenges to ego-defense. First, try to avoid sending the types of messages that force others into defensive positions. For example, be honest with others concerning their opinions without attacking their egos. Imagine how you would feel if someone said to you "That is a stupid idea." Once we utter phrases like that all further communication is doomed. Second, be sensitive enough to recognize ego-defensive behavior. A person criticized for being late to the meeting is likely to respond in a defensive manner by saying "Nothing very important ever happens at these meetings anyway." Try to aid the person and the group during these uncomfortable periods. Finally, be alert to defensive reactions on your own part. If you are the one reprimanded for tardiness, be in touch with yourself so that you can arrest defensive reactions that are likely to impede the group's progress (and make you subject to the development of an ulcer).

2. *We must be aware of individual and perceptual differences that will appear in the group.* Each of us is unique; we come from different backgrounds and therefore bring different personal histories to the group. These individual differences will be manifest in countless ways. What one person finds humorous another may consider offensive. What is "planned growth" to you may appear to be "stifling free enterprise" to the person sitting next to you. From judgments of beauty to issues of truth, our decisions are influenced by our past experiences and thus, having had different experiences, we often reach different conclusions. Effective participants are aware of this truism and are constantly telling themselves that perceptual differences are not only natural, they are beneficial.

3. *The watchful participant is aware of the total communication situation and is cognizant that symbols other than words can send messages.* Therefore, it is important to be alert to all aspects of nonverbal communication—facial expressions, body movements, eye contact, spatial relationships, and seating

arrangements. Someone in the group might well be "talking" with their body as they become upset with the group and slowly edge their chair from the inner circle.

4. *All participants should employ clear and concise feedback.* Respond directly, verbally and nonverbally, to the remarks of others. We all know how frustrating it is when we make a statement to someone and receive only silence. In a group the problem is compounded, for there are now eight or ten persons who are not responding to what is being said. By nodding, smiling, or talking, we let our colleagues know our reactions to what was presented. It not only keeps the group moving, it allows other persons to know we are interested in them and their ideas.

5. *Create an atmosphere conducive to constructive and purposeful discussion.* A relaxed and friendly atmosphere is far more productive than one that is characterized by tension. Simply ask yourself this question: "Is it not true that I am at ease and do my best work when I am in a situation that is free from hostility and anxiety?" If the answer is yes, then do your part to make the communication environment a pleasant one. Discussion should not be conducted in an authoritarian atmosphere, but in a climate where each person is honest and speaks freely. It is a healthy attitude when each person says, "The discussion belongs to all of us—it is a chance to say what we think and feel." This openness and frankness among all participants is not only good for the group, but often helps the individual.

6. *Communication is a two-way process; the listener also plays a key role in discussion.* It is unfair to place the burden for understanding completely on the speaker. Participants in a discussion cannot sit back and contentedly assume they have nothing to do but wait their turns to talk. The listener must pay close attention to what is being said. Participants must ask questions and attempt to narrow and define all ambiguous and nebulous concepts.

7. *"Loaded language" or emotionally toned words and phrases should be avoided in group discussion.* These words bring to mind a variety of meanings and images. When such words are used, they often confuse the real meaning for both sender and receiver. Once again the solution becomes one of using specific words. We are taken off the track and often lose our concentration when someone says "What would she know? She is not only vicious and stupid, but she was once a Communist."

8. *An active participant offers verbal and nonverbal support for the other members.* If by your attitude (facial expressions, posture, utterances), you reveal a lack of interest and enthusiasm, the other members will be inhibited and defensive. No one likes to feel unimportant and without regard. If the receiver of messages lacks expression and animation, the speaker is apt to feel that what is said is futile and not worthy of the group's time. A lack of recognition and support of our ideas hampers a free and spontaneous flow of communication. By our silence and our remarks we can either destroy or aid communication.

9. *Try to employ role-taking (empathy) toward all members of the group.* Understanding the thoughts and feelings of others is an essential ingredient

of successful group participation. Knowing the reasons why people behave as they do enables you to know what to say, when to say it, and how to say it.

10. *Because group discussion employs democratic processes, it is important that each group allow for some deviant behavior.* Not only is it philosophically consistent with democratic principles to accept the deviant, but it also proves beneficial to the group. The deviant is often the one who challenges inconsistent evidence and faulty reasoning. He is often the one who makes us re-evaluate our assumptions and values, and this deviance can, on occasion, force us from apathy and complacency. Welcome and encourage the "oddball"—it could be you.

Styles of Leadership

Learning how to lead a group is much more complex than simply memorizing a series of techniques. Each group, because of its unique personality and choice of topic, requires leadership specifically suited to its needs. While one group may work best with a strong leader, another group might be hampered by such control. Therefore, various styles of leadership have evolved. The best treatment of these styles is offered by William M. Sattler and N. Edd Miller in their book *Discussion and Conference*. They identify five of the most common styles found in discussion groups. Let us briefly examine these five approaches to leadership so that you will be able to decide which style is most appropriate for your particular group. We shall begin with leadership that seeks control of its members and move gradually to a leadership that permits complete and total freedom.

1. At one end of the continuum we have a leadership pattern called *authoritarian.* As the name implies, in this orientation nearly absolute power rests with the leader who not only conducts the meeting and leads the group, but also makes most of the important decisions concerning content.

2. When time is short and group efficiency crucial, *strong supervisory* leadership is often employed. Although this type of leadership is not as radical as the authoritarian approach, it is based on the premise that groups need a strong and aggressive leader. The leader will usually ask specific questions and direct the flow of the meeting in a direction that has been personally predetermined. In essence, the leader is concerned with procedure and solutions and spends little or no time treating issues of group maintenance, member satisfaction, and interpersonal relationships.

3. The *democratic* style of leadership is most often found in group discussion. The leader plays an active role, but sees to it that a democratic atmosphere prevails in the group. This leader encourages participation and stresses individual initiative. Unlike the authoritarian and supervisory leader, the democratic leader is concerned with personalities as well as procedure.

4. *Group-centered* leadership offers the participants freedom to make procedural as well as policy decisions. This leadership is predicated by the belief that each person has the capacity to lead and, therefore the ability to determine goals. Leadership duties are not vested in any one individual, but shared

by all members. For example, if the group would be aided by a running summary, any of the group's members could offer that summary.

5. The most permissive of all styles is *leaderless*. When it prevails there is a total absence of leadership. Leaderless discussions are often characterized by a high degree of member satisfaction, but a low degree of productivity. It takes skilled participants to function in this anarchy.

Leadership in the Group

Research in group discussion and group dynamics has revealed that the so-called born leader is a myth. Leadership is composed of traits and characteristics that can be learned and cultivated. In an ideal group everyone would possess those traits and we would not have to worry about appointing someone to serve as the leader. In this model situation, all the participants would act as leader. They would monitor the group's behavior as well as their own, the roles of leadership would be diffused throughout the group, and leadership tasks would be performed by any person who believed that a particular task would benefit the group. There are, however, many occasions when shared leadership does not work or is inappropriate. For example, the principal of a school would most likely lead the faculty meeting. In such instances, the group must rely on a single leader to guide it and to stimulate participation.

Because the duties of the leader can be shared by all members or vested in one person, the advice that follows applies to an appointed leader or to any participant who perceives a need for leadership in the group and attempts to fulfill that need.

1. *The leader should create a cooperative, democratic climate.* A group atmosphere characterized by demagoguery is less creative and often filled with discontent. You know from your own experience that if you feel uncomfortable due to the actions of an authoritarian leader, you will not do your best work.

2. *The leader should try to remain impartial whenever possible.* There is a tendency among members of a group to view the leader as a boss or someone of superior rank. Viewed in this way, the leader who states personal conclusions at the beginning of the discussion tends to close the door on free and open deliberation. This does not mean that as leader you cannot take part, it simply suggests that you see that all sides get presented and that you do not become a spokesman for one point of view too early in the discussion.

3. *The leader has the responsibility of seeing that the discussion gets started.* This often involves having the group get acquainted. We have all experienced that uneasy silence when forced to interact with strangers. The leader should help us over these periods by making sure there are some introductions and "chatting" before the group begins its serious deliberations. The leader should also state the purpose of the meeting and mention the problem to be discussed.

4. *The leader should get general participation among all members of the group.* This includes changing the communication behavior of the monopolist as well as the shy member of the group. It is the leader's encouragement

and attitude that often determines the frequency of participation among individuals in the group.

5. *The leader should see that a plan, an agenda, or an organizational pattern is followed, and that the main phases of the problem get considered.* If an agenda is used, it is the leader who becomes its particular guardian. The leader must always be asking, "Where have we been?" "Where are we now?" and "Where are we going?"

6. *The leader should make abundant use of transitions and summaries.* By using these two techniques the leader can keep the discussion organized and also keep everyone informed on the group's progress. Imagine how helpful it might be to have someone say, "Now that we have seen the effects of overpopulation, it might be to our advantage to examine some of the causes of this problem."

7. *In an ideal situation the leader should offer the encouragement and support that would allow all members to reach full potential.* This calls for the supplying of extrinsic motivation to each and every person. Praise and reassurance are but two of the techniques available to the leader.

8. *The leader should try to clarify details and contributions whenever possible.* If necessary, contributions should be reworded or rephrased. There will be occasions when the leader might even ask someone else to clarify the point or evidence in question. For example, the leader might ask, "Janet, did your research support the notion just expressed by Paul?"

9. *The leader should see that the group stays on the track and does not wander from point to point.* Personal anecdotes may be interesting, but they seldom do much to keep the discussion moving. On these occasions the leader must help the group return to the issue they were discussing before the irrelevant comment was made.

10. *A group must have successful interpersonal relations if it is to accomplish its goal.* Personal hostilities and pettiness have no place in the problem-solving group discussion. A group of this kind cannot waste its time on therapy; it has too much to do. Therefore, the leader must set a tone that does not allow destructive behavior to develop. If, by chance, conflicts do emerge, the leader must resolve them. A leader may have to change the behavior of a troublesome participant, settle an argument, and at times even offer reprimands.

11. *The leader should bring the discussion to a satisfactory conclusion.* The solution can be summarized if one has been reached or a summary can be offered that highlights the points of agreement. The discussion can also be concluded by reviewing the questions and problems that still remain unanswered.

12. *The leader should be extremely flexible and have a high tolerance for ambiguity.* There will be occasions when the group process becomes frustrating to all the participants, and some might even seek to withdraw. However, the leader must not succumb to this apathy and confusion. He or she must be able to remain flexible and work to overcome the uncertainty within the group. If the leader yields to the ambiguity, it is apt to become conta-

gious. The entire group might lose interest, argue needlessly, or cease working on the problem.

Barriers to Discussion

The most common barriers to successful group discussion are violations of the suggestions for participation and leadership. If the participant, either leader or member, manifests behavior in opposition to what we have just offered, he or she can contribute to the failure of the group.

There are five additional behaviors worth noting as we complete this section on group communication. We have mentioned these barriers earlier in a slightly different context. However, they are important enough to warrant further consideration.

1. *Apathy* among group members is perhaps the most common barrier to successful group discussion. Apathy is a complex phenomenon. It can be brought to the group by specific members or it can even be generated by the group. In either case, apathy and all its external and internal actions can destroy the group. Therefore, all members must make the group an exciting and active encounter for all concerned.
2. *Excessive formality*, whether through rules or attitudes, hampers participation, and often increases tension. Although some rules might be helpful, too many rules appear restrictive and can keep the members stiff in both mind and communication.
3. Closely related to formality is the problem of *control*. A group that tries to control its members will be a group that has unnatural and rigid participation. Lack of freedom will destroy the flow of ideas, feelings, and information.
4. *Dogmatism*, although a corollary to the idea of control, is also a barrier that plagues many discussion groups. If the group, or any of its members, is dogmatic and asserts principles and opinions as if they were gospel, the entire discussion will suffer. Dogmatism is characterized by narrow-mindness and authoritarianism, both of which have no place in group discussion.
5. Our last barrier, *conformity*, seems to be inherent in the discussion process. We are told, and rightly so, that cooperation is crucial and that everyone must work for a common goal. And we also know, from personal experience, that being a member of any group implies that we must conform to the group's structure and norms. But, among other problems, conformity may keep participants from expressing opposing views. And, because conformity is such a strong force, we must be careful that it does not stifle individualism. Do not allow conformity to become a barrier to interaction.

Evaluating the Discussion

Most groups find it useful to evaluate the process they use and the effectiveness of their techniques. Evaluation of the group's behavior and actions can take place at any time and can take a variety of forms. Evaluation allows the group time to measure and isolate its successes and failures; and it points out in a specific manner what happened and why.

Many groups find it helpful to evaluate periodically as they move through the discussion process. They simply stop and ask questions concerning what is happening, why it is happening, what the results are, and what should be done.

Evaluation can examine a host of variables. Members can evaluate group processes, participation, leadership, communication patterns and problems, interaction, tasks, and final products. These evaluations can be made by individual participants or by the group as a whole.

A large number of fill-in forms can be used in group and individual evaluations. *In Appendix B you will find some of the common forms used in evaluation.* Many groups also enjoy developing their own evaluation forms.

Remember that through evaluation and analysis of the group experience we are able to learn from that experience. The insights gained from each discussion can go a long way toward contributing to more effective participation in the next group in which we find ourselves.

Summary

Whether to interact or to solve problems, we find ourselves participating in group deliberations. As discussants we may participate in encounter groups, lecture-forums, symposiums, panels, or problem-solving groups. In all of these situations it is important for the participants to be well informed and well organized.

In problem-solving groups the topic must be selected, worded, and researched. John Dewey's five steps of reflective thinking constitutes one organizational scheme that is quite helpful in solving problems. Defining the problem, analyzing the causes and effects, suggesting solutions, and picking the best solution calls for deliberations that follow a clear-thinking pattern.

Each group member, whether participant or leader, should take an active role, be well informed, cooperate, listen, encourage others, develop empathy, and be brief.

Finally, most groups find it beneficial to evaluate their efforts as a group and as individuals. (See Appendix B for common evaluation forms.)

Suggested Readings

Baird, John E., Jr., and Weinberg, Sanford. *Communication*. Dubuque, IA: Wm. C. Brown Company Publishers, 1977.

Brilhart, John K. *Effective Group Discussion*. 3d ed. Dubuque, IA: Wm. C. Brown Company Publishers, 1978.

Burgoon, Michael; Heston, Judee K.; and McCroskey, James. *Small Group Communication*. New York: Holt, Rinehart and Winston, 1974.

Cathcart, Robert S., and Samovar, Larry A. *Small Group Communication*. 3d ed. Dubuque, IA: Wm. C. Brown Company Publishers, 1979.

Gulley, Halbert, and Leathers, Dale G. *Communication and Group Process*. 3d ed. New York: Holt, Rinehart and Winston, 1977.

Patton, Bobby R., and Giffin, Kim. *Problem-Solving Group Interaction*. New York: Harper and Row, 1973.

Phillips, Gerald M. *Communication and the Small Group*. 2d ed. New York: Bobbs-Merrill, 1973.

Sattler, William M., and Miller, N. Edd. *Discussion and Conference*. 2d ed. Englewood Cliffs, NJ: Prentice-Hall, 1968.

Appendix A
The Job Interview

Discussing the job interview in this text, which stresses public speaking situations, may seem a bit incongruous at first glance. There is an obvious difference in the amount of control of the communication situation exercised by the public speaker compared to the amount of control of the job applicant in an interview. Speaker-listener roles remain relatively fixed in the public speaking situation while they change frequently in the interviewing situation. The greater predictability of message content and structure in the public speaking situation is unlikely to be present in the average interview. The public speaker can present his message from memory, from manuscript, from notes, or impromptu, but the person being interviewed for a job seldom has any option but the impromptu mode. The public speaker can choose when to speak, but the interviewee speaks at the interviewer's pleasure. In view of these differences you may wonder why we are "mixing apples and oranges." The answer will become apparent when we examine some of the similarities of the two situations.

Both are purposeful communication events, not random talking. Like public speaking, interviewing for a job involves attempts to inform and to persuade. The applicant is called upon to present information about a variety of items related to fitness for employment. At the same time, the applicant is attempting to achieve a persuasive impact upon the interviewer through the answering process. Each answer thus becomes a mini-speech with a main point and supporting evidence, with a definite structure and style, with verbal and nonverbal factors operating simultaneously.

We are suggesting that the principles of communication discussed throughout the book are relevant to the interview as well. You should be well organized, conscious of your language, sensitive to the management of your delivery, and particularly alert to the responses (feedback) of your partner. Like good public speaking, successful interviewing involves thorough preparation. When so viewed, the job interview is not the hit-or-miss, matter-of-luck, totally unpredictable event that is often envisioned. We shall now examine some of the ways you can prepare for the interview and then we will discuss the actual conducting of the interview.

Getting Ready for the Interview   Personnel directors agree that the job applicant's chances of conducting a successful interview are enhanced if the applicant has taken the trouble to learn something about the firm or institution and its product or service, about the job itself, and about the criteria employers use when evaluating job applicants. They also agree that a good letter and resume predispose the employer in the applicant's favor. We would add that a knowledge of the forms that questions take and the uses to which they are put in an interview can also be advantageous to the applicant.

Find out about the Firm   We have often stressed the need for careful audience analysis when preparing a speech. A similar need exists when you prepare for the job interview—a need to discover as much information as you can about your future employer, whether that employer be a company, a government agency, an institution, or a one-person business. The information you can gain by such an investigation will be helpful in at least three ways. First, such an inquiry will help you answer the question, "Do I really want to work there?" Second, knowledge of a company will better enable you to show how you can fit into its operation, a crucial element in your forthcoming letter of application and interview. Third, by displaying knowledge of the company, you are saying, in effect, "I have more than a casual interest in working for you." Such an indication of interest is almost certain to be received favorably.

What are some of the things you should find out about the company? We suggest that at least the following factors be investigated: The company's reputation in its field; how its product or service is regarded by those who use it; the company's history of operation; its geographical location(s); its physical facilities; its financial condition; its prospects for growth; the size and composition of its work force; its organizational structure; its chief officers; its personnel policies.

The kind of information you are seeking may be obtained in a variety of ways; such as, letters of inquiry to the company public relations or personnel officer, conversations or interviews with employees or other knowledgeable persons, direct observation by visiting the company, or through resources available in the library. Reference librarians can direct you to specialized volumes that provide a surprising range of factual information about leading business organizations. A thorough investigation takes work, and your efforts to find certain items of information may sometimes prove futile. But the rewards gained from acquiring a thorough knowledge of the prospective employer make the search well worth the effort.

Find out about the Position   "I'll do any kind of work" may suggest a willingness to work, but it hardly suggests competence. In these days of stiff competition for almost all kinds of jobs, the applicant must demonstrate his or her unique fitness for the desired position. In order to do so, the applicant will find it necessary to discover both the general and special requirements of the job.

Among the details with which one should become familiar are (1) general and specific educational requirements for the job; (2) the amount and kind of previous job experience needed; (3) the specific responsibilities the job entails;

(4) the work environment, including any travel involved or prospects of relocation; (5) the associates with whom one will be working; and (6) salary range and prospects for promotion.

Be Aware of the Criteria of Evaluation

Probably the most difficult part of the job applicant's "audience analysis" is trying to determine what criteria of evaluation the employer is likely to use and the relative importance assigned to each criterion. So many subjective factors can influence the interviewer's perception of the applicant during the course of the interview that criteria are changed or rearranged in terms of their importance. A reasonable course for the applicant to follow, therefore, is to compile a list of possible criteria and take a self-test: "How do I measure up in each respect?"

What are some of the possible criteria of evaluation? In their book on interviewing practices, Charles Stewart and William Cash report on a list that Robert Martin gleaned from questioning supervisors of a large aircraft firm. The list is sufficiently general to be applicable to a wide variety of job situations. Highly valued was *ability to communicate*, together with *general intelligence, ambition, integrity, professional competence, creativity, potential for growth, attitude, compatibility, motivation*, and *references*. With this list as a starter, you can add other criteria you deem applicable to the particular job you are seeking. Rate yourself on each item, and try to envision ways you can project your strengths in the letter of application and the ensuing interview.

Compose the Letter and Resume

In most cases the employer's first contact with you as a job applicant will be through your letter of application and resume. The impression you create may very well determine whether or not you are granted an interview. Therefore, careful attention should be given to the preparation of this vital part of your job hunting strategy.

Picture the personnel officer opening the morning's mail. Somewhere in the pile of envelopes is your letter of application. What will be the first thing noticed about your letter? Chances are, its *appearance* will contribute to the first impression. Is it typewritten? Is the type easy to read? Is it neat and free of erasures? Does it display good form? Is it brief? Does it invite closer inspection? The initial impressions are already at work in shaping the personnel officer's attitude toward you. Inconsequential though they may seem, these matters of form and appearance need to be taken into account.

Once the personnel officer begins to read your letter matters of content become the focus. What should go into your letter? In their book, *Effective Speaking in Business*, Huston, Sandberg, and Mills suggest that the application letter be approached in much the same way that one approaches a persuasive speech. It should gain the reader's attention, create a desire, and appeal for action. When viewed in this way, the pattern of organization is apparent.

Like the introduction to a speech, the opening lines of the letter should gain attention and orient the receiver. It has become standard practice to mention the name of a mutual acquaintance or to refer to some person of authority whose name or title will engage the reader's attention and respect. Thus you might open the letter in this fashion: "While attending the recent convention of the Interstate

Advertisers Association in Boston, I met Herbert Buffington of your staff, who told me that you were anticipating an opening for a person with my qualifications." Or perhaps you might write: "Dr. H. S. Knowland, Dean of the College of Engineering at Middle State University, has suggested that I apply for the position that you advertised in the latest placement bulletin."

The body of the letter should show the employer what you have to offer. By indicating how you are *uniquely* qualified for the job, you will create a desire for your services. You should state your case clearly and economically, referring the reader to your resume for additional details. As you compose your case, bear in mind the possible criteria of evaluation that the reader may be applying.

The conclusion should suggest that the reader take some kind of action on your application. Normally, the conclusion will contain a request for an appointment, suggest a date and time when you will be available for an interview.

Like the letter, the resume should be tailored to the needs of the particular job for which you are applying. Among the items of information usually found on resumes are the following:

Personal data—date of birth, address, phone number, marital status, etc.

Educational training—schools attended, degrees obtained

Work experience—name of employer, dates of employment, job category, reason for leaving

Special aptitudes

Scholarships or honors

References

Review the Forms and Uses of Questions

While it is unlikely that you will be able to discover in advance the actual questions that will be put to you during the interview, you can help to reduce uncertainty by reviewing the basic forms in which questions appear and the rationale behind their use.

You will recall that earlier in this text when we examined ways of replying to questions after a speech, we observed that questions may be classified as requests for clarification, requests for elaboration, and as challenges to a position. In the job interview all three classifications may be used by the interviewer—although it is unlikely that the argumentative, or position-challenging, question will appear with any frequency. Most of the time the interviewer is seeking what you know and how much you know, or is attempting to discover what kind of person you are.

The basic types of questions used to elicit such information are the *open question*, the *closed question*, the *mirror question*, the *probing question*, and the *leading question*.

The *open question* invites a relatively unrestricted area of response. "What do you think are the prospects for our field?" allows you to choose the nature of your subject matter and the scope of your response. Similarly, an employer who states, "I'd like to hear about some of your interests," provides you with an opportunity to generalize or to concentrate on just a few items. Your response to such questions can tell the interviewer a lot about you. It may reveal what your values and priorities are and what things you consider important. It may reveal your capacity for analysis—your ability to break a matter down into its component parts. It may reveal how well informed you are or in what areas you lack background. Since the employer has permitted you to "choose the game and the ballpark" you should be sensitive to the amount of time you take in answering. Careful observation of the interviewer's nonverbal behavior can often tell you when it's time to stop.

The *closed question* severely restricts the choices available to the respondent. "Is your spouse employed?" invites a yes or no answer. "How much money do you expect to earn on this job?" gives you little room for anything except to cite a figure. Closed questions are used to elicit brief and specific answers, and, in a rapid-fire series, can draw out a great deal of factual information. Because they discourage any reply not directly to the point they can exert an inhibiting effect upon the person being interviewed. For that reason, most skilled interviewers attempt to put the applicant at ease by posing open questions at the outset of the interview, then posing closed questions after a rapport has been established.

The *mirror question*, as its name suggests, reflects an answer just given by the respondent. "You say you're economically independent?" prompts the applicant to elaborate upon that previous answer. The mirror question, then, is used by the interviewer to secure clarification of some point raised by the applicant.

The *probing question* serves somewhat the same function as the mirror question by seeking elaboration of, or probing, a point already raised. "Why do you say that?" or "How would you go about accomplishing that?" direct the respondent to continue with the present theme. Even a simple "Oh?" or "I see" suggest that the interviewer wants to know more. The interviewer's nonverbal behavior can serve as a kind of probing question. A fixed gaze and a nodding head can tell the applicant, "Go on!"

The *leading question* may be the most insidious kind of question you can encounter. It "leads" you to a specific, expected answer because the answer is implied in the way the question is phrased. "You're opposed to strikes, aren't you?" forces the answerer to take a position from which retreat is difficult without losing face. Leading questions sometimes involve the use of a "loaded word" or expression. For example, "Do you like those ridiculous outfits that the store managers wear?" In the great majority of job interviews, the leading question is a rarity, although it may be used to test an applicant's behavior under stress.

Now that we have examined the principal forms questions take and the uses to which they are put, let us suggest some specific questions that routinely appear in job interviews. Formulating an answer to each of the following questions will be good practice for the "real thing." Before the interview, practice some of the following topics as impromptu speeches.

Why do you wish to work for us?

What do you know about our competitors?

Have you ever been turned down for a position? Why?

How long do you plan to stay in this job?

Are you willing to start at the bottom?

What do you do in your free time?

Tell me about your greatest achievement.

Are you free to travel?

Explain how your educational background applies to this job.

What kind of persons make you uncomfortable?

Did you work your way through school?

What is your ultimate career objective?

Did you enjoy your last job?

In what way do you think you can help us?

Do you have any health problems?

How important is the starting salary to you?

How do you feel about working on weekends?

Is there anything I ought to know about you that is not covered in your resume or letter?

Conducting the Interview

If you have conscientiously applied yourself to the steps of preparation we have outlined, you should be equipped to handle the actual interview. While no one can predict with accuracy everything that might transpire during the course of the interview, a foreknowledge of some of the possibilities can be comforting.

Let us remind you, then, of some of the factors you can control during the interview. They all relate to your behavior and thus may have an effect upon the behavior of the interviewer.

1. Be prompt in meeting your appointment. An important consideration to any employer is how employees regard time. Tardiness, however justifiable the reason might be, is not likely to be well taken.
2. Dress appropriately for the interview. Flashy attire, conspicuous jewelry, or any facet of dress that calls undue attention to itself should be avoided. Similarly, a "laid back," casual attire might be interpreted as a sign of insensitivity toward the interviewer.
3. Greet the interviewer cordially. A sincere smile can be a warming gesture. However, avoid an effusive "hail fellow well met" manner that may be seen as a sign of over-familiarity. A firm handshake is almost always appropriate.
4. Let the interviewer set the tempo and mood of the interview. Avoid talking until it is clear that the interviewer wishes it.
5. Be alert and act alert. Your alertness is signalled nonverbally to the interviewer by such things as your posture, your gaze, and your facial expression. If you are listening intently, these signs of alertness will generally be obvious.
6. Be sincere in your responses. If you are unable to answer a question, say so instead of trying to give an evasive answer. Overstatements, "hard sell" tactics should be avoided at all costs.

7. Avoid slovenly language. Slang expressions or sloppy grammar might be acceptable within a circle of friends but to an interviewer they might suggest a lack of refinement or an inadequate vocabulary. Conversely, attempting to use "big" words in an attempt to impress the interviewer is likely to be recognized as manipulative.
8. Finally, concentrate upon giving rather than getting. Remember, the employer is more interested in what you have to offer the firm than in what the firm has to offer you. This is not to say that you should not raise questions about your legitimate concerns; just make certain that your expressed concerns do not overbalance the employer's concerns.

Good luck!

Summary

The job interview involves both informing and persuading. Prior to the interview the applicant should find out as much as possible about the firm to which application is being made, about the details of the job itself, and about the criteria of evaluation used by the employer. Careful attention to the composition of a letter of application and an accompanying resume is strongly advised. The applicant should be aware of the general forms which questions take and the uses to which they are put in interviews. During the actual interview the applicant should be open and friendly in conduct and should stress the advantages that will accrue to the employer from hiring the applicant.

Suggested Reading

Stewart, Charles J., and Cash, William B. *Interviewing*. 2d ed. Dubuque, IA: Wm. C. Brown Company Publishers, 1978.

Appendix B
Common Forms Used in Evaluation

Speech Evaluation Scale

Speaker_____ Date_____

Subject_____ Round_____

Speech Processes	Ratings and Comments

Content: Purpose, thesis, analysis:
  Specific purpose: clear _____
     narrowed _____
     appropriate to
     audience _____
  Thesis: clear _____
     narrowed _____
     appropriate to
     audience _____
     speaker _____
  Analysis of thesis:
     accurate _____
     thorough _____
  Main points: directly support
     thesis _____ fully develop
     thesis _____
	1 2 3 4 5

Content: Development
  Supporting material:
     clear _____ relevant _____
     specific _____ adequate in
     amount _____
     interesting _____
  Logical reasoning:
     accurate _____
     supported _____	

Speech Processes	Ratings and Comments

Facts: clear _____
    relevant _____
    adequate _____
    interesting _____
Statistics: clear _____
    relevant _____
    adequate _____correctly
    interpreted _____
    interesting _____
Examples: clear _____
    adequate _____
    interesting _____
Testimony: clear _____
    adequate _____
    interesting _____
	1 2 3 4 5

Organization:
    clear _____ effective _____
    Introduction: gets
    attention _____
    orients _____ thesis
    stated _____
    partition _____ creates
    interest _____ proper
    subordination _____
    Body:
    Main points: clear _____
    patterned _____
    Sub-points: clear _____
    patterned _____
    Conclusion: summary _____
    effective _____
    Transitions: smooth _____
    clear _____
    signposts _____
	1 2 3 4 5

Language:
    Grammar: appropriate
    level _____ errors _____
    Rhetorical qualities: oral style
    clear _____
    appropriate _____
    interesting _____
    concrete _____
	1 2 3 4 5

Speech Processes	Ratings and Comments

Delivery:
  Physical presentation:
    appearance _____
    poise _____
    enthusiasm _____
    directness _____
    eye contact _____
    posture _____
    gestures _____
    facial expression _____
  Oral presentation:
    articulation _____
    fluency _____
    pronunciation _____
    variety _____
    pitch _____ rate _____
    loudness _____
    directness _____
	1 2 3 4 5

Speech Outline	1 2 3 4 5

Item markings:	Ratings:
+ —very good	5 very good
(no mark)—average or better	4 good
√ —needs improvement	3 average
	2 poor
	1 unsatisfactory

Speech Evaluation

I. Delivery
 A. Eye contact   good_____
  1. aimless_____   3. windows_____
  2. floor_____   4. other_____
 B. Posture   good_____
  1. stiff_____   3. aimless movement_____
  2. shifting of weight_____   4. other_____
 C. Gestures   good_____
  1. need more_____   3. poor timing_____
  2. larger_____   4. other_____
 D. Vocal variety   good_____
  1. change and vary your   2. pause_____
   a. rate_____   3. enthusiasm_____
   b. force_____   4. other_____
   c. pitch_____
   d. volume_____

II. Content
 A. Audience analysis   good_____
  1. topic too general_____
  2. not for this audience_____
  3. feedback_____
  4. other_____
 B. Imagery and Wording   good_____
  1. more detail_____
  2. poor word choice_____
  3. other_____
 C. Support and evidence   good_____
  1. old sources_____
  2. unrelated to issue_____
  3. weak___, because_____
 D. Motivation (Motive appeals)   good_____
  1. poor audience   3. more development_____
   analysis_____   4. other_____
  2. more detail_____
 E. Introduction   good_____
  weak, because_____
 F. Organization   good_____
  1. no clear pattern_____
  2. weak, because_____

III. Other

Speech to Convince

Speaker_____

Rating Scale: 5—Superior; 4—Above Average; 3—Average; 2—Fair; 1—Poor.

Introduction (circle one) 5 4 3 2 1

    Did the opening words get favorable attention?

    Was the issue under contention introduced tactfully?

    Did the speaker make you feel that the issue was worth considering?

Body 5 4 3 2 1

    Was the central idea (proposition) clear?

    Were the purpose and central idea sufficiently narrowed?

    Did the main points suffice to prove the central idea?

    Were there too many main points? too few? satisfactory number?

    Was each main point supported by evidence?

    Were sources of evidence cited?

    Did the evidence meet the tests of credibility?

    Was the reasoning from the evidence sound?

    Was the speech adapted to audience interests?

    Was the speech adapted to existing audience attitudes toward the topic?

Conclusion 5 4 3 2 1

    Did the conclusion focus the whole speech on the central idea?

Language Usage 5 4 3 2 1

    Clear?

    Correct?

    Appropriate?

    Vivid?

Delivery 5 4 3 2 1

    Visual:

    Vocal:

Dominant Impression of the Speech

Proposition of Policy

Speaker_____

Rating Scale: 5—Superior; 4—Above Average; 3—Average; 2—Fair; 1—Poor.

How Convincingly Does the Speaker Show:

That a problem exists? _____

That it is significant enough to warrant correction? _____

That it is caused by an inherent weakness in the present system? _____

That the proposed solution will correct the problem? _____

That the solution will be feasible? _____

That any disadvantages will be outweighed by advantages? _____

That the proposed solution is the best solution to the problem? _____

How Effectively Does the Speaker Employ:

Evidence of fact and opinion? _____

(Underline any appropriate categories: Evidence was insufficient in quantity; poor in quality; improperly applied; not clearly related to the point supposedly being proved; sources not given; credibility of sources not always established) _____

Forms of reasoning? _____

(Underline any appropriate categories: Faulty reasoning from examples; from axiom, from cause to probable effect; from effect to probable cause; from analogy) _____

Factors of attention and interest? _____

Signposts for organizational clarity? _____

Language? _____

Visual aspects of delivery? _____

Vocal aspects of delivery? _____

Dominant Impression of the Speech

Speech to Inform

Speaker _____

Rating Scale: 5—Superior; 4—Above Average; 3—Average; 2—Fair;
    1—Poor

Choice of Subject   _____

Introduction

    Did the opening statements effectively gain attention?   _____

    Did the speaker make you feel a need for information?   _____

    Did the speaker establish his or her right to inform,   _____
        directly or indirectly?

    Graceful transition into the body of the speech?   _____

Body

    Clarity of organization?   _____

    Information made interesting?   _____

    Information made understandable?   _____

    Visual aid capably handled?   _____

Conclusion

    Speech gracefully concluded?   _____

Language Usage

    Clear?   _____

    Grammatically correct?   _____

    Vivid?   _____

    Appropriate?   _____

Use of Voice (Check the appropriate blank)

    Pitch level: Too high _____ Too low _____ OK _____

    Variation of pitch: Varied _____ Monotonous to a degree _____

    Very monotonous _____

    Rate: Too fast _____ Too slow _____ OK _____

    Variation of rate: Too little _____ Too much _____ OK _____

    Loudness: Too loud _____ Too soft _____ OK _____

    Variation of loudness: Too little _____ Too much _____ OK _____

    Pronunciation: Generally correct _____ Frequently faulty _____

    Words mispronounced: _____

    Enunciation: Clear _____ Indistinct _____

Visual Aspects of Delivery

    Posture: Alert but at ease _____ All weight on one foot _____

    Leaning on lectern _____ Stiff _____ Shifting weight constantly _____

Gestures: Too few _____ Too many _____ OK in quantity _____

Quality of gestures: Properly motivated _____ Affected _____ Clumsy _____

Movements: Immobile _____ Distracting movements _____ Satisfactory in quantity and quality _____

Facial expression: Very animated _____ Occasionally animated _____ Never animated _____

Eye contact: Looked at everyone _____ Favored one section _____ Avoided audience _____

Total Impression Left by Speech (Use rating scale) _____

Evaluation and Criticism of Speeches

1. Has the speaker made an attempt to be objective and fair to himself or herself, the audience, and the subject?

2. Did the speaker have a worthwhile purpose? Was it of college caliber? Was the purpose easy to follow and logically developed?

3. Was there evidence that the speaker had analyzed the audience and the speaking occasion?

4. Did the speaker know the subject? Did he or she seem to be prepared both in terms of research and in terms of oral practice?

5. Was the speech structurally sound? Did the subdivisions, both major and minor, relate to and support the main ideas? Were the transitions between ideas clear?

6. Did the speaker use language meaningfully? Did he or she employ words or phrases that were clear and adequately defined? Did he or she make effective use of imagery and word pictures? Did he or she avoid cliches, slang, and poor grammar? Was the speaker's usage appropriate to the audience, the occasion, and the subject?

7. Did the speaker use factors of attention and interest in both the content and delivery of the speech?

8. Did the speaker's illustrations, examples, statistics, testimony, and analogies meet the tests of sound evidence? Was enough evidence employed to support each point?

9. Did the speaker reflect a "sense of communication?" Did he or she maintain eye contact? Did he or she employ vocal variety? Was there adequate movement?

10. What was the *total* impression left by the speech?

11. How successfully did the speaker fulfill the demands of the specific speech assignment?

The following factors are just a few of the characteristics that will influence an audience's perception and response to your message. (The term "audience" is used in this context to stand for one receiver or a large audience.)

Age_____Sex_____ Approximately how many present _____

Educational level _____Occupation _____

Economic status _____Group allegiances _____

_____

Political affiliation _____ Attitude toward me _____

Attitude toward the communication situation _____

Knowledge of the specific subject _____

Primary interests_____

Primary goals_____

Primary attitudes and beliefs _____

_____

Other important data _____

_____

_____

_____

Out-of-Class Listening Report

Supply the information requested below regarding a speech you heard presented before a religious, civic, academic group, etc. Hand this report to your instructor during the first class meeting following the speaking event.

Do Not Complete the Report During the Speech.

1. Speaker's name _____ Subject _____

2. General end _____ Specific purpose _____

3. Occasion _____ Time _____ Place _____

4. Type of audience _____ Number _____

5. How effective was he or she in beginning and ending the speech?____

_____

6. List the major points developed in the speech _____

_____

7. How was the speaker's delivery?_____

_____

_____

_____

8. Did the speaker adapt the speech to *this* audience? (explain) _____

_____

9. Did he or she prove (or explain if informative speech) the main points? (explain) _____

_____

_____

10. Criticize his or her language in terms of clarity, interest, ambiguity, etc.

_____

_____

11. Did the speaker achieve his or her purpose? _____Why or why not__

_____

Note: Use more paper if needed.

Observation of a Formal Speaking Situation

Name_____ Date_____

Topic_____ Date observed_____

1. What was the speaker's key idea or thesis sentence?

2. What was the purpose of his or her speech (To inform or to persuade)?

3. How did he or she explain or prove the main points? (Be specific.)

4. How did he or she maintain attention and interest?

5. What type of conclusion did the speaker use?

6. Comment on the speaker's general effectiveness.

Evaluating Group Discussion

1. How effective was the group in accomplishing its *overall objective*?

1	2	3	4	5	6	7
very effective			moderately effective			not effective

2. Did the members of the group seem *well prepared*?

1	2	3	4	5	6	7
very well prepared			moderately prepared			not at all prepared

3. Did the group follow an *organizational pattern*?

1	2	3	4	5	6	7
very well organized			moderately organized			poorly organized

4. Was there an effective *flow of communication* between all participants in the discussion? Comment and evaluate.

5. What were the strong points and the weak points of the group in the area of *participation*?

6. What were the strong points and the weak points of the group in the area of *leadership*?

Observation of a Group Discussion

Name_____   Date_____

Place of observation_____

1. Describe the occasion, the subject under discussion, and the participants.

2. Type of discussion: (Problem / Solution)?

3. Why was the discussion performed and were the participants motivated?

4. Was this discussion effective in its pursuit? If so, how?

5. Was there evidence of good feedback between participants? Explain.

6. What was the effect of the feedback?

7. Did the discussion proceed in a purposeful manner?

8. Did all participants discuss? Why or why not?

9. Describe the leader's role.

Critic's Discussion Evaluation Sheet

Name_____ Date_____

Evaluation of individuals in the group.

Some criteria for evaluating individual participation:
  1. Information (understanding facts and values involved in the problem)
  2. Analysis (use of evidence and ability to locate main issues)
  3. Cooperative thinking (contributes to group opinion and synthesizes opinion)
  4. Speaking (conversational attitude, clarity in voice and diction)
  5. Courteousness (treatment of others, their opinions and attitudes)

Instructions: List participants, in column A, rate them; in column B, rank them in order of their effectiveness in the group.

Name of participant	A rate 1, 2, 3, or 4	B rank 1, 2, 3, . . . 8
1. _____	_____	_____
2. _____	_____	_____
3. _____	_____	_____
4. _____	_____	_____
5. _____	_____	_____
6. _____	_____	_____
7. _____	_____	_____
8. _____	_____	_____

Rating: 1—Poor, 2—Average, 3—Good, 4—Superior

Evaluate the group.

Some criteria for evaluating group participation:
  1. Group Information. Does the group possess extensive, comprehensive, and accurate knowledge of the information on the discussion topic?
  2. Group Processes. Does the group exhibit knowledge of the basis of cause, generalization, theory, inference making, and logical reasoning in the discussion process?
  3. Group Relations. Does the group demonstrate the ability to integrate and synthesize individual contributions into common purposes within the group?

Evaluation of this group _____

Rating: 1—Poor, 2—Average, 3—Good, 4—Superior

Comments: (Use more paper if needed.)

End-of-Discussion Suggestion Slip

What is your overall rating of today's discussion for each of the items? Please circle appropriate number.

	Very Low	Low	Av	High	Very High
1. Physical arrangement and comfort	1	2	3	4	5
2. Orientation	1	2	3	4	5
3. Group atmosphere	1	2	3	4	5
4. Interest and motivation	1	2	3	4	5
5. Participation	1	2	3	4	5
6. Productiveness	1	2	3	4	5
7. Choice	1	2	3	4	5

Please answer the following questions:

1. How would you rate this discussion? (check)
   poor ___ mediocre ___ all right ___ good ___ excellent ___

2. What were the strong points?

3. What were the weak points?

4. What improvements would you suggest?

Index

Notes

Notes

Notes

Notes

Notes

Notes

Notes